Networking For Dummies
6th Edition

W9-CEJ-549

Cheat Sheet

My Network and Welcome to It

Write down important stuff about your own network in the spaces provided below.

Network server type:
(Check One)

___ NetWare (Version: ___)
___ Windows 2000 Server
___ Windows NT 4

___ Windows XP / Me / 98
___ Other: _____

Account Information

My user ID: _____

My password: <u>DON'T WRITE IT HERE!</u>

Domain Name: _____

Network Administrator

Name: _____

Phone number: _____

E-mail name: _____

Favorite snack food: _____

My Network Drives

Drive Letter	Description
_____	_____
_____	_____
_____	_____
_____	_____

My Network Printers

Printer Name	Description
_____	_____
_____	_____
_____	_____

Coax Cabling Rules

- Segment limited to 185 meters (600 feet)
- Uses BNC connectors
- T-connectors used to connect cable to computers
- Terminators required at both ends of segment

For Dummies: Bestselling Book Series for Beginners

Networking For Dummies, 6th Edition

Cheat Sheet

Twisted-Pair Cabling Rules

- Maximum cable length: 100 meters (330 feet).
- All computers cabled to central wiring hub.
- Terminators not required.
- RJ-45 connector wired as follows:
  - Pin 1 White/orange
  - Pin 2 Orange/white
  - Pin 3 White/green
  - Pin 6 Green/white
- Up to three hubs may be daisy-chained together.
- Some hubs may also be linked using thin or thick coax.

Help, Mr. Wizard!

Before calling the network guru, try this:

- Make sure that everything is plugged in.
- Make sure that the network cable is properly attached. For twisted-pair cable, the little light on the back of your computer where the cable plugs in should be glowing.
- If your computer is frozen solid, try restarting it by pressing Ctrl+Alt+Delete.
- Press Ctrl+S if error messages fly by so fast you can't read them. Press it again to resume.
- Try the Windows Network Troubleshooter. (Click Start⇨Help and then look under "Troubleshooting.")
- If all else fails, try restarting the entire network (but have everyone log off first).

Private IP Address Ranges

10.0.0.0	to	10.255.255.255
172.16.0.0	to	172.31.255.255
192.168.0.0	to	192.168.255.255

E-mail Shorthand

BTW	By the Way
FWIW	For What It's Worth
IMO	In My Opinion
IMHO	In My Humble Opinion
IOW	In Other Words
PMJI	Pardon Me for Jumping In
ROFL	Rolling on the Floor Laughing
ROFL,PP	Rolling on the Floor Laughing, Peeing My Pants
TIA	Thanks in Advance
TTFN	Ta Ta for Now
TTYL	Talk to You Later
<g>	Grin
<bg>	Big Grin
<vbg>	Very Big Grin

Secrets to Network Happiness

- Back up religiously.
- Document your network layout and keep your documentation up-to-date.
- Keep an adequate supply of spare parts and tools on hand.
- Never turn off or restart the server while users are logged in.
- Don't be afraid, Luke.

Copyright © 2002 Wiley Publishing, Inc.
All rights reserved.

Item 1677-9.

For more information about Wiley Publishing, call 1-800-762-2974.

For Dummies: Bestselling Book Series for Beginners

Networking

FOR

DUMMIES®

6TH EDITION

Networking

FOR

DUMMIES®

6TH EDITION

by Doug Lowe

Wiley Publishing, Inc.

Networking For Dummies, 6th Edition

Published by
Wiley Publishing, Inc.
909 Third Avenue
New York, NY 10022
www.wiley.com

Copyright © 2003 by Wiley Publishing, Inc., Indianapolis, Indiana

Published by Wiley Publishing, Inc., Indianapolis, Indiana

Published simultaneously in Canada

For general information on our other products and services or to obtain technical support, please contact our Customer Care Department within the U.S. at 800-762-2974, outside the U.S. at 317-572-3993, or fax 317-572-4002.

Wiley also publishes its books in a variety of electronic formats. Some content that appears in print may not be available in electronic books.

Library of Congress Control Number: 2002110279

ISBN: 0-7645-1677-9

Manufactured in the United States of America

10 9 8 7 6 5 4 3 2

6B/QU/RQ/QS/IN

Wiley Publishing, Inc. is a trademark of Wiley Publishing, Inc.

About the Author

Doug Lowe has written a whole bunch of computer books, including more than 30 *For Dummies* books including *PowerPoint 2002 For Dummies*, *Internet Explorer 6 For Dummies*, and *Microsoft Office 2002 For Dummies Quick Reference*. He lives in that sunny All-American City of Fresno, California, where the motto is, "Go Dogs! (The Other Bulldogs, that is)" with his wife, two teenage daughters, and one elderly female Golden Retriever. He's one of those obsessive-compulsive decorating nuts who puts up tens of thousands of lights at Christmas and creates computer-controlled Halloween decorations that rival Disney's Haunted Mansion. Maybe his next book should be *Tacky Holiday Decorations For Dummies*.

Dedication

To Debbie, Rebecca, Sarah, and Bethany

Author's Acknowledgments

The list of thank-yous for this book is long and goes back several years. I'd like to first thank John Kilcullen, David Solomon, Janna Custer, Erik Dafforn, Greg Robertson, and Ray Marshall for all of their help with the first edition. Then came the second edition, for which I would like to thank Tim Gallan, Mary Goodwin, and Joe Salmeri. For the third edition, I'd like to thank Jennifer Ehrlich, Constance Carlisle, and Jamey L. Marcum. The fourth edition enlisted the help of Jeanne S. Criswell, Ted Cains, and Jamey L. Marcum. And the fifth edition was accomplished with help from Dana Lesh, Rebekah Mancilla, Becky Huehls, Amy Pettinella, Suzanne Thomas, and Garrett Pease.

Wow. For this, the sixth edition, I'd like to thank project editor Andrea Boucher, who did a great job overseeing all the editorial work that was required to put this book together. I'd also like to thank Garrett Pease, who once again gave the entire manuscript a thorough technical look-through and offered many excellent suggestions, and Andrea Boucher again as the copy editor, who made sure the i's were crossed and the t's dotted (oops, reverse that!). And, as always, thanks to all the behind-the-scenes people who chipped in with help I'm not even aware of.

Publisher's Acknowledgments

We're proud of this book; please send us your comments through our online registration form located at www.dummies.com/register/.

Some of the people who helped bring this book to market include the following:

Acquisitions, Editorial, and Media Development

Project Editor: Andrea C. Boucher

 (Previous Edition: Dana Rhodes Lesh)

Acquisitions Editor: Greg Croy

Technical Editor: Garrett Pease

Editorial Manager: Carol Sheehan

Editorial Assistant: Amanda Foxworth

Cartoons: Rich Tennant, www.the5thwave.com

Production

Project Coordinator: Dale White

Layout and Graphics: Amanda Carter, Carrie Foster, Joyce Haughey, Stephanie D. Jumper, Barry Offringa

Proofreaders: John Greenough; TECHBOOKS Production Services, Inc.

Indexer: TECHBOOKS Production Services, Inc.

Publishing and Editorial for Technology Dummies

 Richard Swadley, Vice President and Executive Group Publisher

 Mary C. Corder, Editorial Director

 Andy Cummings, Vice President and Publisher

Publishing for Consumer Dummies

 Diane Graves Steele, Vice President and Publisher

 Joyce Pepple, Acquisitions Director

Composition Services

 Gerry Fahey, Vice President of Production Services

 Debbie Stailey, Director of Composition Services

Contents at a Glance

Table of Contents

Introduction

- -

*W*elcome to the sixth edition of *Networking For Dummies,* the book
that's written especially for people who have this nagging feeling in
the back of their minds that they should network their computers but haven't
a clue as to how to start or where to begin.

Do you often copy a spreadsheet file to a floppy disk and give it to the person
in the next office so that he or she can look at it? Are you frustrated because
you can't use the fancy laser printer that's on the financial secretary's computer? Do you wait in line to use the computer that has the customer database? You need a network!

Or maybe you already have a network, but you have just one problem: They
promised that the network would make your life easier, but instead, it's
turned your computing life upside down. Just when you had this computer
thing figured out, someone popped into your office, hooked up a cable, and
said, "Happy networking!" Makes you want to scream.

Either way, you've found the right book. Help is here, within these humble
pages.

This book talks about networks in everyday — and often irreverent — terms.
The language is friendly; you don't need a graduate education to get through
it. And the occasional potshot will help unseat the hallowed and sacred tradi-
tions of networkdom, bringing just a bit of fun to an otherwise dry subject.
The goal is to bring the lofty precepts of networking down to earth where you
can touch them and squeeze them and say, "What's the big deal? I can do this!"

About This Book

This isn't the kind of book you pick up and read from start to finish, as if it
were a cheap novel. If I ever see you reading it at the beach, I'll kick sand in
your face. This book is more like a reference, the kind of book you can pick
up, turn to just about any page, and start reading. You have 31 chapters, and
each one covers a specific aspect of networking — such as printing on the
network, hooking up network cables, or setting up security so that bad guys
can't break in. Just turn to the chapter you're interested in and start reading.

Each chapter is divided into self-contained chunks, all related to the major theme of the chapter. For example, the chapter on hooking up the network cable contains nuggets like these:

- What Is Ethernet?
- Two Types of Ethernet Cable
    - Coax cable
    - Twisted Pair cable
- Installing Network Cable
    - Getting the tools that you need
    - Attaching a BNC connector to coax cable
    - Attaching an RJ-45 connector to UTP cable
- Professional Touches

You don't have to memorize anything in this book. It's a "need-to-know" book: You pick it up when you need to know something. Need to know what 100baseT is? Pick up the book. Need to know how to create good passwords? Pick up the book. Otherwise, put it down and get on with your life.

How to Use This Book

This book works like a reference. Start with the topic you want to find out about. Look for it in the table of contents or in the index to get going. The table of contents is detailed enough that you should be able to find most of the topics you're looking for. If not, turn to the index, where you can find even more detail.

After you've found your topic in the table of contents or the index, turn to the area of interest and read as much as you need or want. Then close the book and get on with it.

Of course, the book is loaded with information, so if you want to take a brief excursion into your topic, you're more than welcome. If you want to know the big security picture, read the whole chapter on security. If you just want to know how to make a decent password, read just the section on passwords. You get the idea.

If you need to type something, you'll see the text you need to type like this: **Type this stuff**. In this example, you type **Type this stuff** at the keyboard and press Enter. An explanation usually follows, just in case you're scratching your head and grunting, "Huh?"

Whenever I describe a message or information that you see on the screen, I present it as follows:

```
A message from your friendly network
```

This book rarely directs you elsewhere for information — just about everything that you need to know about networks is right here. For more information about Windows, try *Windows XP For Dummies* by Andy Rathbone (Wiley Publishing, Inc.). Andy also has excellent books about previous editions of Windows. For even more basic information about PCs, see *PCs For Dummies* by Dan Gookin. You can also find plenty of other *For Dummies* books that cover just about every program known to humanity.

What You Don't Need to Read

Much of this book is skippable. I've carefully placed extra-technical information in self-contained sidebars and clearly marked them so that you can steer clear of them. Don't read this stuff unless you're really into technical explanations and want to know a little of what's going on behind the scenes. Don't worry; my feelings won't be hurt if you don't read every word.

Foolish Assumptions

I'm going to make only two assumptions about who you are: *(1)* You're someone who works with a PC, and *(2)* you either have a network or you're thinking about getting one. I hope that you know (and are on speaking terms with) someone who knows more about computers than you do. My goal is to decrease your reliance on that person, but don't throw away his or her phone number quite yet.

Is this book useful for Macintosh users? Absolutely. Although the bulk of this book is devoted to showing you how to link Windows-based computers to form a network, you can find information about how to network Macintosh computers as well.

How This Book Is Organized

Inside this book, you find chapters arranged in six parts. Each chapter breaks down into sections that cover various aspects of the chapter's main subject. The chapters are in a logical sequence, so reading them in order (if you want to read the whole thing) makes sense. But the book is modular enough that you can pick it up and start reading at any point.

Here's the lowdown on what's in each of the six parts.

Part 1: The Absolute Basics: A Network User's Guide

The chapters in this part present a layperson's introduction to what networking is all about. This is a good place to start if you're clueless about what a network is. It's also a great place to start if you're a hapless network user who doesn't give a whit about optimizing network performance, but you want to know what the network is and how to get the most out of it.

The best thing about this part is that it focuses on how to use a network without getting into the technical details of setting up a network or maintaining a network server. In other words, this part is aimed at ordinary network users who have to learn how to get along with a network.

Part II: Building Your Own Network

Uh-oh. The boss just gave you an ultimatum: Get a network up and running by Friday or pack your things. The chapters in this section cover everything you need to know to build a network, from picking the network operating system to installing the cable.

Part III: The Dummies Guide to Network Management

I hope that the job of managing the network doesn't fall on your shoulders, but in case it does, the chapters in this part can help you out. You find out all about backup, security, performance, dusting, mopping, and all the other stuff network managers have to do.

Part IV: Webifying Your Network

After you get your network up and running, the first thing your users do is bang on your door and demand Internet access. The chapters in this part show you how to grant their request. Not only that, but you find out how to set up your own Web server so that you can create a Web site of your own. And you discover how to turn your network into an intranet so that your LAN users can access information on a local Web server.

Part V: More Ways to Network

The chapters in this part present additional information about networking, such as setting up a wireless network, dialing in to your network from another computer while you're away from the office, welcoming Macintosh computers and older MS-DOS computers into your network fold, and setting up a Linux server for your network.

Part VI: The Part of Tens

This wouldn't be a *For Dummies* book without a collection of lists of interesting snippets: ten network commandments, ten network gizmos only big networks need, ten big network mistakes, and more!

Icons Used in This Book

Hold it — technical stuff is just around the corner. Read on only if you have your pocket protector.

Pay special attention to this icon; it lets you know that some particularly useful tidbit is at hand — perhaps a shortcut or a little-used command that pays off big.

Did I tell you about the memory course I took?

Danger Will Robinson! This icon highlights information that may help you avert disaster.

Information specific to NetWare. Skip this stuff if you don't use, or do not plan to use, NetWare.

Windows 2000 Server information is in the vicinity.

Shines the spotlight on information about the latest version of Windows.

Where to Go from Here

Yes, you can get there from here. With this book in hand, you're ready to plow right through the rugged networking terrain. Browse through the table of contents and decide where you want to start. Be bold! Be courageous! Be adventurous! And above all, have fun!

Part I
The Absolute Basics: A Network User's Guide

The 5th Wave   By Rich Tennant

"You the guy having trouble staying connected to the network?"

In this part . . .

One day the Network Thugs barge into your office and shove a gun in your face. "Don't move until we've hooked you up to the network!" one of them says while the other one rips open your PC, installs a sinister-looking electronic circuit card, closes the PC back up, and plugs a cable into its back. "It's done," they say as they start to leave. "Now . . . don't call the cops. We know who you are!"

If this has happened to you, you'll appreciate the chapters in this part. They provide a gentle introduction to computer networks written especially for the reluctant network user.

What if you don't have a network yet, and you're the one who's supposed to do the installing? Then the chapters in this part clue you in to what a network is all about. That way, you're prepared for the unfortunately more technical chapters contained in Part II.

Chapter 1

Networks Will Not Take Over the World, and Other Network Basics

Computer networks get a bad rap in the movies. In *War Games,* Matthew Broderick plays a nerdy computer-whiz kid who nearly starts World War III by playing a game called "Global Thermonuclear War" on a Defense Department computer. In the *Terminator* movies, a computer network of the future called "Skynet" takes over the planet, builds deadly terminator robots, and sends them back through time to kill everyone unfortunate enough to have the name Sarah Connor. And in *The Matrix,* a vast and powerful computer network enslaves humans and keeps them trapped in a simulation of the real world.

Fear not. These bad networks exist only in the dreams of science fiction writers. Real-world networks are much more calm and predictable. They don't think for themselves, they can't evolve into something you don't want them to be, and they won't hurt you — even if your name is Sarah Connor.

Now that you're over your fear of networks, you're ready to breeze through this chapter. It's a gentle, even superficial, introduction to computer networks, with a slant toward the concepts that can help you use a computer that's attached to a network. This chapter isn't very detailed; the really detailed and boring stuff comes later.

What Is a Network?

A *network* is nothing more than two or more computers connected by a cable (or in some cases, by a wireless connection) so that they can exchange information.

Of course, computers can exchange information in other ways besides networks. Most of us have used what computer nerds call the *sneakernet*. That's where you copy a file to a floppy disk and then walk the disk over to someone else's computer. (The term *sneakernet* is typical of computer nerds' feeble attempts at humor.)

The whole problem with the sneakernet is that it's slow; plus, it wears a trail in your carpet. One day, some penny-pinching computer geeks discovered that connecting computers together with cables was actually cheaper than replacing the carpet every six months. Thus, the modern computer network was born.

You can create a computer network by hooking all the computers in your office together with cables and installing a special *network interface card* (an electronic circuit card that goes inside your computer — ouch!) in each computer so that you have a place to plug in the cable. Then you set up your computer's operating system software to make the network work, and — voilà — you have a working network. That's all there is to it.

If you don't want to mess with cables, you can create a *wireless network* instead. In a wireless network, each computer is equipped with a special wireless network adapter that has little rabbit-ear antennas. Thus, the computers can communicate with each other without the need for cables.

Figure 1-1 shows a typical network with four computers. You can see that all four computers are connected with a network cable to a central network device called a *hub*. You can also see that Ward's computer has a fancy laser printer attached to it. Because of the network, June, Wally, and the Beaver can also use this laser printer. (Also, you can see that the Beaver has stuck yesterday's bubble gum to the back of his computer. Although not recommended, the bubble gum shouldn't adversely affect the network.)

Computer networking has its own strange vocabulary. Fortunately, you don't have to know every esoteric networking term. Here are a few basic buzzwords to get you by:

> ✔ Networks are often called LANs. *LAN* is an acronym that stands for *local area network*. It's the first *TLA*, or *three-letter acronym,* that you see in this book. You don't need to remember it, or any of the many TLAs that follow. In fact, the only three-letter acronym you need to remember is TLA.

- ✔ You may guess that a four-letter acronym is called an *FLA*. Wrong! A four-letter acronym is called an *ETLA,* which stands for *extended three-letter acronym.*

- ✔ Every computer connected to the network is said to be *on the network.* The technical term (which you can forget) for a computer that's on the network is a *node.*

- ✔ When a computer is turned on and can access the network, the computer is said to be *online.* When a computer can't access the network, it's *offline.* A computer can be offline for several reasons. The computer can be turned off, the user may have disabled the network connection, the computer may be broken, the cable that connects it to the network can be unplugged, or a wad of gum can be jammed into the disk drive.

- ✔ When a computer is turned on and working properly, it's said to be *up.* When a computer is turned off or broken, it's said to be *down.* Turning off a computer is sometimes called *taking it down.* Turning it back on is sometimes called *bringing it up.*

- ✔ Don't confuse local area networks with the Internet. The *Internet* is a huge amalgamation of computer networks strewn about the entire planet. Networking the computers in your home or office so that they can share information with one another and connecting your computer to the worldwide Internet are two entirely separate things. If you want to use your local area network to connect your computers to the Internet, you can consult Chapter 18 for instructions.

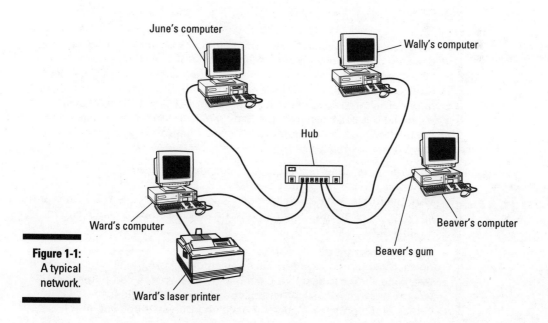

Figure 1-1:
A typical
network.

Why Bother?

Frankly, computer networks are a bit of a pain to set up. So, why bother? Because the benefits of having a network make the pain of setting one up bearable. You don't have to be a Ph.D. to understand the benefits of networking. In fact, you learned everything you need to know in kindergarten: Networks are all about sharing. Specifically, networks are about sharing three things: files, resources, and programs.

- ✔ **Sharing files:** Networks enable you to share information with other computers on the network. Depending on how you set up your network, you can share files with your network friends in several different ways. You can send a file from your computer directly to a friend's computer by attaching the file to an e-mail message and then mailing it. Or, you can let your friend access your computer over the network so that your friend can retrieve the file directly from your hard drive. Yet another method is to copy the file to a disk on another computer, and then tell your friend where you put the file so that he or she can retrieve it later. One way or the other, the data travels to your friend's computer over the network cable, and not on a floppy disk as it does in a sneakernet.

- ✔ **Sharing resources:** You can set up certain computer resources — such as a hard drive or a printer — so that all the computers on the network can access them. For example, the laser printer attached to Ward's computer in Figure 1-1 is a shared resource, which means that anyone on the network can use it. Without the network, June, Wally, and the Beaver would have to buy their own laser printers.

  Hard drives can be shared resources, too. In fact, you must set up a hard drive as a shared resource in order to share files with other users. Suppose Wally wants to share a file with the Beaver, and a shared hard drive has been set up on June's computer. All Wally has to do is copy his file to the shared hard drive in June's computer and tell the Beaver where he put it. Then, when the Beaver gets around to it, he can copy the file from June's computer to his own. (Unless, of course, Eddie Haskell deletes the file first.)

  You can share other resources, too, such as modems (which enable you to access the Internet) and CD-ROM or DVD drives (devices that store vast quantities of data and are most useful for large clip-art libraries and encyclopedias and for playing tunes or watching movies while you're supposed to be working).

- ✔ **Sharing programs:** Rather than keeping separate copies of programs on each person's computer, sometimes putting programs on a drive that everyone shares is best. For example, if you have ten computer users who all use a particular program, you can purchase and install ten copies of the program — one for each computer. Or you can purchase a ten-user license for the program and then install just one copy of the program on a shared drive. Each of the ten users can then access the program from the shared hard drive.

In most cases, however, running a shared copy of a program over the network is unacceptably slow. A more common way of using a network to share programs is to copy the program's installation disks or CDs to a shared network drive. Then you can use that copy to install a separate copy of the program onto each user's local hard drive. For example, Microsoft Office enables you to do this, if you purchase a license from Microsoft for each computer on which you install Office.

The advantage of installing Office from a shared network drive is that you don't have to lug around the installation disks or CDs to each user's computer. And the system administrator can customize the network installation so that the software is installed the same way on each user's computer. (However, these benefits are significant only for larger networks. If your network has fewer than about ten computers, you're probably better off installing the program separately on each computer directly from the installation disks or CDs.)

Remember that purchasing a single-user copy of a program and then putting it on a shared network drive, so that everyone on the network can access it, is illegal. If you have five people who use the program, you need to either purchase five copies of the program or purchase a network license that specifically allows five or more users.

Another benefit of networking is that networks enable computer users to communicate with one another over the network. The most obvious way networks allow computer users to communicate is by passing messages back and forth using e-mail programs or instant messaging programs. But networks also offer other ways to communicate: For example, you can hold online meetings over the network. Network users who have inexpensive video cameras attached to their computers can have video conferences. You can even play a friendly game of Hearts over a network — during your lunch break, of course.

Servers and Clients

The network computer that contains the hard drives, printers, and other resources that are shared with other network computers is called a *server.* This term comes up repeatedly, so you have to remember it. Write it on the back of your left hand.

Any computer that's not a server is called a *client.* You have to remember this term, too. Write it on the back of your right hand.

Only two kinds of computers are on a network: servers and clients. Look at your left hand and then look at your right hand. Don't wash your hands until you have these terms memorized.

The distinction between servers and clients in a network would be somewhat fun to study in a sociology class, because it's similar to the distinction between the haves and the have-nots in society.

- ✔ Usually, the most powerful and expensive computers in a network are the servers. This fact makes sense because every user on the network shares the server's resources.

- ✔ The cheaper and less powerful computers in a network are the clients. Clients are the computers used by individual users for everyday work. Because clients' resources don't have to be shared, they don't have to be as fancy.

- ✔ Most networks have more clients than servers. For example, a network with ten clients can probably get by with one server.

- ✔ In many networks, a clean line of segregation exists between servers and clients. In other words, a computer is either a server or a client, and not both. A server can't become a client, nor can a client become a server.

- ✔ Other networks are more progressive, allowing any computer in the network to be a server and allowing any computer to be both server and client at the same time. The network illustrated in Figure 1-1 is this type of network.

Dedicated Servers and Peers

In some networks, a server computer is a server computer and nothing else. This server computer is dedicated solely to the task of providing shared resources, such as hard drives and printers, to be accessed by the network client computers. Such a server is referred to as a *dedicated server* because it can perform no other task besides network services.

Other networks take an alternative approach, enabling any computer on the network to function as both a client and a server. Thus, any computer can share its printers and hard drives with other computers on the network. And while a computer is working as a server, you can still use that same computer for other functions such as word processing. This type of network is called a *peer-to-peer network,* because all the computers are thought of as peers, or equals.

Here are some points to ponder concerning the difference between dedicated server networks and peer-to-peer networks while you're walking the dog tomorrow morning:

✔ Peer-to-peer networking features are built into Windows. Thus, if your computer runs Windows, you don't have to buy any additional software to turn your computer into a server. All you have to do is enable the Windows server features.

✔ The network server features that are built into Windows 9*x*/Me/XP aren't very efficient because these versions of Windows were not designed primarily to be network servers. If you're going to dedicate a computer to the task of being a full-time server, you should use a special network operating system instead of the standard Windows operating system. A network operating system, also known as a *NOS,* is specially designed to handle networking functions efficiently. The two most commonly used network operating systems are Microsoft's Windows 2000 Server (which used to be known as Windows NT Server) and Novell's NetWare. I describe them both in the next section, "The NOS Choice."

✔ Many networks are both peer-to-peer and dedicated server networks at the same time. These networks have one or more server computers that run Windows 2000 Server or some other NOS, as well as client computers that use the server features of Windows to share their resources with the network.

✔ Besides being dedicated, it's helpful if your servers are also sincere.

The NOS Choice

Most dedicated network servers do not run a desktop version of Windows such as Windows XP, Me, or 98. Instead, dedicated network servers usually run a network operating system or NOS. A network operating system is specially designed to efficiently carry out the tasks of coordinating the access to shared network resources among the network client computers.

Although you have several network operating systems to choose from, the two most popular are NetWare and Windows 2000 Server.

✔ One of the most popular network operating systems is NetWare, from a company called Novell. NetWare is very advanced but also very complicated. So complicated, in fact, that it has an intensive certification program that rivals the bar exam. The lucky ones that pass the test are awarded the coveted title *Certified Novell Engineer,* or *CNE,* and a lifetime supply of pocket protectors. Fortunately, a CNE is really required only for large networks with dozens or even hundreds of computers attached. Building a NetWare network with just a few computers isn't too difficult.

✔ Windows 2000 Server is a special network server version of Windows the popular Windows operating system from Microsoft. Windows 2000 Server used to be known as Windows NT Server. Thanks to the familiar Windows interface, Windows 2000 Server is a bit easier to set up and use than NetWare. (Throughout this book, I'll use the term *Windows Server* to refer to the various server version of Windows.)

Not wanting to be left out, Microsoft has its own certification program for Windows 2000 specialists. If you pass the full battery of certification tests, you get to wear an MCSE badge, which lets the whole world know that you are a *Microsoft Certified Systems Engineer.*

✔ Other network operating system choices include UNIX, Linux, and IBM's OS/2 Warp Server. Apple also makes its own network server operating system called Mac OS X Server, designed specially for Macintosh computers.

What Makes a Network Tick?

To use a network, you don't really have to know much about how it works. Still, you may feel a little bit better about using the network if you realize that it doesn't work by voodoo. A network may seem like magic, but it isn't. The following is a list of the inner workings of a typical network:

✔ **Network interface cards:** Inside any computer attached to a network is a special electronic circuit card called a *network interface card.* The TLA for network interface card is *NIC.*

Using your network late into the evening is not the same as watching NIC at night.

On newer computers, you can use an external network interface that connects to the computer via the computer's USB port.

✔ **Network cable:** The network cable is what physically connects the computers together. It plugs into the network interface card at the back of your computer.

The most common type of network cable looks something like telephone cable. However, appearances can be deceiving. Many phone systems are wired using a lower grade of cable that won't work for networks. For a computer network, each pair of wires in the cable must be twisted in a certain way. That's why this type of cable is called a *twisted-pair cable.* Standard phone cable doesn't have the right twists.

Older networks often use another type of cable, called *coaxial cable* or just *coax.* Coax is similar to the cable used to bring Nick at Nite to your TV. The cable used for cable TV is not the same as the cable used for computer networks, though. So don't try to replace a length of broken network cable with TV cable. It won't work. Networks require a higher grade of cable than is used for cable TV.

Of the two cable types, twisted-pair cable is the best kind to use for new networks. Coax cable is found in plenty of older networks, but if you are building a new network, you want to use twisted-pair cable. For the complete lowdown on networking cables, refer to Chapter 10.

You can do away with network cable by creating a wireless network. You find information about wireless networking in Chapter 20.

✔ **Network hub:** If your network is set up using twisted-pair cable, your network also needs a network hub. A *hub* is a small box with a bunch of cable connectors. Each computer on the network is connected by cable to the hub. The hub, in turn, connects all the computers to each other. If your network uses coax cable, the cable goes directly from computer to computer, so a network hub isn't used.

Instead of hubs, some networks use a faster device known as a *switch*. The term *hub* is often used to refer to both true hubs and switches.

✔ **Network software:** Of course, the software really makes the network work. To make any network work, a whole bunch of software has to be set up just right. For peer-to-peer networking with Windows, you have to play with the Control Panel to get networking to work. And network operating systems such as Windows 2000 Server or Novell's NetWare require a substantial amount of tweaking to get them to work just right. For more information about choosing which network software to use for your network, refer to Chapter 8. To find out what you need to know to configure the software so that your network runs smoothly, refer to Chapters 12 through 16.

It's Not a Personal Computer Anymore!

If I had to choose one point that I want you to remember from this chapter more than anything else, it's this: Once you hook up your personal computer (PC) to a network, it's not a personal computer anymore. You are now part of a network of computers, and in a way, you've given up one of the key things that made PCs so successful in the first place: independence.

I got my start in computers back in the days when mainframe computers ruled the roost. *Mainframe computers* are big, complex machines that used to fill entire rooms and had to be cooled with chilled water. My first computer was a water-cooled Binford Power-Proc Model 2000. Argh, argh, argh. (I'm not making up the part about the water. A plumber was frequently required to install a mainframe computer. In fact, the really big ones were cooled by liquid nitrogen. I am making up the part about the Binford 2000.)

Mainframe computers required staffs of programmers and operators who wore white lab coats just to keep them going. They had to be carefully managed. A whole bureaucracy grew up around managing mainframes.

Mainframe computers used to be the dominant computer in the workplace. Personal computers changed all that. Personal computers took the computing power out of the big computer room and put it on the user's desktop, where it belongs. PCs severed the tie to the centralized control of the mainframe computer. With a PC, a user could look at the computer and say, "This is mine . . . all mine!" Mainframes still exist, but they're not nearly as popular as they once were.

Networks are changing everything all over again. In a way, it's a change back to the mainframe computer way of thinking. True, the network isn't housed in the basement and doesn't have to be installed by a plumber. But you can no longer think of your PC as your own. You're part of a network, and like the mainframe, the network has to be carefully managed.

Here are a few ways in which a network robs you of your independence:

- ✔ You can't just indiscriminately delete files from the network. They may not be yours.

- ✔ The network forces you to be concerned about security. For example, a server computer has to know who you are before it will let you access its files. So you'll have to know your user-id and password to access the network. This is to prevent some 15-year-old kid from hacking his way into your office network via its Internet connection and stealing all of your computer games.

- ✔ Just because Wally sends something to Ward's printer doesn't mean it immediately starts to print. The Beave may have sent a two-hour print job before that. Wally just has to wait.

- ✔ You may try to retrieve an Excel spreadsheet file from a network drive, only to discover that someone else is using it. Like Wally, you just have to wait.

- ✔ If you copy a 600MB database file to a server's drive, you may get calls later from angry coworkers complaining that no room is left on the server's drive for their important files.

- ✔ Someone may pass a virus to you over the network. You may then accidentally infect other network users.

- ✔ You have to be careful about saving sensitive files on the server. If you write an angry note about your boss and save it on the server's hard drive, your boss may find the memo and read it.

- ✔ If you want to access a file on Ward's computer but Ward hasn't come in and turned his computer on yet, you have to go into his office and turn it on yourself. To add insult to injury, you have to know Ward's password if Ward decided to password-protect his computer. (Of course, if you're the Beave, you probably already know Ward's password and everyone else's too, for that matter. If you don't, you can always ask Eddie Haskell.)

✔ If your computer is a server, you can't just turn it off when you're finished using it. Someone else may be accessing a file on your hard drive or printing on your printer.

✔ Why does Ward always get the best printer? If *Leave It to Beaver* were made today, I bet the good printer would be on June's computer.

The Network Manager

Because so much can go wrong, even with a simple network, designating one person as the *network manager* (sometimes also called the *network administrator*) is important. This way, someone is responsible for making sure that the network doesn't fall apart or get out of control.

The network manager doesn't have to be a technical genius. In fact, some of the best network managers are complete idiots when it comes to technical stuff. What's important is that the manager be organized. The manager's job is to make sure that plenty of space is available on the file server, the file server is backed up regularly, new employees can access the network, and so on.

The network manager's job also includes solving basic problems that the users themselves can't solve and knowing when to call in an expert when something really bad happens.

✔ Part III of this book is devoted entirely to the hapless network manager. So if you're nominated, read that section. If you're lucky enough that someone else is nominated, celebrate by buying him or her a copy of this book.

✔ In small companies, picking the network manager by drawing straws is common. The person who draws the shortest straw loses and becomes manager.

✔ Of course, the network manager can't really be a complete technical idiot. I was lying. (For those of you in Congress, that means I was "testifying.") I exaggerated to make the point that organizational skills are more important than technical skills. The network manager needs to know how to do various maintenance tasks. This knowledge requires at least a little technical know-how, but the organizational skills are more important.

What Have They Got That You Don't Got?

With all this stuff to worry about, you may begin to wonder if you're smart enough to use your computer after it's attached to the network. Let me assure you that you are. If you're smart enough to buy this book because you know that you need a network, you're more than smart enough to use the network after it's put in. You're also smart enough to install and manage a network yourself. This isn't rocket science.

I know people who use networks all the time. And they're no smarter than you are. But they do have one thing that you don't have: a certificate. And so, by the powers vested in me by the International Society for the Computer Impaired, I present you with the certificate in Figure 1-2, confirming that you've earned the coveted title, Certified Network Dummy, better known as *CND.* This title is considered much more prestigious in certain circles than the more stodgy CNE or MSCE badges worn by real network experts.

Congratulations, and go in peace.

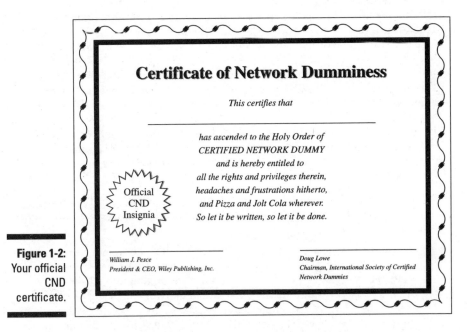

Certificate of Network Dumminess

This certifies that

_____

has ascended to the Holy Order of
CERTIFIED NETWORK DUMMY
and is hereby entitled to
all the rights and privileges therein,
headaches and frustrations hitherto,
and Pizza and Jolt Cola wherever.
So let it be written, so let it be done.

Official
CND
Insignia

William J. Pesce
President & CEO, Wiley Publishing, Inc.

Doug Lowe
Chairman, International Society of Certified
Network Dummies

Figure 1-2:
Your official
CND
certificate.

Chapter 2

Life on the Network

After you hook up your PC to a network, it's not an island anymore — separated from the rest of the world like some kind of isolationist fanatic waving a "Don't tread on me" flag. The network connection changes your PC forever. Now your computer is a part of a system, connected to other computers on the network. You have to worry about annoying network details, such as using local and shared resources, logging in and accessing network drives, using network printers, logging off, and who knows what else.

Oh, bother.

This chapter brings you up to speed on what living with a computer network is like. Unfortunately, this chapter gets a little technical at times, so you may need your pocket protector.

Distinguishing between Local Resources and Network Resources

In case you didn't catch this in Chapter 1, one of the most important differences between using an isolated computer and using a network computer is the distinction between *local resources* and *network resources*. Local resources are things such as hard drives, printers, modems, and CD-ROM drives that are connected directly to your computer. You can use local resources whether you're connected to the network or not. Network resources are the hard drives, printers, modems, and CD-ROM drives that are connected to the network's server computers. You can use network resources only after your computer is connected to the network.

The whole trick to using a computer network is to know which resources are local resources (they belong to you) and which are network resources (they belong to the network). In most networks, your C drive is a local drive. And if a printer is sitting next to your PC, it's probably a local printer. You can do anything you want with these resources without affecting the network or other users on the network (as long as the local resources aren't shared on the network).

✔ You can't tell just by looking at a resource whether it's a local resource or a network resource. The printer that sits right next to your computer is probably your local printer, but then again, it may be a network printer. The same holds for hard drives: The hard drive in your PC is probably your own, but it may be a network drive, which can be used by others on the network.

✔ Because dedicated network servers are full of resources, you may say that they aren't only dedicated (and sincere) but also resourceful. (Groan. Sorry, this is yet another in a tireless series of bad computer-nerd puns.)

What's in a Name?

Just about everything on a computer network has a name: The computers themselves have names, the people that use the computers have names, and the hard drives and printers that can be shared on the network have names. Knowing all the names that are used on your network isn't essential, but you do need to know some of them.

✔ Every person who can use the network has a *user identification* (*user ID* for short). You need to know your user ID in order to log on to the network. You also need to know the user IDs of your buddies, especially if you want to steal their files or send them nasty notes. You can find more information about user IDs and logging on in the section "Logging On to the Network" later in this chapter.

✔ Letting the folks on the network use their first names as their user IDs is tempting, but not a good idea. Even in a small office, you eventually run into a conflict. (And what about that Mrs. McCave — made famous by Dr. Seuss when she had 23 children and named them all Dave?) I suggest that you come up with some kind of consistent way of creating user IDs. For example, you may use your first name plus the first two letters of your last name. Then Wally's user ID would be wallycl and Beaver's would be beavercl. Or you may use the first letter of your first name followed by your complete last name. Then Wally's user ID would be wcleaver and Beaver's would be bcleaver. (Note that in most networks, capitalization does matter in the user name. Thus, bcleaver is different from BCleaver.)

✔ Every computer on the network must have a unique computer name. You don't have to know the names of all the computers on the network, but it helps if you know your own computer's name and the names of any server computers you need to access. The computer's name is often the user ID of the person who uses the computer most often. Sometimes the names indicate the physical location of the computer, such as office-12 or back-room. Server computers often have names that reflect the group that uses the server most, like acctng-server or cad-server.

Then again, some network nerds like to assign techie-sounding names like BL3K5-87a.

Or you may want to use names from science fiction movies. HAL, Colossus, M5, and Data come to mind. Cute names like Herbie are not allowed. (However, Tigger and Pooh are entirely acceptable. Recommended, in fact. Tiggers like networks.)

✔ Network resources such as hard drives and printers have names, too. For example, a network server may have two printers, named laser and inkjet (to indicate the type of printer), and two hard drives, named C drive and D drive.

✔ In NetWare, names of hard drives are called volume names. Often, they are names such as SYS1, SYS2, and so on. NetWare administrators frequently lack sufficient creativity to come up with more interesting volume names.

✔ Networks that use a network operating system such as Windows Server or Novell's NetWare have a user ID for the network administrator. If you log on using the administrator's user ID, you can do anything you want: add new users, define new network resources, change Wally's password — anything. The supervisor's user ID is usually something very clever, such as ADMINISTRATOR.

Logging On to the Network

To use network resources, you must connect your computer to the network, and you must go through a super-secret process called *logging on*. The purpose of logging on is to let the network know who you are so that it can decide if you're one of the good guys.

Logging on is a little bit like cashing a check: The process requires two forms of identification. The first form is your *user ID*, the name by which the network knows you. Your user ID is usually some variation of your real name, like "Beave" for "The Beaver." Everyone who uses the network must have a user ID.

Your *password* is a secret word that only you and the network know. If you type the correct password, the network believes you are who you say you are. Every user has a different password, and the password should remain a secret.

In the early days of computer networking, you had to type a logon command at a stark MS-DOS prompt and then supply your user ID and password. Nowadays, the glory of Windows is that you get to log on to the network through a special network logon dialog box, which appears when you start your computer, as shown in Figure 2-1.

If you're stuck using an old MS-DOS based computer, you may still have to type a logon command to access your network. Your network administrator can cheerfully show you how to do this. (If he or she grumbles, offer a jelly doughnut.)

Here are some more logon points to ponder:

✔ The terms *user name* and *logon name* are sometimes used instead of user ID. They mean the same thing.

✔ As long as we're talking about words that mean the same thing, *log in* and *log on* mean the same thing.

✔ As far as the network is concerned, you and your computer aren't the same thing. Your user ID refers to you, not to your computer. That's why you have a user ID and your computer has a computer name. You can log on to the network using your user ID from any computer that's attached to the network. And other users can log on at your computer using their own user IDs.

When others log on at your computer using their own user IDs, they can't access any of your network files that are protected by your password. However, they *are* able to access any local files that you haven't protected. So be careful which people you allow to use your computer.

✔ Windows XP has a cool new feature that displays icons for each of the users registered on your computer. When this feature is enabled, you can log on by clicking your name and then typing your password.

✔ If you are logging on to a Windows Server network, the logon dialog box includes a field in which you can enter the domain name you want to log on to. Hopefully, a suitable default value appears for the domain name so that you can safely ignore this field. If not, your network administrator will be happy to tell you how to enter this information.

✔ For NetWare networks, the logon dialog box may indicate the tree and context you are using to log on. Hopefully, your network administrator already configured the tree and context to the correct values. If not, he or she will tell you how to set the correct tree and context values. (On older NetWare networks, you may be asked to enter the name of the NetWare Login Server. Again, your network administrator will tell you what name to enter.)

✔ Your computer may be set up so that it logs you on automatically whenever you turn it on. In that case, you don't have to type your user ID and password. This setup makes the task of logging on more convenient, but takes the sport out of it. And it's a terrible idea if you're the least bit worried about bad guys getting into your network or personal files.

✔ Guard your password with your life. I'd tell you mine, but then I'd have to shoot you.

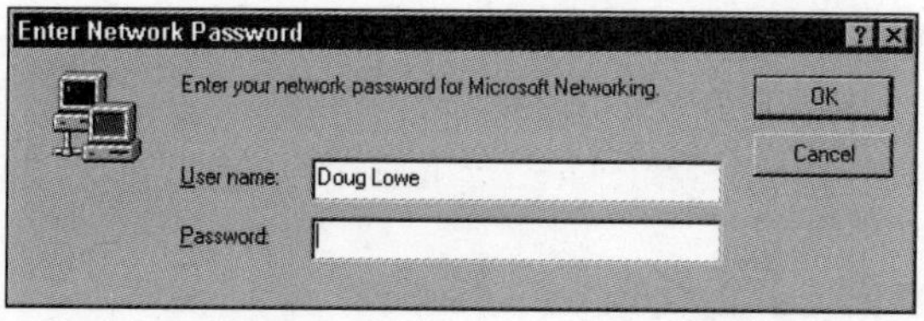

Figure 2-1:
You have to enter your user ID and password to access the network.

Enter Network Password	? X
Enter your network password for Microsoft Networking.	OK
	Cancel
User name: Doug Lowe	
Password:	

Understanding Shared Folders

Before Network (B.N.), your computer probably had just one hard drive, known as C drive. Maybe two, C and D. In any case, these drives are physically located inside your PC. They are your local drives.

Now that you're on a network, you probably have access to drives that aren't located inside your PC but are located instead in one of the other computers on the network. These network drives can be located on a dedicated server computer or, in the case of a peer-to-peer network, on another client computer.

In some cases, you can access an entire network drive over the network. But in most cases, you can't access the entire drive. Instead, you can access only certain folders (*directories* in old MS-DOS lingo) on the network drives. Either way, the shared drives or folders are known in Windows terminology as *shared folders*.

Shared folders can be set up with restrictions on how you may use them. For example, you may be granted full access to some shared folders so that you can copy files to or from them, delete files on them, create or remove folders on them, and so on. On other shared folders, your access may be limited in certain ways. For example, you may be able to copy files to or from the shared folder, but not delete files, edit files, or create new folders. You may also be asked to enter a password before you can access a protected folder. The amount of disk space you are allowed to use on a shared folder may also be limited. For more information about file-sharing restrictions, refer to Chapter 13.

Keep in mind that in addition to accessing shared folders that reside on other people's computers, you can also designate your computer as a server to enable other network users to access folders that you share. To learn how to share folders on your computer with other network users, refer to Chapter 4.

Oh, the Network Places You'll Go

 Windows enables you to access network resources, such as shared folders, by opening the My Network Places icon that resides on your desktop. When you first open My Network Places, you're greeted by icons that represent the shared resources you can access from your computer, as shown in Figure 2-2.

As you can see from Figure 2-2, each of the four computers on the network has been set up as a shared drive. You can open any of these shared drives and access the files they contain as if they were on your local computer.

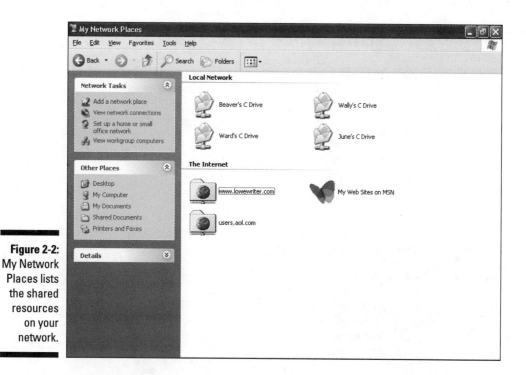

Figure 2-2:
My Network
Places lists
the shared
resources
on your
network.

You can summon a list of all the computers that are available on your network by clicking View Workgroup Computers in the Network Tasks section of the My Network Places window. This action displays an icon for each computer on your network, as shown in Figure 2-3. (If your computer is on a large network, you may not have a View Workgroup Computers link. In that case, your network administrator can set up shortcuts to the network resources you need, or tell you how to set up the shortcuts yourself.)

You can also access My Network Places from any Windows application program. For example, suppose that you're working with Microsoft Word and would like to open a document file that has been stored in a shared folder on your network. All you have to do is choose the File⇨Open command to bring up an Open dialog box. Near the top of the Open dialog box is a list box labeled *Look In.* From this list, choose the My Network Places icon. This displays a list of shared network resources you can access, as shown in Figure 2-4. Then, locate the document file that you want to open on the network.

If you are using Windows 95 or 98, My Network Places is referred to as the Network Neighborhood. When you call up the Network Neighborhood in Windows 95 or 98, you are immediately greeted by a list of the computers available on your network. You can then click one of the computers to access its shared drives and folders.

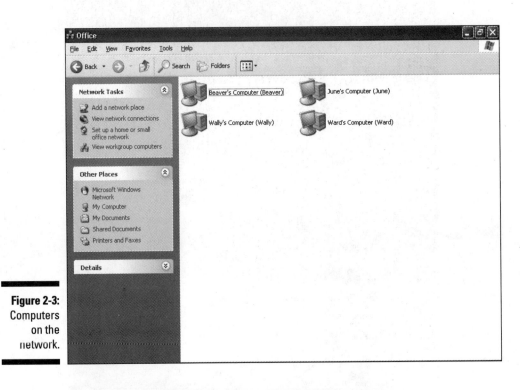

Figure 2-3:
Computers
on the
network.

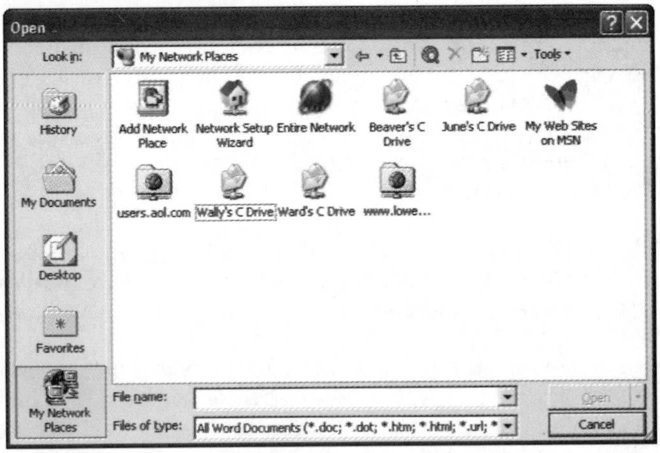

Figure 2-4:
You can
access My
Network
Places
from any
Windows
program.

Here are a few points to ponder concerning My Network Places:

✔ Viewing the resources that are available on the network by way of My
Network Places is also known as *browsing the network*. Unfortunately,

browsing the network through My Network Places may be painfully slow if a large number of computers are connected to your local network workgroup.

✔ If your network has fewer than 32 computers, Windows automatically displays icons for each shared network resource when you open My Network Places. If you are on a larger network, you may need to set up icons for the network resources you use. You can do so by clicking Add a Network Place in the My Network Places window. Contact your network guru for details about how to use the Add a Network Place wizard to set up your network places.

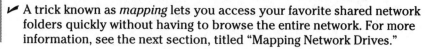

✔ A trick known as *mapping* lets you access your favorite shared network folders quickly without having to browse the entire network. For more information, see the next section, titled "Mapping Network Drives."

Mapping Network Drives

If you find yourself accessing a particular shared folder frequently, you may want to use a special trick called *mapping* to access the shared folder more efficiently. Mapping assigns a drive letter to a shared folder. Then you can use the drive letter to access the shared folder as if it were a local drive. In this way, you can access the shared folder from any Windows program without having to navigate through the Network Neighborhood.

For example, you can map a shared folder named \Wal's Files to drive G on your computer. Then, to access files stored in the shared \Wal's Files folder, you would look on drive G.

To map a shared folder to a drive letter, follow these steps:

1. **Use the Network Neighborhood to locate the shared folder you want to map to a drive.**

   If you're not sure how to do this, refer to the section "Oh, the Network Places You'll Go" earlier in this chapter.

2. **Right-click the shared folder and then choose the Map Network Drive command from the pop-up menu that appears.**

   This action summons the Map Network Drive dialog box, shown in Figure 2-5.

3. **Change the drive letter in the Drive drop-down list if you want to.**

   You probably don't have to change the drive letter that Windows selects (in Figure 2-5, drive Z). But if you're picky, you can select the drive letter from the Drive drop-down list.

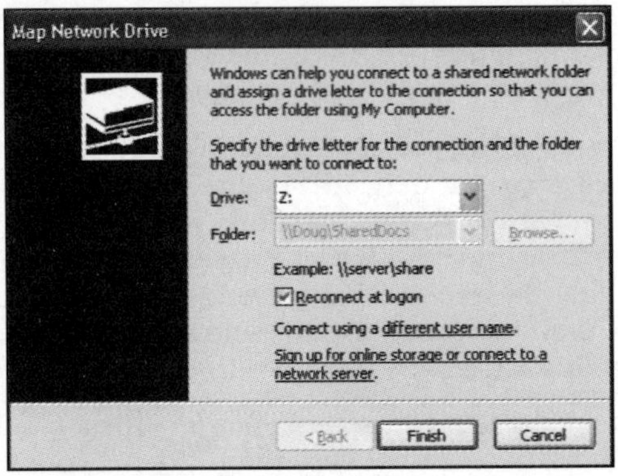

Figure 2-5:
Mapping a
network
drive.

4. **If you want this network drive to be automatically mapped each time you log on to the network, check the Reconnect at Logon option.**

If you leave the Reconnect at Logon option unchecked, the drive letter is available only until you shut Windows down or log off the network. If you check this option, the network drive automatically reconnects each time you log on to the network.

Be sure to check the Reconnect at Logon option if you use the network drive often.

5. **Click OK.**

That's it! You're done.

Your network administrator may have already set up your computer with one or more mapped network drives. If so, you can ask him or her to tell you which network drives have been mapped. Or you can just open My Computer and have a look. (Mapped network drives are listed in My Computer using the icon shown in the margin.)

✔ Assigning a drive letter to a network drive is called *mapping the drive,* or *linking the drive* by network nerds. "Drive H is mapped to a network drive," they say.

✔ The drive letter that you use to map a drive on a network server doesn't have to be the same drive letter that the server uses to access the file. For example, suppose that you use drive H to link to the server's C drive. (This is confusing, so have another cup of coffee.) In this scenario, drive H on your computer is the same drive as drive C on the server computer. This shell game is necessary for one simple reason: You can't access the server's C drive as drive C because your computer has its own drive C! You have to pick an unused drive letter and map or link it to the server's C drive.

✔ Network drive letters don't have to be assigned the same way for every computer on the network. For example, a network drive that is assigned drive letter H on your computer may be assigned drive letter Q on someone else's computer. In that case, your drive H and the other computer's drive Q are really the same drive. This can be very confusing. If your network is set up this way, put pepper in your network administrator's coffee.

✔ Accessing a shared network folder through a mapped network drive is much faster than accessing the same folder via the Network Neighborhood. That's because Windows has to browse the entire network to list all available computers whenever you open the Network Neighborhood window. In contrast, Windows does not have to browse the network at all to access a mapped network drive.

✔ If you choose the Reconnect at Logon option for a mapped drive, you'll receive a warning message if the drive is not available when you log on. In most cases, the problem is that the server computer isn't turned on. Sometimes, however, this message is caused by a broken network connection. For more information about fixing network problems such as this, refer to Chapter 6.

Four Good Uses for a Shared Folder

After you know which shared network folders are available, you may wonder what you're supposed to do with them. Here are four good uses for a network folder.

Use it to store files that everybody needs

A shared network folder is a good place to store files that more than one user needs to access. Without a network, you have to store a copy of the file on everyone's computer, and you have to worry about keeping the copies synchronized (which you can't do, no matter how hard you try). Or you can keep the file on a disk and pass it around. Or you can keep the file on one computer and play musical chairs — whenever someone needs to use the file, he or she goes to the computer that contains the file.

With a network, you can keep one copy of the file in a shared folder on the network, and everyone can access it.

Dealing with programs that don't like to share

If you're trying to share a file that's accessed by an older program — for example, an ancient DOS version of a spreadsheet program like Lotus 1-2-3 — you may have a problem. You have to make sure that two people don't try to update the file at the same time. For example, suppose that you retrieve a spreadsheet file and start to work on it and then another user retrieves the same file a few minutes later. That user won't see the changes you've made so far because you haven't saved the file on the drive yet. Now, suppose you finish making your changes and you save the file while the other user is still staring at the screen. Guess what happens when the other user saves his or her changes a few minutes later? All the changes you made are gone, lost forever in the Black Hole of Unprotected Concurrent Access.

The root cause of this problem is that older programs don't *reserve* the file while they're working on it. As a result, other programs aren't prevented from working on the file at the same time. The result is a jumbled mess. Fortunately, programs that are designed to work with Windows 95 or later are much more understanding about networks, so they do reserve files when you open them. These programs are much safer for network use.

Use it to store your own files

You can also use a shared network folder as an extension of your own hard drive storage. For example, if you've filled up all the free space on your hard drive with pictures, sounds, and movies that you've downloaded from the Internet, but the network server has billions and billions of gigabytes of free space, you have all the drive space you need. Just store your files on the network drive!

Here are a few guidelines for storing files on network drives:

✔ Using the network drive for your own files works best if the network drive is set up for private storage that other users can't access. That way, you don't have to worry about the nosy guy down in Accounting who likes to poke around in other people's files.

✔ Don't overuse the network drive. Remember that other users have probably filled up their own hard drives, so they want to use the space on the network drive, too.

✔ Before you store personal files on a network drive, make sure that you have permission. A note from your mom will do.

Use it as a pit stop for files on their way to other users

"Hey, Wally, could you send me a copy of last month's baseball stats?"

"Sure, Beave." But how? If the baseball stats file resides on Wally's local drive, how does Wally send a copy of the file to Beaver's computer? Wally can do this by copying the file to a network folder. Then Beaver can copy the file to his local hard drive.

Here are some tips to keep in mind when you use a network drive to exchange files with other network users:

- ✔ Don't forget to delete files that you've saved to the network folder after they've been picked up! Otherwise, the network folder quickly fills up with unnecessary files.

- ✔ Creating a directory on the network drive specifically intended for holding files en route to other users is a good idea. Call this directory PIT-STOP or something similar to suggest its function.

- ✔ Most e-mail programs also let you deliver files to other users. This is called "sending a file attachment." The advantage of sending a file via e-mail is that you don't have to worry about details like where to leave the file on the server and who's responsible for deleting the file.

Use it to back up your local hard drive

If enough drive space is available on the file server, you can use it to store backup copies of the files on your hard drive. Just copy the files that you want to back up to a shared network folder.

Obviously, copying all your data files to the network drive can quickly fill up the network drive. You'd better check with the network manager before you do it. The manager may have already set up a special network drive that is designed just for backups. And, if you're lucky, your network manager may be able to set up an automatic backup schedule for your important data so you don't have to remember to back it up manually.

Hopefully, your network administrator also routinely backs up the contents of the network server's disk to tape. That way, if something happens to the network server, the data can be recovered from the backup tapes.

Using a Network Printer

Using a network printer is much like using a network hard drive. You can print to a network printer from any Windows program by choosing File➪Print to call up a Print dialog box from any program and choosing a network printer from the list of available printers.

Keep in mind, however, that printing on a network printer isn't exactly the same as printing on a local printer. When you print on a local printer, you're the only one who is using that printer. But when you print to a network printer, you're sharing that printer with other network users. This complicates things in several ways:

- ✔ If several users print to the network printer at the same time, the network has to keep the print jobs separate from one another. If it didn't, the result would be a jumbled mess, with your 168-page report being mixed up with the payroll checks. That would be bad. Fortunately, the network takes care of this situation by using a fancy feature called *print spooling.*

- ✔ Invariably, when I get in line at the hardware store, the person in front of me is trying to buy something that doesn't have a product code on it. I end up standing there for hours waiting for someone in Plumbing to pick up the phone for a price check. Network printing can be like that. If someone sends a two-hour print job to the printer before you send your half-page memo, you have to wait. Network printing works on a first-come, first-served basis, unless you know some of the tricks that I discuss in Chapter 3.

- ✔ Before you were forced to use the network, your computer probably had just one printer attached to it. Now, you may have access to a local printer and several network printers. You may want to print some documents on your cheap (oops, I mean local) inkjet printer but use the network laser printer for really important stuff. To do that, you have to find out how to use your programs' functions for switching printers.

- ✔ Network printing is really too important a subject to squeeze into this chapter. So Chapter 3 goes into this topic in more detail.

Logging Off the Network

After you finish using the network, you should log off. Logging off the network makes the network drives and printers unavailable. Your computer is still physically connected to the network (unless you cut the network cable with pruning shears — bad idea! Don't do it!), but the network and its resources are unavailable to you.

- ✔ After you turn off your computer, you're automatically logged off the network. After you start your computer, you have to log in again. Logging off the network is a good idea if you're going to leave your computer unattended for a while. As long as your computer is logged in to the network, anyone can use it to access the network. And because unauthorized users can access it under your user ID, you get the blame for any damage they do.

- ✔ In Windows, you can log off the network by clicking the Start button and choosing the Log Off command. This process logs you off the network without restarting Windows. (In some versions of Windows 95, you must choose the Start⇨Shut Down command to log off the network.)

Chapter 3

Using a Network Printer

*I*f you come to hate anything about using a network, it's using a network printer. Oh, for the good ol' days when your slow but simple dot-matrix printer sat on your desk right next to your computer for you, and nobody else but you, to use. Now you have to share the printer down the hall. It may be a neat printer, but now you can't watch it all the time to make sure that it's working.

Now you have to send your 80-page report to the network printer, and when you go check on it 20 minutes later, you discover that it hasn't printed yet because someone else sent an 800-page report before you. Or the printer's been sitting idle for 20 minutes because it ran out of paper. Or all 80 pages of your report printed on the company letterhead that someone accidentally left in the paper tray. Or your report just disappeared into Network-Network Land.

What a pain. This chapter can help you out. It clues you in to the secrets of network printing and gives you some Network Pixie Dust (NPD) to help you find those lost print jobs. (This chapter may also convince you to spend $69 of your own money to buy your own little inkjet printer so that you won't have to mess around with the network printer!)

What's So Special about Network Printing?

Why is network printing such a big deal? In Chapter 3, I talk about sharing network drives and folders and show that sharing is really pretty simple. After everything is set up right, using a network drive is hardly different from using a local drive.

The situation would be great if sharing a printer were just as easy. But it isn't. The problem with network printing is that printers are slow and finicky devices. They run out of paper. They eat paper. They run out of toner or ink. And sometimes they just croak. Dealing with all these problems is hard enough when the printer is right next to the computer on your desk, but using the printer that's accessed remotely via a network is even harder.

A printer in every port

Before I delve into the details of network printing, I want to review some printing basics. A *port* is a connection on the back of your computer. You use ports to connect devices to the computer. You plug one end of a cable into the port and plug the other end of the cable into a connector on the back of the device that you want to connect. Nearly all computers have at least two devices connected to ports: a keyboard and a mouse. Many computers also have a printer attached to a port, and some computers have other devices, such as a modem or a scanner.

There are two types of ports you can attach printers to: *parallel* and *USB*. (Certain types of older printers used serial port connections, but most of these printers have long since been used to make beehives.) The serial port is mostly used nowadays to connect a mouse or a modem to the computer. (Actually, USB ports are a new, improved version of serial port that may soon become more popular than parallel ports for printers. For more information about USB, see the sidebar "Hop on the Universal Serial Bus.")

Another type of port that your computer may or may not have is a SCSI port. *SCSI* (pronounced *skuzzy*), which stands for *Small Computer System Interface*, is a special type of high-speed parallel port that's used mostly to connect disk drives, tape drives, CD-ROM drives, and other devices, such as scanners, to your computer. Because you don't use the SCSI port to connect a printer, you can ignore it for now.

Here are some additional points to ponder concerning the mysteries of printer ports:

- After the introduction of the first IBM Personal Computer way back in 1492, the names LPT1, LPT2, and LPT3 were assigned to the parallel ports (LPT stands for "Line Printer"). The first parallel port (and the only parallel port on most computers) is LPT1. LPT2 and LPT3 are the second and third parallel ports. Even today, Windows uses these same names.

- LPT1 has a pseudonym: PRN. The names LPT1 and PRN both refer to the first parallel port and are used interchangeably.

- COM1, COM2, COM3, and COM4 are the names used for the four serial ports. (COM stands for *communications,* a subject that the people who came up with names like LPT1 and COM1 needed to study more closely.)

- Hopefully, the name assigned to each port on your computer is printed next to the port's connector on the back of your computer. If not, you have to check your computer's manual to find out which port is which.

Some network printers don't connect to a port on a computer at all. Instead, these printers have an Ethernet port and connect directly to the network.

Printer configuration

All you have to do to use a printer is plug it into the parallel port (or the USB port) on the back of your computer, right? Nope. You must also configure Windows to work with the printer. To do this, you must install a special piece of software called a *printer driver,* which tells Windows how to print to your printer.

Each type of printer has its own type of printer driver. Drivers for the most common printers come with Windows. For printers that are more exotic — or for newer printers that weren't available at the time you purchased Windows — the printer manufacturer supplies the driver on a disk that comes with the printer.

To find out what printers are already configured in Windows XP, click the Start button and open the Control Panel. Then, double-click the Printers and Faxes icon. The Printers and Faxes folder appears, as shown in Figure 3-1. (To call up this folder in Windows 98 or Windows Me, choose Start⇨Settings⇨Printers.)

The Printers and Faxes folder shows an icon for each printer installed on your computer. In the case of Figure 3-1, only one printer has been installed: a Hewlett-Packard HP PSC-750. If you have more than one printer installed on your computer, you see a printer icon for each printer.

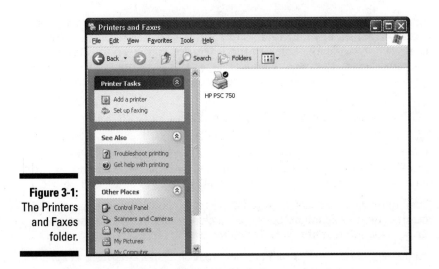

Figure 3-1:
The Printers
and Faxes
folder.

You can configure a new printer for your computer by double-clicking the Add Printer icon. Doing so starts the Add Printer Wizard, which adds a printer driver for a new printer to your computer. For more information about using this Wizard, see the section "Adding a Network Printer" later in this chapter.

Spooling and the print queue

Printers are far and away the slowest part of any computer. As far as your computer's central processing unit (CPU) is concerned, the printer takes an eternity to print a single line of information. To keep the CPU from twiddling its microscopic thumbs, computer geeks invented *spooling*.

Spooling is really pretty simple. Suppose that you use Microsoft Word to print a 200-page report. Without spooling, Word would send the report directly to the printer. You'd have to play Solitaire until the printer finished printing.

With spooling, Word doesn't send the report directly to the printer. Instead, Word sends the report to a disk file. Because the disk drives are so much faster than printers, you have to wait only a few seconds for the print job to finish. After your 200-page report is sent to the spool file, you can continue to use Word for other work, even though the printer hasn't actually finished your report yet.

Suppose you turn right around and send another 200-page report to the printer, while the printer is still busy printing the first 200-page report. The second report must wait for the printer to finish the first report. The place where the report waits is called the *print queue.* Print queue is the computer-nerd term for the line in which your print job has to wait while other print jobs that reached the line sooner are printed. Your print job isn't actually printed until it gets to the front of the line; that is, until it gets to the front of the queue.

Here are a few more spooling tidbits:

✔ The people who invented network printing way back in the 1960s thought that calling the line that print jobs wait in a *line* would be uncool. The Beatles and anything British were popular back then, so they picked the British-sounding word *queue* instead.

✔ Although considered rude, cutting to the front of the queue is possible. You find out how to do that later in this chapter. This trick is good to know — especially if you're the only one who knows.

✔ Brits always use too many letters. They like to throw extra letters into words like *colour.* The word *queue* is pronounced like "cue," not "cue-you." "Cue-you" is spelled "queueue," and is often used by Certified Network Dummies as an insult.

✔ Believe it or not, the word *spool* is actually an acronym — a five-letter acronym, or EETLA ("Expanded Extended Three-Letter Acronym") to be precise. Brace yourself, because this acronym is really nerdy: Spool stands for "Simultaneous Peripheral Output On-Line."

What is a print job?

I've used the term *print job* several times without explaining what it means, so you're probably already mad at me. I'd better explain before it's too late. A print job is a collection of printed pages that are kept together and treated as a set. If you print a 20-page document from Word, the entire 20-page printout is a single print job. Every time you use Word's Print command (or any other program's Print command), you create a print job.

How does the network know when one print job ends and the next one begins? Because the programs that do the printing send out a special code at the end of each Print command that says, "This is the end of the print job. Everything up to this point belongs together, and anything I print after this point belongs to my next print job."

Analogy alert! You can think of this code as the little stick you use at the gro-cery-store checkout stand to separate your groceries from the groceries that belong to the person in line behind you. The stick tells the clerk that all the groceries in front of the stick belong together, and the groceries behind the stick belong to the next customer.

Hop on the Universal Serial Bus

Nearly all new computers now include one or more ports called USB ports. *USB,* which stands for *Universal Serial Bus,* is designed to eventually replace most, if not all, of the external connections required by your computer.

Think about all the external devices that you may have to connect to a typical computer: keyboard, monitor, mouse, printer, and perhaps a scanner, modem, video camera, speakers, and maybe even an external CD-ROM or tape drive. Each of these devices needs its own type of cable, and it's up to you to figure out which of the many receptacles on the back of your computer to plug each cable into.

Now, with USB, you can replace all of these components (except the monitor and speakers) with USB-compatible devices and plug them all into USB ports. Most newer computers have two or more USB ports on the back for hooking up your keyboard, mouse, and printer, and a couple of USB ports on the front for connecting devices such as digital cameras. And many USB keyboards also have one or two USB connections. So if you use up all of your computer's USB ports, you can plug additional USB devices into the keyboard's USB port. If you still don't have enough USB ports for all your USB devices, you can purchase an inexpensive USB hub, which lets you plug four or more USB devices into a single USB port.

Besides saving you the hassle of untangling a multitude of cables and connectors, USB devices also automatically reconfigure themselves after you attach them to your computer. You no longer have to fuss with detailed configuration settings such as IRQ numbers and DMA addresses. You can even add or remove USB devices without turning off your computer or restarting Windows. When you plug a USB device into your computer, Windows automatically recognizes the device and configures it for use.

You can also use the USB to connect to the network without having to install a separate network interface card inside your computer by using a USB Ethernet adapter, although that's not generally a very efficient route to go as the slower USB port slows down your network connection.

When you print over a network, you can do lots of neat stuff with print jobs. You can tell the print server to print more than one copy of your job. You can tell it to print a full-page banner at the beginning of your job so that your job will be easy to find in a big stack of print jobs. Or you can tell it to stop printing when your job gets to the front of the line so that you can change from plain paper to preprinted invoices or checks. You handle these tricks from the standard Windows Print dialog boxes.

Adding a Network Printer

 Before you can print to a network printer, you have to configure your computer to access the network printer that you want to use. From the Start

menu, choose Settings⇨Printers to open the Printers folder. If your computer
is already configured to work with a network printer, an icon for the network
printer appears in the Printers folder (see the icon in the margin). You can
tell a network printer from a local printer by the shape of the printer icon.
Network printer icons have a pipe attached to the bottom of the printer.

If you don't have a network printer configured for your computer, you can
add one by using the Add Printer Wizard. Open the Add Printer icon in the
Printers folder to start the Add Printer Wizard. When the Wizard asks
whether you want to add a local or a network printer, choose network. Then,
when the Wizard asks you to specify a printer, choose the Browse option and
click Next. button. A dialog box similar to the one in Figure 3-2 appears, showing the computers and shared resources available in My Network Places.

Figure 3-2:
The Add
Printer
Wizard
wants to
know which
network
printer you
want to use.

Add Printer Wizard	
Browse for Printer	
When the list of printers appears, select the one you want to use.	

Printer:

Shared printers:

- Microsoft Windows Network
  - OFFICE
    - \\DOUG\HP DeskJet 855C   HP DeskJet 855C
    - \\DOUG\HP PSC 750   HP PSC 750
    - DOUG

Printer information

Comment:

Status: Documents waiting:

< Back   Next >   Cancel

Sniff around in this dialog box until you find the printer you want to use from
your computer. Click this printer and then click OK to return to the Add
Printer Wizard.

If you can't find the printer you want to use, ask your network administrator
for the printer's network name. Then, instead of browsing for the printer,
type the printer's network name when the Add Printer Wizard asks you to
specify a printer.

Next, the Wizard copies the correct printer driver for the network printer to
your computer. Depending on the operating system that your computer uses
and the Windows version that you use, you may be asked to insert your
Windows CD-ROM so that Windows can locate the driver files, or you may
have to insert the driver disk that came with the printer. In many cases, however, Windows copies the driver files directly from the server computer that

the printer is attached to, so you won't have to bother with the Windows CD or the printer's driver disks.

Finally, the Add Printer Wizard asks whether you want to designate the printer as your default printer, as shown in Figure 3-3. Check Yes if this is the printer you will use most of the time. If you have a local printer that you use most of the time and are just creating a connection to a network printer that you will use only on special occasions, check No. Then click Next to continue and finish the Wizard.

Many network printers, especially newer ones, are connected directly to the network via a built-in Ethernet card. Setting up these printers can be tricky. You may need to ask the network administrator for help setting up this type of printer. (Some printers that are connected directly to the network have their own Web address, such as Printer.CleaverFamily.com. If that's the case, you can often set up the printer by using your Web browser to go to the printer's Web page, then clicking a link that lets you install the printer.)

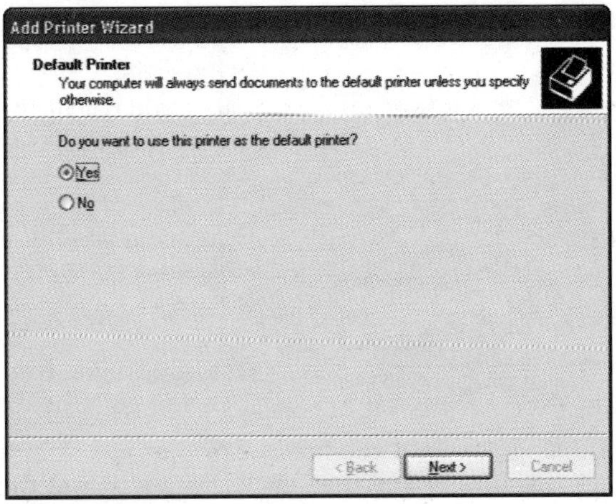

Figure 3-3:
Deciding
whether to
use this
printer as
your default
printer.

Using a Network Printer

After you have installed the network printer in Windows, printing to the network printer is a snap. You can print to the network printer from any Windows program by using the File➪Print command to summon the Print dialog box. For example, Figure 3-4 shows the Print dialog box for WordPad — the free word processing program that comes with Windows. Near the top of this dialog box is a drop-down list titled Name, which lists all the printers that are installed on your computer. Choose the network printer from this list and then click OK to print your document. That's all there is to it!

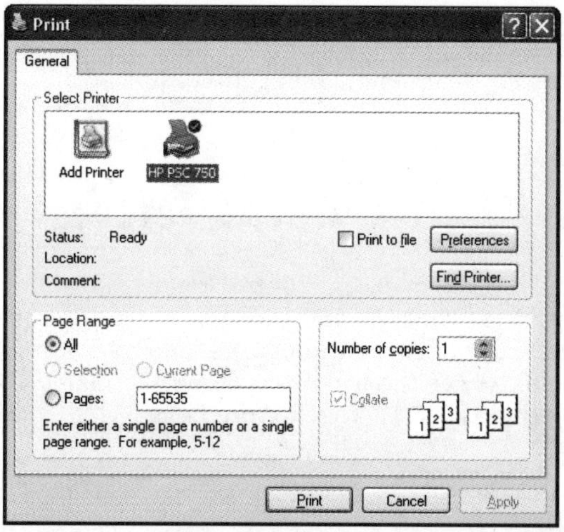

Figure 3-4:
A typical
Print
dialog box.

Playing with the Print Queue

After you send your document to a network printer, you usually don't have to worry about it. You just go to the network printer, and — voilà! — your printed document is waiting for you.

That's what happens in the ideal world. In the real world where you and I live, all sorts of things can happen to your print job between the time you send it to the network printer and the time it actually prints:

- ✔ You discover that someone else already sent a 50-trillion-page report ahead of you that isn't expected to finish printing until the national debt is completely paid off.

- ✔ The price of framis valves goes up $2 each, rendering foolish the recommendations you made in your report.

- ✔ Your boss calls and tells you that his brother-in-law will be attending the meeting, so won't you please print an extra copy of the proposal for him. Oh, and a photocopy won't do. Originals only, please.

- ✔ You decide to take lunch, so you don't want the output to print until you get back.

Fortunately, your print job isn't totally beyond your control just because you've already sent it to the network printer. You can easily change the status of jobs that you've already sent. You can change the order in which jobs print, hold a job so that it won't print until you say so, or cancel a job altogether.

You can probably make your network print jobs do other tricks, too — such as shake hands, roll over, and play dead. But the basic tricks — hold, cancel, and change the print order — are enough to get you started.

Using Windows Print Queue Tricks

To play with the printer queue, open the Control Panel (Start➪Control Panel) and click Printers and Faxes. Then, open the icon for the printer that you want to manage. A window similar to the one shown in Figure 3-5 appears. If you happen to be Wally, you can see the bad news: Some user named Beaver has slipped in a 145-page report from Microsoft Word before your little 1-page memo.

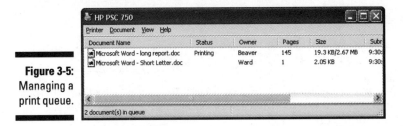

Figure 3-5:
Managing a print queue.

To manipulate the print jobs that appear in the print queue or in the printer itself, use the following tricks:

- ✔ To temporarily stop a job from printing, select the job and choose the Document➪Pause Printing command. Choose the same command again to release the job.

- ✔ To delete a print job, select the job and choose the Document➪Cancel Printing command.

- ✔ To stop the printer, choose the Printer➪Pause Printing command. To resume, choose the command again.

- ✔ To delete all print jobs, choose the Printer➪Purge Print Documents command.

- ✔ To cut to the front of the line, drag the print job that you want to print to the top of the list.

Note that depending on how your network is set up, you may not be able to mess with other users' print jobs. Sigh.

The best thing about Windows printer management is that it shelters you from the details of working with different network operating systems. Whether you print on a NetWare printer, a Windows 2000 network printer, or a shared Windows XP printer, the Printer window icon manages all print jobs in the same way.

What to Do When the Printer Jams

The only three sure bets in life: The original *Star Wars* movies are better than the prequels, old actors like Harrison Ford always play across from leading ladies that are thirty years younger, and the printer always jams shortly after your job reaches the front of the queue.

What do you do when you walk in on your network printer while it's printing all 133 pages of your report on the same line?

1. **Start by yelling "Fire!"**

   No one comes to your rescue if you yell "Printer!"

2. **Find the printer's online button and press it.**

   This step takes the printer offline so that the server stops sending information to it and the printer stops. This doesn't cure anything, but it stops the noise. If you must, turn the printer off.

3. **Pull out the jammed paper and reinsert the good paper into the printer. Nicely.**

4. **Press the online button so that the printer resumes printing.**

If the printer completely crumbles up one or more pages of your document, you can reprint just the pages that were messed up by calling up the Print dialog box from the program you used to print the document and selecting the pages you want to reprint. If the printer ate the entire print job, you'll have to reprint the entire thing. (If you're using Windows 2000, you can use the Print Queue to restart the print job from the first page.)

If you don't want to mess with clearing the printer jam, just cancel the print job. Then, print your document again using another printer. Then act surprised when you hear someone shouting that the first printer is full of crumpled paper.

Chapter 4

Becoming a Server

. . . .

In This Chapter

▶ Transforming your computer into a network server

▶ Sharing folders with network users

▶ Sharing your printer

. . . .

As you probably know, networks consist of two types of computers: client computers and server computers. In the economy of computer networks, *client computers* are the consumers — the ones who use network resources such as shared printers and disk drives. *Servers* are the providers — the ones that offer their own printers and hard drives to the network so that the client computers can use them.

This chapter shows you how to turn your humble Windows client computer into a server computer so that other computers on your network can use your printer and any folders that you decide you want to share. In this way, your computer functions as both a client and a server computer at the same time. Your computer is a client when you send a print job to a network printer or when you access a file stored on another server's hard drive. Your computer is a server when someone else sends a print job to your printer or accesses a file stored on your computer's hard drive.

Enabling File and Printer Sharing

Before you can share your files or your printer with other network users, you must set up a Windows feature known as *File and Printer Sharing*. Without this feature installed, your computer can be a network client but not a server.

If you are lucky, the File and Printer Sharing feature is already set up on your computer. To find out, double-click the My Computer icon on your desktop. Select the icon for your C drive and then click File in the menu bar to reveal the File menu. If the menu includes a Sharing command, then File and Printer Sharing is already set up, so you can skip the rest of this section. If you can't find a Sharing command in the File menu, then you have to install File and Printer Sharing before you can share a file or a printer with other network users.

File and Printer Sharing is usually installed on Windows XP systems. To install File and Printer Sharing on a Windows 9x/Me computer, follow these steps:

1. **From the Start menu, choose Settings⇨Control Panel.**

   The Control Panel comes to life.

2. **Double-click the Network icon.**

   The Network dialog box appears, as shown in Figure 4-1.

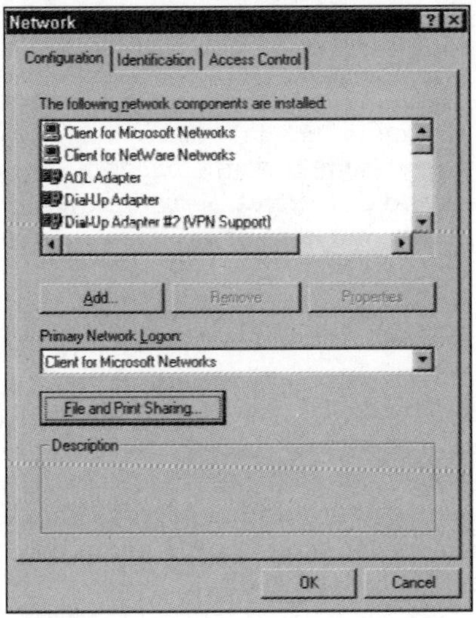

Figure 4-1:
The
Network
dialog box.

3. **Click the File and Print Sharing button.**

   This action summons the File and Print Sharing dialog box, as shown in Figure 4-2.

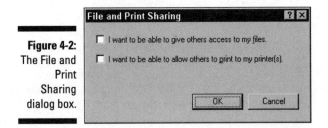

Figure 4-2:
The File and
Print
Sharing
dialog box.

4. **Click the File and Print Sharing options you want to enable for your computer.**

   The first option enables you to share your files with other network users; the second allows you to share your printer. To share both your files and your printer, check both options.

5. **Click OK to dismiss the File and Print Sharing dialog box.**

   You return to the Network dialog box.

6. **Click OK to dismiss the Network dialog box.**

   The Network dialog box vanishes, and a Copy Progress dialog box appears to let you know that Windows is copying the files required to enable File and Print Sharing. If you're prompted to insert the Windows CD-ROM, do so with a smile.

   After all the necessary files have been copied, you see a dialog box informing you that you must restart your computer for the new settings to take effect.

7. **Click Yes to restart your computer.**

   Your computer shuts down and then restarts. Your computer may take a minute or so to restart, so be patient. When your computer comes back to life, you're ready to share files or your printer.

While you are in the Network dialog box, do not mess around with any of the other network settings. You can safely change the File and Print Sharing options, but you should leave the rest of the settings on the Network dialog box well enough alone.

Sharing a Hard Drive or Folder

To enable other network users to access files that reside on your hard drive, you must designate either the entire drive or a folder on the drive as a shared drive or folder. If you share an entire drive, other network users can access all the files and folders on the drive. If you share a folder, network users can access only those files that reside in the folder you share. (If the folder you share contains other folders, network users can access files in those folders, too.)

I recommend against sharing an entire hard drive, unless you want to grant everyone on the network the freedom to sneak a peek at every file on your hard drive. Instead, you should share just the folder or folders that contain the specific documents that you want others to be able to access. For example, if you store all your Word documents in the My Documents folder, you can share your My Documents folder so that other network users can access your Word documents.

To share a folder on a Windows XP computer, follow these steps:

1. **Double-click the My Computer icon on your desktop.**

   The My Computer window comes to center stage.

2. **Select the folder that you want to share.**

   Click the icon for the drive that contains the folder that you want to share, and then find the folder itself and click it.

3. **Choose the File⇨Sharing and Security command.**

   The Properties dialog box for the folder that you want to share appears. Notice that the sharing options are grayed out.

4. **Click the Share This Folder on the Network option.**

   After you click this option, the rest of the sharing options come alive, as shown in Figure 4-3.

   If you prefer, you can skip Steps 2 through 4. Instead, just right-click the folder you want to share and then choose Sharing and Security from the pop-up menu that appears.

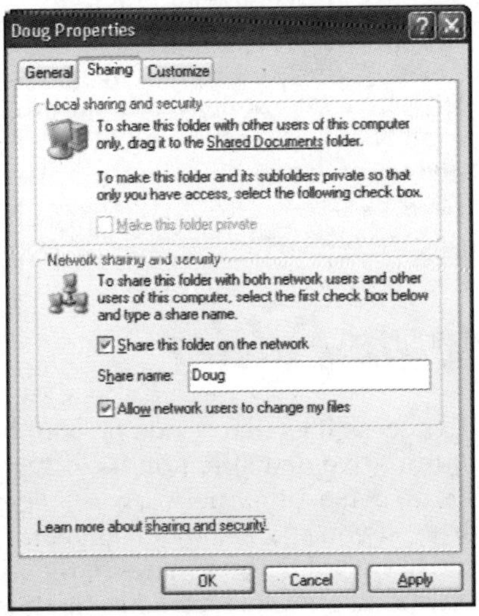

Figure 4-3:
The Sharing options come to life when you click the Share This Folder On the Network option.

5. **Change the Share Name if you don't like the name that Windows proposes.**

   The *Share Name* is the name that other network users use to access the shared folder. You can use any name you want, but the name can be no more than 12 characters in length. Uppercase and lowercase letters are treated the same in a share name, so the name MY Documents is the same as MY DOCUMENTS.

Windows proposes a share name for you based on the actual folder name. If the folder name is 12 or fewer characters, the proposed share name is the same as the folder name. But if the folder name is longer than 12 characters, Windows abbreviates it. For example, the name Multimedia Files becomes MULTIMEDIA F.

If the name that Windows chooses doesn't make sense or seems cryptic, you can change the share name to something better. For example, I would probably use MEDIA FILES instead of MULTIMEDIA F.

6. **If you want to allow other network users to change the files in this folder, check the Allow Network Users to Change My Files option.**

   If you leave this option unchecked, other network users will be able to open your files, but they won't be able to save any changes they make.

7. **Click OK.**

The Properties dialog box vanishes, and a hand is added to the icon for the folder to show that the folder is shared, as shown in the margin.

If you change your mind and decide that you want to stop sharing a folder, double-click the My Computer icon, select the folder or drive that you want to stop sharing, and choose the File⇨Sharing command to summon the Properties dialog box. Uncheck the Share This Folder on the Network option and then click OK.

The procedure for sharing folders in previous versions of Windows is similar, but the command is called Sharing instead of Sharing and Security.

Sharing a Printer

Sharing a printer is much more traumatic than sharing a hard drive. When you share a hard drive, other network users access your files from time to time. When they do, you hear your drive click a few times, and your computer may hesitate for a half-second or so. The interruptions caused by other users accessing your drive are sometimes noticeable, but rarely annoying.

But when you share a printer, your co-worker down the hall is liable to send a 40-page report to your printer just moments before you try to print a 1-page memo that has to be on the boss's desk in two minutes. The printer may run out of paper or, worse yet, it may jam during someone else's print job — and you'll be expected to attend to the problem.

Although these interruptions can be annoying, sharing your printer makes a lot of sense in some situations. If you have the only decent printer in your office or workgroup, everyone is going to be bugging you to let them use it anyway. You may as well share the printer on the network. At least this way, they won't be lining up at your door asking you to print their documents for them.

The following procedure shows you how to share a printer in Windows:

1. **From the Start menu, choose Control Panel; then choose Printers and Faxes.**

   The Printers and Faxes folder appears, as shown in Figure 4-4. In this example, the Printers folder lists a single printer, named HP PSC 750.

2. **Select the printer that you want to share.**

   Click the icon for the printer to select the printer.

3. **Choose the File⇨Sharing command.**

   You're right: This doesn't make sense. You're sharing a printer, not a file, but the Sharing command is found under the File menu. Go figure.

   When you choose the File⇨Sharing command, the Properties dialog box for the printer appears.

4. **Click the Share This Printer option.**

   Figure 4-5 shows the Printer Properties dialog box that appears after you click the Shared As option.

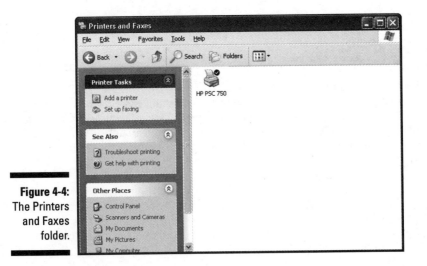

Figure 4-4:
The Printers and Faxes folder.

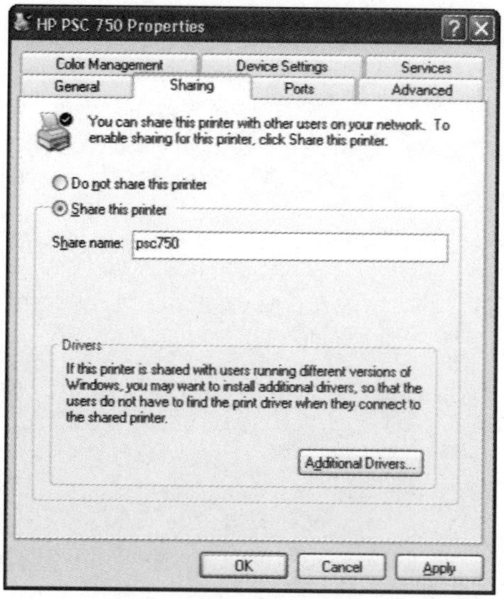

Figure 4-5:
The
Properties
dialog box
for a shared
printer.

5. **Change the Share Name if you don't like the name suggested by Windows.**

   Other computers use the share name to identify the shared printer, so choose a meaningful or descriptive name.

6. **Click OK.**

   You return to the Printers folder, where a hand is added to the printer icon, as shown in the margin, to show that the printer is now a shared network printer.

To take your shared printer off the network so that other network users can't access it, follow the above procedure through Step 3 to call up the Printer Properties dialog box. Check Do Not Share This Printer, then click OK. The hand disappears from the printer icon to indicate that the printer is no longer shared.

Chapter 5

Mr. McFeeley's Guide to E-mail

. . . .

In This Chapter

▶ Using e-mail

▶ Reading and sending e-mail messages

▶ Scheduling and conferencing electronically

▶ Watching smileys and e-mail etiquette

. . . .

Do you often return to your office after a long lunch to find your desk covered with those little pink "While You Were Out" notes and your computer screen plastered with stick-on notes?

If so, maybe the time has come for you to bite the bullet and find out how to use your computer network's electronic mail, or *e-mail,* program. Most computer networks have one. If yours doesn't, bug the network manager until he or she gets one.

This chapter introduces you to what's possible with a good e-mail program. So many e-mail programs are available that I can't possibly show you how to use all of them, so I'm focusing on Microsoft Outlook, the e-mail program that comes with Microsoft Office. Other e-mail programs are similar.

E-mail and Why It's So Cool

E-mail is nothing more than the computer-age equivalent of Mr. McFeeley, the postman from *Mr. Rogers' Neighborhood.* E-mail enables you to send messages to and receive messages from other users on the network. Instead of writing the messages on paper, sealing them in an envelope, and then giving them to Mr. McFeeley to deliver, e-mail messages are stored on disk and electronically delivered to the appropriate user.

Sending and receiving e-mail

To send an e-mail message to another network user, you must activate the e-mail program, compose the message by using a text editor, and provide an address, which is usually the network user ID of the user that you want the message sent to. Most e-mail programs also require that you create a short comment that identifies the subject of the message.

When you receive a message from another user, the e-mail program copies the message to your computer and then displays it on-screen so you can read it. You can then delete the message, print it, save it to a disk file, or forward it to another user. You can also reply to the message by composing a new message to be sent back to the user who sent the original message.

Here are some additional thoughts about sending and receiving e-mail:

- ✔ When someone sends a message to you, most e-mail programs immediately display a message on your computer screen or make a sound to tell you to check your e-mail. If your computer isn't on the network when the message is sent, then you're notified the next time that you log on to the network.

- ✔ E-mail programs can be set up to check for new e-mail automatically when you log on to the network and periodically throughout the day, say every 10 or 15 minutes.

- ✔ You can easily attach files to your messages. You can use this feature to send a word-processing document, a spreadsheet, or a program file to another network user.

    Be careful about attachments other people send to you. E-mail attachments are how computer viruses are spread. So don't open an attachment you weren't expecting or from someone you don't know.

- ✔ You can keep a list of users that you commonly send e-mail to in an address book. That way you don't have to retype the user ID every time.

- ✔ You can address a message to more than one user — the electronic equivalent of a carbon copy. Some programs also enable you to create a list of users and assign a name to this list. Then you can send a message to each user in the list by addressing the message to the list name. For example, June may create a list including Ward, Wally, and Beaver, and call the list Boys. To send e-mail to all the boys on her family network, she simply addresses the message to Boys.

- ✔ Some e-mail programs can handle your Internet e-mail as well as your LAN e-mail. There are subtle differences between Internet and LAN e-mail, however. LAN email is exchanged with other users on your local

network. To send a message to another user on your network, you just
specify that person's user name. In contrast, you can exchange Internet
e-mail with anyone in the world who has an Internet connection and an
Internet e-mail account. To send Internet e-mail, you must address the
message to the recipient's Internet e-mail address.

Understanding the mail server

E-mail programs rely on a network server computer that is set up as a mail
server, which works kind of like an electronic post office where messages are
stored until they can be delivered to the recipient. A network server that is
used as a mail server doesn't have to be dedicated to this purpose, although
this is sometimes true for larger networks. In smaller networks, a network file
and print server can also act as the mail server.

Here are some details that you should know about mail servers:

✔ Windows 2000 and NetWare come with basic mail server programs that
let you set up an e-mail system for your network. For more advanced
e-mail functions, you can purchase and install a separate mail server,
such as Microsoft Exchange Server. (Unfortunately, the mail server that
comes with Windows 2000 is considerably more difficult to set up and
use than the one that comes with Windows NT.)

✔ Disk space on a mail server is often at a premium. Be sure to delete
unneeded messages after you read them.

✔ Managing the mail server can become one of the most time-consuming
tasks of managing a network. Be prepared to spend time managing user
accounts, fixing broken message folders, and tinkering with various settings and options.

Microsoft Outlook

Because it is a part of Microsoft Office, Microsoft Outlook is one of the most
popular programs for accessing e-mail. Although many other e-mail programs
are available, most of them work much like Outlook for the basic chores of
reading and creating e-mail messages.

Internet Explorer (which comes with Windows) includes a scaled-back version of Outlook called *Outlook Express*. Outlook Express is designed to work
only with e-mail that you send and receive over the Internet, not for e-mail

that you exchange with other users over a local area network. As a result, Outlook Express is generally not used as an e-mail program for network users. (However, if each network user has an Internet connection and an Internet e-mail account, Outlook Express works fine.)

The following sections describe some basic procedures for using Microsoft Outlook to send and receive e-mail.

Sending e-mail

To send an e-mail message to another network user, start Microsoft Outlook by choosing Microsoft Outlook from the Start⇨Programs menu. Outlook appears in its own window, as shown in Figure 5-1.

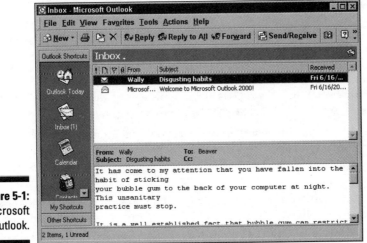

Figure 5-1: Microsoft Outlook.

To create a message to send to another user, click the New Mail Message button. A window appears in which you may type the e-mail address of the recipient (usually the recipient's network user ID), the subject of the message, and then the message itself.

Figure 5-2 shows a message that has been composed and is now ready to be delivered.

After you finish typing the message, click the Send button. The message is delivered to the user listed in the To field.

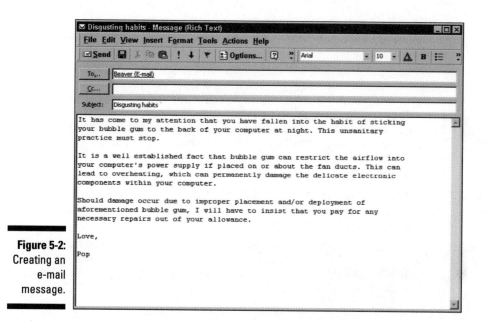

It has come to my attention that you have fallen into the habit of sticking your bubble gum to the back of your computer at night. This unsanitary practice must stop.

It is a well established fact that bubble gum can restrict the airflow into your computer's power supply if placed on or about the fan ducts. This can lead to overheating, which can permanently damage the delicate electronic components within your computer.

Should damage occur due to improper placement and/or deployment of aforementioned bubble gum, I will have to insist that you pay for any necessary repairs out of your allowance.

Love,

Pop

Figure 5-2:
Creating an
e-mail
message.

Here are a few additional points about sending e-mail:

✔ The recipient must run Outlook or another e-mail program on his or her computer to check for incoming e-mail. When the recipient runs his or her e-mail program, your message is delivered.

✔ You can keep a personalized address list using the Address Book, which is available from the Tools menu in Outlook.

✔ You can use Outlook to send e-mail to other users of your local network and to send to and receive e-mail from Internet users. However, a modem or some other type of connection to the Internet is necessary to send e-mail to an Internet e-mail address.

Reading your e-mail

To read e-mail sent to you by other users, simply start Microsoft Outlook by choosing it from the Start➪Programs menu. After you start Outlook, the program automatically checks to see if you have any new e-mail and automatically checks for new messages on a regular basis. Any new messages that you receive appear in the main Outlook window, highlighted with boldface type. In addition, Outlook plays a special sound to inform you whenever you receive new e-mail.

To read a message that has been sent to you, just double-click the message in the Outlook main window. The text of the message appears in a separate window.

After you read the message, you have several options for handling it:

- ✔ If the message is worthy of a reply, click the Reply button. A new message window appears, enabling you to compose a reply. The new message is automatically addressed to the sender of the original message, and the text of the original message is inserted at the bottom of the new message.

- ✔ If the message was addressed to more than one recipient, the Reply to All button lets you send a reply that is addressed to all the recipients listed on the original message.

- ✔ If the message was intended for someone else, or if you think that someone else should see it (maybe it contains a juicy bit of gossip), click the Forward button. A new message window appears, enabling you to type the name of the user that you want the message forwarded to.

- ✔ If you want a hard copy of the message, click the Print button.

- ✔ If the message is unworthy of even filing, click the Delete button. Poof! The message is whisked away to a folder called Deleted Items. (You can use the Edit⇨Empty "Deleted Items" Folder command to permanently delete everything in the Deleted Items folder.)

- ✔ If you have more than one message waiting, you can read the next message in line by clicking the Next button.

Dealing with attachments

An *attachment* is a file that is sent along with an e-mail message. An attachment can be any kind of file: a Word document, a spreadsheet, a program, a database file, or any other type of file.

To send an attachment as part of an outgoing message, just click the Insert File button (which looks like a paper clip) to summon the Insert File dialog box. Then select the file you want to attach and click OK.

If someone sends you e-mail with an attachment, a paper-clip appears next to the message in your Inbox and you see an icon representing the attached file when you read the message. You can open the file by double-clicking the icon. However, before you do so, make sure you know who sent you the attachment and what the attachment is. Attachments are the main way computer viruses are spread, so be suspicious of any unexpected attachments.

To protect your computer (and your network) from e-mail viruses, consider installing an anti-virus program such as Norton AntiVirus (www.symantec.com) or McAfee VirusScan (www.mcafee.com).

E-mail Etiquette

Communicating with someone via e-mail is different from talking with that person face-to-face or over the telephone. You need to be aware of these differences, or you may end up insulting someone without meaning to. Of course, if you do mean to insult someone, pay no attention to this section.

The following paragraphs summarize the salient points of e-mail etiquette:

✓ Always remember that e-mail isn't as private as you'd like it to be. It's not that difficult for someone to electronically steam open your e-mail and read it. So be careful about what you say, to whom you say it, and about whom you say it.

✓ Don't forget that all the rules of social etiquette and office decorum apply to e-mail, too. If you wouldn't pick up the phone and call the CEO of the company, don't send him or her e-mail, either.

✓ When you reply to someone else's e-mail, keep in mind that the person you're replying to may not remember the details of the message that he or she sent to you. Providing some context for your reply is polite. Most e-mail systems (including Outlook) do this for you by automatically tacking on the original message at the end of the reply. If yours doesn't do this, be sure to provide some context, such as including a relevant snippet of the original message in quotation marks, so that the recipient knows what you're talking about.

✓ E-mail doesn't have the advantage of voice inflections. This limitation can lead to all kinds of misunderstandings. You have to make sure that people know when you're joking and when you mean it. E-mail nerds have developed a peculiar way to convey tone of voice: They string together symbols on the computer keyboard to create smileys. Table 5-1 shows some of the more commonly used (or abused) smileys.

Table 5-1	Commonly Used and Abused Smileys
Smiley	*What It Means*
:-)	Just kidding
;-)	Wink

(continued)

Table 5-1 *(continued)*

Smiley	What It Means
: - (	Bummer
: - O	Well, I never!
: - x	My lips are sealed.

✔ If you don't get it, tilt your head to the left and look at the smiley sideways.

✔ E-mail nerds also like to use shorthand abbreviations for common words and phrases, like FYI for "For Your Information" and ASAP for "As Soon As Possible." Table 5-2 lists the more common ones.

Table 5-2   Common E-mail Abbreviations

Abbreviation	What It Stands For
BTW	By the Way
FWIW	For What It's Worth
IMO	In My Opinion
IMHO	In My Humble Opinion
IOW	In Other Words
PMJI	Pardon Me for Jumping In
ROFL	Rolling on the Floor, Laughing
ROFL,PP	Rolling on the Floor Laughing, Peeing My Pants
TIA	Thanks in Advance
TTFN	Ta Ta for Now (quoting Tigger)
TTYL	Talk to You Later
<g>	Grin
<bg>	Big Grin
<vbg>	Very Big Grin

✔ Note that the abbreviations referring to gestures or facial expressions are typed between a less-than sign and a greater-than sign: <g>. Other gestures are spelled out, like <sniff>, <groan>, or <sigh>.

✔ You're not able to italicize or underline text on many e-mail programs (although you can do so in Exchange, Outlook, or Outlook Express). Type an asterisk before and after a word you *wish* you could italicize. Type an underscore _before_ and _after_ a word that you'd like to underline.

✔ Be aware that if you do use italics, underlining, or any other formatting features that are available in Exchange, Outlook, or Outlook Express, the person receiving your mail may not be able to see the formatting if they use a different e-mail program.

✔ Capital letters are the electronic equivalent of SHOUTING. TYPING AN ENTIRE MESSAGE IN CAPITAL LETTERS CAN BE VERY ANNOYING AND CAN CAUSE YOU TO GET THE ELECTRONIC EQUIVALENT OF LARYNGITIS.

✔ Don't be gullible about hoaxes and chain letters. If you receive an e-mail with a warning about some new virus that wipes out your hard drive if you sneeze near your computer or an e-mail that claims that you'll make eleven billion dollars if you forward the message to ten of your best friends, just delete the e-mail. Don't forward it.

✔ Frequently sending e-mail with large attachments can be annoying.

Chapter 6

Help! The Network's Down!

. . . .

. . . .

*F*ace it: Networks are prone to break.

They have just too many "C" parts. Cables. Connectors. Cards. All these parts must be held together in a delicate balance; the network equilibrium is all-too-easy to disturb. Even the best-designed computer networks sometimes act as if they're held together with baling wire, chewing gum, and duct tape.

To make matters worse, networks breed suspicion. After your computer is attached to a network, you're tempted to blame the network every time something goes wrong, regardless of whether the problem has anything to do with the network. You can't get columns to line up in a Word document? Must be the network. Your spreadsheet doesn't add up? The @#$% network's acting up again.

This chapter doesn't even begin to cover everything that can go wrong with a computer network. If it did, you'd take this book back and demand a refund after you got about 40 pages into "Things that can go wrong with IPX.COM."

Instead, this chapter focuses on the most common things that can go wrong with a network that an ordinary network user (that's you) can fix. And best of all, I point you in the right direction when you come up against a problem that you can't fix yourself.

When Bad Things Happen to Good Computers

What do you do when your computer goes on the blink? Here are some general ideas for identifying the problem and deciding whether you can fix it yourself:

1. **Make sure that your computer and everything attached to it is plugged in.**

   Computer geeks love it when a user calls for help and they get to tell the user that the computer isn't plugged in. They write it down in their geek logs so that they can tell their geek friends about it later. They may even want to take your picture so that they can show it to their geek friends. (Most "accidents" involving computer geeks are a direct result of this kind of behavior.)

2. **Make sure that your computer is properly connected to the network.**

3. **Note any error messages that appear on the screen.**

4. **Try the built-in Windows network troubleshooter.**

   For more information, see the section "The Windows Networking Troubleshooter" later in this chapter.

5. **Do a little experimenting to find out whether the problem is indeed a network problem or just a problem with your computer.**

   See the section "Time to Experiment" later in this chapter for some simple things you can do to isolate a network problem.

6. **Try restarting your computer.**

7. **Try restarting the network server.**

   This is something you should attempt only if you know how and only if you are authorized to do so. See the section "How to Restart a Network Server" later in this chapter.

8. **If none of these steps corrects the problem, scream for help.**

   Have a suitable bribe prepared to encourage your network guru to work quickly. (You can find a handy list of suitable bribes at the end of this chapter.)

My Computer's Dead!

If your computer seems totally dead, here are some things to check:

✔ Is it plugged in?

✔ If your computer is plugged into a surge protector or a power strip, make sure that the surge protector or power strip is plugged in and turned on. If the surge protector or power strip has a light, it should be glowing.

✔ Make sure that the computer's On/Off switch is turned on. This sounds too basic to even include here, but many computers are set up so that the computer's actual power switch is always left in the On position and the computer is turned on or off by means of the switch on the surge protector or power strip. Many computer users are surprised to find out that their computers have On/Off switches on the back of the cases.

✔ To complicate matters, newer computers have a Sleep feature, in which they appear to be turned off but really they're just sleeping. All you have to do to wake such a computer is jiggle the mouse a little. (I used to have an uncle like that.) It's easy to assume that the computer is turned off, press the power button, wonder why nothing happened, then press the power button and hold it down, hoping it will take. If you hold down the power button long enough, the computer will actually turn itself off. Then, when you turn the computer back on, you'll get a message saying the computer wasn't shut down properly. Arghhh! The moral of the story is to jiggle the mouse if the computer seems to have nodded off.

✔ If you think your computer isn't plugged in but it looks like it is, listen for the fan. If the fan is turning, the computer is getting power and the problem is more serious than an unplugged power cord. (If the fan isn't running, but the computer is plugged in and power is on, the fan may be out to lunch.)

✔ If the computer is plugged in, turned on, and still not running, plug a lamp into the outlet to make sure that power is getting to the outlet. You may need to reset a tripped circuit breaker or replace a bad surge protector. Or you may need to call the power company. (If you live in California, don't bother calling the power company. It probably won't do any good.)

Surge protectors have a limited life span. After a few years of use, many surge protectors continue to provide electrical power for your computer, but the components that protect your computer from power surges no longer work. If you are using a surge protector that is more than two or three years old, replace the old surge protector with a new one.

✔ The monitor has a separate power cord and switch. Make sure that the monitor is plugged in and turned on. (The monitor actually has two cables that must be plugged in. One runs from the back of the monitor to the back of the computer; the other is a power cord that comes from the back of the monitor and must plug into an electrical outlet.)

✔ Your keyboard, monitor, mouse, and printer are all connected to the back of your computer by cables. Make sure that these cables are all plugged in securely.

✔ Make sure that the other ends of the monitor and printer cables are plugged in properly, too.

✔ Most monitors have knobs that you can use to adjust the contrast and brightness of the monitor's display. If the computer is running but your display is dark, try adjusting these knobs. They may have been turned all the way down.

Ways to Check Your Network Connection

Network gurus often say that 95 percent of all network problems are cable problems. The cable that connects your computer to the rest of the network is a finicky beast. It can break at a moment's notice, and by "break," I don't necessarily mean "to physically break in two." Sure, sometimes the problem with the cable is that Eddie Haskell got to it with pruning shears. But cable problems aren't usually visible to the naked eye.

✔ If your network uses *twisted-pair cable* (the cable that looks something like phone wire and is sometimes called "10baseT," "UTP," or "Cat-5" cable), you can quickly tell whether the cable connection to the network is good by looking at the back of your computer. A small light is near where the cable plugs in. If this light is glowing steadily, the cable is good. If the light is dark or if it's flashing intermittently, you have a cable problem.

   If the light is not glowing steadily, try removing the cable from your computer and reinserting it. This action may cure the weak connection.

✔ Detecting a cable problem in a network that's wired with *coaxial cable,* the kind that looks like cable-TV cable, is more difficult. The connector on the back of the computer forms a T. The base end of the T plugs into your computer. One or two coaxial cables plug into the outer ends of the T. If you use only one coaxial cable, you must use a special plug called a *terminator* instead of a cable at the other end of the T. If you can't find a terminator, try conjuring one up from the twenty-first century. *Warning:* Do not do this if your name happens to be Sarah Connor.

Don't unplug a coaxial cable from the network while the network is running. Data travels around a coaxial network the way the baton travels around the track in a relay race. If one person drops it, the race is over. The baton never gets to the next person. Likewise, if you unplug the network cable from your computer, the network data never gets to the computers that are "down the line" from your computer.

Well, actually, Ethernet — see Chapter 10 — isn't dumb enough to throw in the towel at the first sign of a cable break. You can disconnect the cable for a few seconds without permanently scattering network messages across the galaxy, and you can disconnect the T connector itself from the network card so long as you don't disconnect the cables from the T connector. But don't attempt either action unless you have a good reason and a really good bribe for the network manager, who is sure to find out that you've been playing with the cables.

✔ Some networks are wired so that your computer is connected to the network with a short (six feet or so) patch cable. One end of the patch cable plugs into your computer, and the other end plugs into a cable connector mounted on the wall. Try quickly disconnecting and reconnecting the patch cable. If that doesn't do the trick, try to find a spare patch cable that you can use.

If you can't find a spare patch cable, try borrowing a fellow network user's patch cable. If the problem goes away when you use your neighbor's patch cable, you can assume that your patch cable has gone south and needs to be replaced. The good news is that you can purchase a replacement patch cable from your local computer store for about $15.

✔ If you come in late at night while no one is around, you can swap your bad patch cable with someone else's good cable, and no one will ever know. The next day, that particular neighbor will want to borrow this book from you so that he or she can find out what's wrong with the network. The day after that, someone else will need the book. You may never get your book back. You'd better buy a copy for everyone now.

Notice: Neither the author nor the publisher endorses such selfish behavior. We mention it here only so that you'll know what happened when one day someone down the hall has a network problem, and you suddenly have a network problem the next day.

✔ In some networks, computers are connected to one another via a small box called a *hub*. The hub is prone to cable problems, too — especially those hubs that are wired in a "professional manner" involving a rat's nest of patch cables. Don't touch the rat's nest. Leave problems with the rat's nest to the rat — er, that is, the network guru.

A Bunch of Error Messages Just Flew By!

Did you notice any error messages on your computer screen when you started your computer? If so, write them down. They are invaluable clues that can help the network guru solve the problem.

If you see error messages when you start up your computer, keep the following points in mind:

✔ Don't panic if you see lots of error messages fly by. Sometimes a simple problem that's easy to correct can cause a plethora of error messages when you start your computer. The messages may look as if your computer is falling to pieces, but the fix may be very simple.

✔ If the messages fly by so fast that you can't see them, press your computer's Pause key. Your computer comes to a screeching halt, giving you a chance to catch up on your error-message reading. After you've read enough, press the Pause key again to get things moving. (On some computers, the Pause key is labeled "Hold." On computers that don't have a Pause key, pressing Ctrl+Num Lock or Ctrl+S does the same thing.)

✔ If you missed the error messages the first time, restart your computer and watch them again.

✔ Better yet, press F8 when you see the message Starting Windows. This displays a menu that allows you to select from several startup options, including one that processes each line of your CONFIG.SYS file separately so that you can see the messages displayed by each command before proceeding to the next command.

The Windows Networking Troubleshooter

Windows comes with a built-in troubleshooter that can often help you pin down the cause of a network problem. Figure 6-1 shows the Windows XP version. Answer the questions asked by the troubleshooter and click Next to move from screen to screen. The Networking Troubleshooter can't solve all networking problems, but it does point out the causes of the most common problems.

The procedure for starting the Networking Troubleshooter depends on which version of Windows you are using:

✔ For Windows 98, click the Start button; then choose Help⇨Troubleshooting⇨Windows 98 Troubleshooters, and finally click Networking.

✔ For Windows Me, choose Start⇨Help⇨Troubleshooting⇨Home Networking & Network Problems. Finally, click Home Networking Troubleshooter.

✔ For Windows XP, choose Start⇨Help and Support⇨Networking and the Web⇨Fixing Network or Web problems; then click Home and Small Office Networking Troubleshooter.

Windows 95 also came with a network troubleshooter, but it is not as thorough.

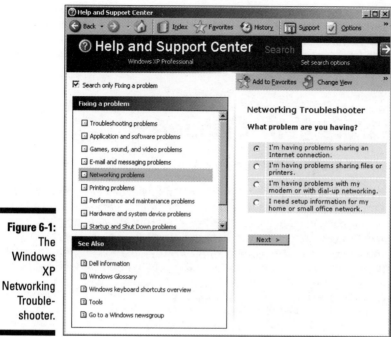

Figure 6-1:
The
Windows
XP
Networking
Trouble-
shooter.

Time to Experiment

If you can't find some obvious explanation for your troubles — like the computer's unplugged — you need to do some experimenting to narrow down the possibilities. Design your experiments to answer one basic question: Is this a network problem or a local computer problem?

Here are some ways you can narrow down the cause of the problem:

✔ Try performing the same operation on someone else's computer. If no one on the network can access a network drive or printer, something is probably wrong with the network. On the other hand, if you're the only one having trouble, the problem is with your computer alone. Your computer may not be reliably communicating with the network or configured properly for the network, or the problem may have nothing to do with the network at all.

✔ If you're able to perform the operation on someone else's computer without problems, try logging on to the network with someone else's computer, using your own user ID. Then see whether you can perform the operation without error. If you can, the problem is probably on your computer rather than on the server computer. Your network guru will want to know.

> ✔ If you can't log on at another computer, try waiting for a bit. Your account may be temporarily locked out. This can happen for a variety of reasons, the most common being trying to log on with the wrong password several times in a row. If you're still locked out an hour later, call the network administrator and offer a doughnut.

How to Restart Your Computer

Sometimes trouble gets your computer so tied up in knots that the only thing you can do is reboot. In some cases, your computer just starts acting weird. Strange characters appear on the screen, or Windows goes haywire and won't let you exit a program. Sometimes your computer gets so confused that it can't even move. It just sits there, like a deer staring at oncoming headlights. It won't move, no matter how hard you press the Esc key or the Enter key. You can move the mouse all over your desktop, or you can even throw it across the room, but the mouse pointer on the screen stays perfectly still.

When your computer starts acting strange, you need to reboot. If you must reboot, you should do so as cleanly as possible. Try the following steps:

1. **Save your work if you can.**

   Use the File⇨Save command, if you can, to save any documents or files that you were editing when things started to go haywire. If you can't use the menus, try clicking the Save button in the toolbar. If that doesn't work, try pressing Ctrl+S — the standard keyboard shortcut for the Save command.

2. **Close any running programs if you can.**

   Use the File⇨Exit command or click the Close button in the upper-right corner of the program window. Or press Alt+F4.

3. **Choose the Start⇨Shut Down command from the taskbar.**

   For Windows XP, choose Start⇨Turn Off Computer.

   The Shut Down Windows dialog box appears.

4. **Select the Restart option and then click OK.**

   Your computer restarts itself.

If restarting your computer doesn't seem to fix the problem, you may need to turn your computer all the way off and then turn it on again. To do so, follow the previous procedure until Step 4. Choose the Shut Down option instead of the Restart option and then click OK. Depending on your computer, Windows either turns off your computer or displays a message that says you can now safely turn off your computer. If Windows doesn't turn the computer off for you, flip the On/Off switch to turn your computer off. Wait a minute or so and then turn the computer back on.

Most newer computers won't immediately shut themselves off when you press the Power button. Instead, you must hold the Power button down for a few seconds to actually turn off the power. This is a precaution designed to prevent you from accidentally powering down your computer.

Here are a few things to try if you have trouble restarting your computer:

✔ If your computer refuses to respond to the Start⇨Shut Down command, try pressing the Ctrl, Alt, and Delete keys at the same time. This is called the "three-finger salute." It's appropriate to say "Queueue" as you do it.

When you press Ctrl+Alt+Delete, Windows 9*x* and later versions attempt to display a dialog box that enables you to close any running programs or shut down your computer entirely. Unfortunately, sometimes Windows 9*x* becomes so confused that it can't display the restart dialog box, in which case pressing Ctrl+Alt+Delete may restart your computer.

✔ If Ctrl+Alt+Delete doesn't do anything, you've reached the last resort. The only thing left to do is press the Reset button on your computer.

Pressing the Reset button is a drastic action that you should take only after your computer becomes completely unresponsive. Any work you haven't yet saved to disk is lost. (Sniff.) (If your computer doesn't have a Reset button, turn the computer off, wait a few moments, and then turn the computer back on again.)

✔ If at all possible, save your work before restarting your computer. Any work you haven't saved is lost. Unfortunately, if your computer is totally tied up in knots, you probably can't save your work. In that case, you have no choice but to push your computer off the digital cliff.

How to Restart a Network Server

If you think the network is causing your trouble, you can restart the network server to see whether the problem goes away.

Restarting a NetWare or Windows 2000 server is not a good idea unless your network administrator has shown you how to do it and has given you permission to do so. If you don't know what you're doing, you may not be able to get the server running again. In that case, you have to tuck your tail between your legs, call the network administrator, and apologize profusely for messing with the network when you know you shouldn't have.

Here is the basic procedure for restarting a network server. Keep in mind that for NetWare or Windows 2000 servers, you may need to take additional steps to get things going again. Check with your network administrator to be sure.

1. **Have all users log off the network.**

   It isn't necessary to make everyone actually turn off their computers. Just have them log off.

2. **After you're sure the users have logged off, shut down the network server.**

   You want to do this behaving like a good citizen if possible — decently and in order. If you use Novell NetWare, type **down** on the server's keyboard and then reboot the server. For Windows NT or Windows 2000 Server, use the Start⇨Shut Down command.

3. **Reboot the server computer or turn it off and then on again. Watch the server start up to make sure that no error messages appear.**

4. **Tell everyone to log back on, and make sure everyone can now access the network.**

Remember the following when you consider restarting the network:

   ✔ Restarting the network server is more drastic than restarting your individual computer. Make sure that everyone saves his or her work and logs off the network before you do it! You can cause major problems if you blindly turn off the server computer while users are logged on.

   ✔ Obviously, restarting the network is a major inconvenience to every network user. Better offer treats.

   ✔ Restarting the network is a job for the network guru. Don't do it yourself unless the network guru isn't around, and even then, do it only after asking his or her permission in writing, preferably in triplicate.

The Care and Feeding of Your Network Guru

Your most valuable asset when something goes wrong with the network is your network guru. If you're careful to stay on good terms with your guru, you're way ahead of the game when you need his or her help.

Make an effort to solve the problem yourself before calling in the cavalry. Check the network connection. Try rebooting. Try using someone else's computer. The more information that you can provide the guru, the more appreciation you get.

Be polite, but assertively tell your guru what the problem is, what you tried to do to fix it, and what you think may be causing the problem (if you have a clue). Say something like this:

"Hi, Joe. I've got a problem with the network: I can't log in from my computer. I tried a few things to try to figure out the problem. I was able to log in from Wally's computer using my user ID, so I think the problem may be just with my computer.

"To be sure, I checked some other things. The green light on the back of my computer where the network cable plugs in is glowing, so I don't think it's a cable problem. I also rebooted my computer, but I still couldn't log on. My guess is that something may be wrong with my computer's network driver, but maybe we should try restarting the server first."

Blow into your guru's ear like that, and he or she will follow you anywhere. (Of course, that may be an undesirable result.)

Here are a few other ways you can be nice to your computer guru, if you are so inclined:

- ✔ Always remember your manners. No one likes to be yelled at, and even computer geeks have feelings (believe it or not). Be polite to your network guru, even if you're mad or you think the problem is his or her fault. This suggestion may sound obvious, but you want your guru to like you.

- ✔ Don't call your guru every time the slightest little thing goes wrong. Computer experts hate explaining that the reason the computer is only printing in capital letters is that you pressed the Caps Lock key.

- ✔ Read the manual. It probably won't help, but at least your guru thinks you tried. Gurus like that.

- ✔ Humor your network guru when he or she tries to explain what's going on. Nod attentively when she describes what the bindery is or when he says something is wrong with the File Allocation Table. Smile appreciatively when she tries to simplify the explanation by using a colorful metaphor. Wink when he thinks that you understand.

- ✔ Mimic your guru's own sense of humor, if you can. For example, most computer geeks like the old *Saturday Night Live* routine with the copier guy. So say something like, "It's Joe, fixin' the network. Crimpin' the cable. Jumpin' Joe, the Net-o-Rama, rentin' an apartment at eight oh two dot three Ethernet Lane. Captain Joe of the Good Ship NetWare, goin' down with the server." Don't worry if it's not funny. He'll think it is.

Computer Bribes for Serious Network Trouble

A *For Dummies* book wouldn't be complete without a bribe list. You probably know already about the common foodstuffs most computer gurus respond to: Cheetos, Doritos, Jolt Cola, Diet Coke (I wish they made Diet Jolt — twice the caffeine, and twice the NutraSweet), Twinkies, and so on.

Bribes of this sort are suitable for small favors. But if you're having a serious problem with your network, you may need to lay it on a bit thicker. More serious bribes include the following:

- ✔ Computer games, especially 3D shoot-em-ups.

- ✔ Videotapes of any Pink Panther, Monty Python, or Mel Brooks movies.

- ✔ T-shirts, hats, or coffee mugs with strange stuff written on them. Shirts, hats, or mugs from computer companies are even better.

- ✔ *Star Trek* paraphernalia. A high percentage of computer gurus are also Trekkies, or as they sometimes prefer to be called, Trekkers. Most of them like the original *Star Trek, The Next Generation,* and *Deep Space Nine.* Most don't care for *Voyager.* And the jury is still out on *Enterprise.*

  If you want to really impress a guru, use the three-letter acronyms for each series: *TOS* for The Original Series, *TNG* for *The Next Generation,* and *DS9* for *Deep Space Nine.* (*VOY* is for *Voyager,* but because nobody likes *Voyager,* it doesn't matter. *Enterprise* is *ENT.*)

- ✔ MP3 files of songs that computer geeks like. Anything by the Monkees will do. At the time I wrote this, the most popular place to get MP3 files was Morpheus (www.morpheus.com).

- ✔ Short films burned onto a CD-ROM are great. Especially things like *Star Wars* parodies. There are a bunch of them on the Internet. Download one, burn it onto a CD, and you'll make an instant friend. (Two good sources for online films are www.ifilm.com and www.movieflix.com.)

Part II
Building Your
Own Network

The 5th Wave — By Rich Tennant

"I guess you could say this is the hub of our network."

In this part . . .

You discover how to build a network yourself, which includes planning it and installing it. And you find out what choices are available for cable types, network operating systems, and all the other bits and pieces that you have to contend with.

Yes, some technical information is included in these chapters. But fear not! I bring you tidings of great joy! Lo, a working network is at hand, and you, yea even you, can design it and install it yourself.

Chapter 7

The Bad News: You Have to Plan Ahead

Okay, so you're convinced that you need to network your computers. What now? Do you stop by Computers-R-Us on the way to work, install the network before morning coffee, and expect the network to be fully operational by noon?

I don't think so.

Networking your computers is just like any other worthwhile endeavor: To do it right requires a bit of planning. This chapter helps you think through your network before you start spending money. It shows you how to come up with a networking plan that's every bit as good as the plan that a network consultant would charge $1,000 for. See? This book is already saving you money!

Making a Network Plan

If you pay a consultant or a company that specializes in network design to study your business and prepare a networking plan, the result is a 500-page proposal with the sole purpose, aside from impressing you with bulk, of preventing you from understanding just exactly what the consultant is proposing.

The truth is, you don't have to be a computer science major to make a good network plan. Despite what computer consultants want you to think, designing a small computer network isn't rocket science. You can do it yourself. Just follow these simple guidelines:

✔ Don't rush through the planning phase. The most costly networking mistakes are the ones that you make before you install the network. Think things through and consider alternatives.

✔ Write down the network plan. The plan doesn't have to be a fancy, 500-page document. (If you want to make it look good, pick up a ½ inch, three-ring binder. The binder is big enough to hold your network plan with room to spare.)

✔ Ask someone else to read your network plan before you buy anything; preferably, ask someone who knows more about computers than you do.

Taking Stock

One of the most challenging parts of planning a network is figuring out how to work with the computers that you already have. In other words, how do you get from here to there? Before you can plan how to get "there," you have to know where "here" is. In other words, you have to take a thorough inventory of your current computers.

What you need to know

You need to know the following information about each of your computers:

✔ **The processor type and, if possible, its clock speed.** Hope that all your computers are 1GHz MHz Pentium 4's or better. But in most cases, you find a mixture of computers, some new, some old, some borrowed, some blue. You might even find a few archaic pre-Pentium computers.

You can't usually tell what kind of processor that a computer has just by looking at the computer's case. Most computers, however, display the processor type when you turn them on or reboot them. If the information on the startup screen scrolls too quickly for you to read it, try pressing the Pause key to freeze the information. After you finish reading it, press the Pause key again so that your computer can continue booting.

✔ **The size of the hard drive and the arrangement of its partitions.** In Windows, you can find out the size of your computer's hard drive by opening the My Computer window, right-clicking the drive icon, and choosing the Properties command from the shortcut menu that appears. Figure 7-1 shows the Properties dialog box for a 24.4GB hard drive that has 4.06GB of free space.

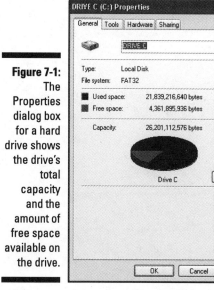

Figure 7-1:
The
Properties
dialog box
for a hard
drive shows
the drive's
total
capacity
and the
amount of
free space
available on
the drive.

If your computer has more than one hard drive, Windows lists an icon for each drive in the My Computer window. Jot down the size and amount of free space available on each of the drives.

✔ **The amount of memory.** In Windows, you can find out this information easily enough by right-clicking the My Computer desktop icon and choosing the Properties command. The amount of memory on your computer appears in the dialog box that appears. For example, Figure 7-2 shows the System Properties dialog box for a computer running Windows XP Professional with 256MB of RAM.

✔ **The operating system version.** If you are running Windows 95 or later, you can determine the version by checking the System Properties dialog box. For example, Figure 7-2 shows the System Properties dialog box for a computer running Windows XP Professional.

✔ **What kind of printer, if any, is attached to the computer.** Usually, you can tell just by looking at the printer. You can also tell by examining the Printers and Faxes folder (in Windows XP, choose Start➪Control Panel and then double-click Printers and Faxes).

✔ **What software is used on the computer.** Microsoft Office? WordPerfect? Lotus 1-2-3? Make a complete list, and include version numbers.

✔ **Any other devices connected to the computer.** A CD, DVD, or CD-RW drive? Scanner? Zip or Jazz drive? Tape drive? Video camera? Battle droid? Hot tub?

Figure 7-2:
The System
Properties
dialog box
for a
computer
running
Windows
XP
Professional
with 256MB
of RAM.

Programs that gather information for you

Gathering information about your computers is a lot of work if you have more than a few computers to network. Fortunately, several available software programs can automatically gather the information for you. These programs inspect various aspects of a computer, such as the CPU type and speed, amount of RAM, and the size of the computer's hard drives. Then they show the information on the screen and give you the option of saving the information to a hard drive file or printing it.

Windows comes with just such a program, which is called Microsoft System Information. Microsoft System Information gathers and prints information about your computer. You can start Microsoft System Information by choosing Start⇨Programs⇨Accessories⇨System Tools⇨System Information.

When you fire up Microsoft System Information, you see a window similar to the one shown in Figure 7-3. Initially, Microsoft System Information displays basic information about your computer, such as your version of Microsoft Windows, the processor type, the amount of memory on the computer, and the free space on each of the computer's hard drives. You can obtain information that is more detailed by clicking Hardware Resources, Components, Software Environment, or Applications in the left side of the window.

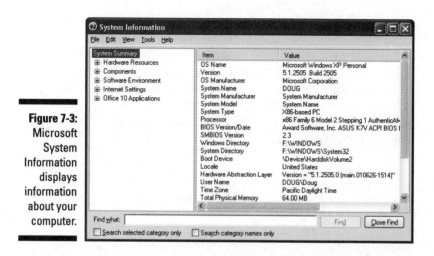

Figure 7-3: Microsoft System Information displays information about your computer.

If you have Windows 95, don't panic. You may have Microsoft System Information anyway: Microsoft includes it with Office. To start Microsoft System Information from any of the Office programs (Word, Excel, or PowerPoint), choose the Help⇨About command. When the About dialog box appears, click the System Info button.

Considering Why You Need a Network, Anyway

An important step in planning your network is making sure that you understand why you want the network in the first place. Here are some of the more common reasons for needing a network, all of them quite valid:

- ✔ My coworker and I exchange files using a floppy disk just about every day. With a network, we could trade files without using the floppies.

- ✔ I don't want to buy everyone a laser printer when I know the one we have now just sits there taking up space most of the day. So wouldn't buying a network be better than buying a laser printer for every computer?

- ✔ I want to provide an Internet connection for all of your computers. There are many networks, especially smaller ones, that exist solely for the purpose of sharing an Internet connection.

> ✔ Someone figured out that we're destroying seven trees a day by printing interoffice memos on paper, so we want to save the rainforest by setting up an e-mail system.
>
> ✔ Business is so good that one person typing in orders eight hours each day can't keep up. With a network, I can have two people entering orders, and I won't have to pay either one overtime.
>
> ✔ My brother-in-law just put in a network at his office, and I don't want him to think I'm behind the times.

Make sure that you identify all the reasons why you think you need a network, and then write them down. Don't worry about winning the Pulitzer Prize for your stunning prose. Just make sure that you write down what you expect a network to do for you.

If you were making a 500-page networking proposal, you'd place the description of why a network is needed in a tabbed section labeled "Justification." In your ½ inch network binder, file the description under "Why."

As you consider the reasons why you need a network, you may conclude that you don't need a network after all. That's okay. You can always use the binder for your stamp collection.

Making Three Basic Network Decisions That You Can't Avoid

When you plan a computer network, you're confronted with three inescapable network decisions. You can't install the network until you make these decisions. The decisions are weighty enough that I devote a separate section in this chapter to each one.

I haven't introduced a new TLA (three-letter acronym) in a while, so I call these basic network decisions *BNDs,* which stands for — you guessed it — "basic network decisions."

Do you need a dedicated server computer?

If the only reason for your network is to share a printer and exchange an occasional file, you may not need a dedicated server computer. In that case, you can create a peer-to-peer network using the computers you already have. However, all but the smallest networks benefit from having a separate, dedicated server computer.

✔ Using a dedicated server computer makes the network faster, easier to work with, and more reliable. Consider what happens when the user of a server computer, which doubles as a workstation, decides to turn the computer off, not realizing that someone else is accessing files on his or her hard drive.

✔ You don't necessarily have to use your biggest and fastest computer as your server computer. I've seen networks where the slowest computer on the network is the server. This is especially true when the server is mostly used to share a printer. So if you need to buy a computer for your network, consider promoting one of your older computers to be the server and using the new computer as a client.

✔ When you plan your server configuration, you must also plan how your data and program files will be dispersed on the network. For example, will all users have copies of Microsoft Office on their local drives, or will one copy of Office be stored on the server drive? (Within the limits of your software license, of course.)

✔ Planning your server configuration also means planning which folders will be shared and how security will be set up.

✔ Server configuration is heady enough to merit its own chapter: Chapter 9.

If you need a dedicated server, what operating system should it use?

You have many network operating systems from which to choose, but from a practical point of view, your choices are limited to the following:

✔ Windows 2000 Server, which is probably the most popular choice. Windows 2000 Server is a special version of Windows that is specially optimized to run efficiently as a network server. One of the benefits of Windows 2000 Server is that because it is actually a version of Windows, you can use it to run Windows software such as Microsoft Office.

✔ Novell NetWare, which was once the most popular server computer operating system. NetWare requires that you dedicate at least one computer to act as a network server, and it can be a challenge for a novice user to install. Because NetWare is not a version of Windows, it cannot run Windows software. NetWare may be a better choice if your network consists of older client computers that still run DOS.

✔ Linux, which is an inexpensive of the popular Unix operating system. Linux is sometimes the best choice if you plan on using the server to host an Internet Web site, because many of the most popular Web server tools are designed to run on Linux.

✔ If you don't want to dedicate a computer to function as a server, you can build the entire network using Windows 95, 98, Windows Me, Windows XP, or Windows 2000 Professional on your client computers.

✔ You can start with a simple peer-to-peer network using Windows 95/98, Windows Me, Windows XP, or Windows 2000 Professional now and then upgrade to NetWare or Windows NT/2000 Server later. All the networks listed in this section use the same cable, network interface cards, hubs, and so on. Changing from one to another is a matter of reconfiguring the software. (Of course, to change from a peer-to-peer network to NetWare or Windows NT/2000 Server, you must have a dedicated server computer.)

✔ If the server computer is an older computer — say, a first generation Pentium — you may want to consider Linux or Netware. These operating systems tend to run more efficiently than Windows on slower computers.

✔ Chapter 8 describes the advantages and disadvantages of each of these systems so that you can decide which is the best choice for your network.

How should you connect the computers?

The third basic networking decision is how to connect your computers.

✔ The most popular way to cable your network is to use twisted-pair cable, also known as UTP cable. An alternative is to use coaxial cable, also known as thinnet cable. However, UTP is easier to install, easier to fix if something should go wrong, and allows for faster transfer speeds. Because of these advantages, I recommend you use UTP for all new networks. (For information about the differences between UTP and thinnet cable, refer to Chapter 1.)

✔ You must also pick the network interface cards to install into each computer. Using the same card in each computer is best, although you can also mix and match them. The card that you select must be compatible with the cable you select. For example, if you opt to use twisted-pair cable, make sure all of your network cards work with twisted-pair cable.

✔ If you use twisted-pair cable, you also need one or more network hubs.

✔ You have to decide where and how to route the cable so that it reaches each of the computers that you need to network, what type of wall jacks to use, and how to manage the cables where they come together at the network hubs. As you plan the cabling, you need to draw a floor plan showing the location of each computer and the route of the cables.

✔ If drilling holes through the walls is not an option, you may opt to use a wireless network instead. For more information, see Chapter 20.

✔ I give you the gory details of network cabling in Chapter 10.

Using a Network Starter Kit — Networks to Go

For me, one of the most fun parts of building a network is going to my local computer store and filling a shopping cart full of stuff. I love to wander the aisles and pick out a network switch, network interface cards, cables, connectors, a case of Diet Coke, and other goodies.

If shopping isn't your bag, you can buy in a single box all the pieces you need to network two or three computers. A typical network starter kit for two computers includes two Ethernet network interface cards, a small hub, two twisted pair cables with connectors already attached (so that you can connect both computers to the hub), and instructions for hooking everything up. A kit of this sort costs between $75 and $250, depending on where you purchase it, who manufactures the individual components in the kit, and the capacity of the hub.

The starter kit accommodates the first two computers in your network. For each additional computer that you want to connect, you need to purchase an add-on kit that contains a network interface card and a cable.

Here are a couple of additional points to ponder concerning network starter kits:

✔ The cable that comes with the starter kit is generally 25 feet long. This is usually enough cable to connect computers that are located in the same room. If the computers are in separate rooms, you probably need additional network cable.

✔ The hub that comes with twisted-pair starter kits usually has ports for connecting as many as four or five computers. If you know you need to network more than that, you should probably purchase the hub and other network components separately.

Looking at a Sample Network Plan

Consider a typical family business: Cleavers' Baseball Card Emporium, which buys and sells valuable as well as worthless baseball cards and other baseball memorabilia.

The Cleavers' computer inventory

The Cleavers have four computers:

- ✔ Ward's computer is a brand-new 2 MHz Pentium 4 with 512MB of RAM and an 80GB hard drive. Ward runs Microsoft Windows XP Professional and Office XP for spreadsheet analysis (Excel) and occasional word processing (Word). He also has a high-speed laser printer.

- ✔ June's computer is an older 1.2GHz MHz Pentium 4 with 128MB of RAM and an 20GB hard drive. June runs Windows 98 Second Edition and does most of the company's word processing with an old version of Word for Windows. She has a little inkjet printer that she bought at a garage sale for $20, but it doesn't work well, so she would like to use Ward's laser printer to print letters.

- ✔ Wally's computer is a 486 with 4MB of RAM, a 300MB hard drive, and Windows 3.1.

- ✔ The Beaver has a 700MHz Pentium III computer with 64MB of RAM, a 12GB hard drive, and a built-in Ethernet port. The computer originally belonged to Eddie Haskell, but Beave traded a Joe DiMaggio, a Barry Bonds, and a Sammy Sosa for it. The Beaver keeps the company's inventory records on his computer by using a database program that he created himself using Java.

Why the Cleavers need a network

The Cleavers want to network their computers for three simple reasons:

- ✔ So that everyone can access the laser printer.
- ✔ So that everyone can access the inventory database.
- ✔ So that everyone can access the Internet via a high-speed cable connection.

Without the second and third reason, the Cleavers wouldn't need a network. They can share the laser printer by purchasing a simple printer-sharing switch that would enable all four computers to access the printer (see the sidebar "Stupid stuff about printer switches"). But to give everyone access to the inventory database or to share an Internet connection requires a network.

The network operating system

The Cleavers aren't computer whizzes, so they opt for a simple peer-to-peer network operating system based on Windows. This network operating system enables them to share the printer and the hard drive containing the inventory database — so it adequately meets their needs.

After Ward decides that a Windows network is the way to go, he realizes that Wally's computer just won't cut the mustard. Ward considered upgrading Wally's computer by adding more memory, but he decided instead to sell the computer at a garage sale (he hopes to get $10) and buy Wally a brand new laptop computer that runs Windows XP.

The server configuration

Because the Cleavers can't afford a separate computer to use as a server, two of the computers do double duty as both clients and servers. Ward's computer is set up as a client/server so that everyone can access his printer, and the Beaver's computer is set up as a client/server so that everyone can access the inventory database.

Stupid stuff about printer switches

If your only reason for networking is to share a printer, there may be a cheaper way: Buy a switch box instead of a network. Switch boxes let two or more computers share a single printer. Instead of running a cable directly from one computer to the printer, you run cables from each computer to the switch box and then run one cable from the switch box to the printer. Only one of the computers has access to the printer at a time; the switch decides which one.

You can find two kinds of printer switches:

✔ **Manual printer switches:** These have a knob on the front that enables you to select which computer is connected to the printer. When you use a manual switch, you first must make sure that the knob is set to your computer before you try to print. Turning the knob while someone else is printing probably will cost you a bag of doughnuts.

✔ **Automatic printer switches:** These have a built-in electronic ear that listens to each computer. When it hears one of the computers trying to talk to the printer, the electronic ear automatically connects that computer to the printer. The switch also has an electronic holding pen called a *buffer* that can hold printer output from one computer if another computer is using the printer. Automatic switches aren't foolproof, but they work most of the time.

Naturally, a good automatic switch costs more than a manual switch. For example, a manual switch that can enable four computers to share one printer costs about $20. A decent automatic switch to enable four computers to share a printer can set you back about $75. Still, that's a lot cheaper and easier to set up than a full-blown network.

After the network is up and running, Ward considers moving the inventory database from the Beaver's computer to his own computer. That way, only one server computer has to be managed. Because Ward doesn't use his computer often, he probably won't mind the small reduction in performance as other users access his hard drive. (Of course, because Ward is both company CEO and the head of the household, he won't consider trading his high-powered computer with June, who uses her computer six or seven hours every day. Sigh.)

Network cabling

For simplicity's sake, the Cleavers opt to wire their network with twisted-pair cable. Three of the four computers are located in the spacious den, so the floor plan presents no unusual wiring problems. The hub can be placed on a desk next to any of the four computers.

Fortunately, only three of the computers need networking cards, because Beaver's computer has a built-in network port. To simplify shopping, the Cleavers decide to purchase a network starter kit for Ward's and June's computer.

For Wally's brand new laptop, the Cleavers decide to go wireless so that Wally can use the laptop from anywhere in the house. So they purchase a wireless networking card for the laptop and a gadget called a *wireless access point* to connect the laptop to the network. The wireless access point happens to double as a four-port hub and an Internet firewall router that will enable them to share their Internet connection.

After the Cleavers get everything up and running, they'll be able to share the printer, the database, and the Internet connection with ease.

Chapter 8

Choosing Your Weapon (Or, Which Server Operating System Should You Use?)

In This Chapter

▶ Considering Novell NetWare

▶ Considering Windows NT Server and Windows 2000 Server

▶ Considering other server operating systems, including OS/2, UNIX, Linux, and the Mac OS X Server

▶ Considering peer-to-peer networking with Windows

*O*ne of the basic choices that you must make before you go too far is to decide which network operating system to use as the foundation for your network. This chapter provides an overview of the advantages and disadvantages of the most popular network operating systems.

Microsoft's Server Operating Systems

Microsoft currently supports two versions of its flagship server operating system: Windows NT Server 4 and Windows 2000 Server. Windows 2000 Server is the newer and more advanced version. Although Microsoft still supports Windows NT Server 4, it no longer sells this operating system. Still, there are plenty of networks chugging along just fine with NT.

As this book went to press, Microsoft was preparing a new version to be called Windows .NET Server. For the time being, however, Windows 2000 Server is the top of the line.

NTFS drives

NT Server can use hard drives that are formatted in the same way as standard Windows and MS-DOS drives. (The technical term for this type of drive formatting is *FAT,* which stands for File Allocation Table.) But for better performance, Windows NT Server enables you to format your hard drives using a different type of disk format, called *NTFS* (for NT File System). NTFS drives have the following advantages over FAT drives:

✔ NTFS drives can be larger than FAT drives. FAT uses 32-bit disk addresses, which means that the largest hard drive can be 4GB. NTFS uses 64-bit disk addresses, which can theoretically support drives that are several million times larger than the biggest drives made today.

✔ NTFS is much more efficient at using the space on your hard drive. As a result, NTFS can cram more data onto a given hard drive than FAT.

✔ NTFS drives provide better security features than FAT drives. NTFS stores security information on disk for each file and directory. In contrast, FAT has only rudimentary security features.

✔ NTFS drives are more reliable because NTFS keeps duplicate copies of important information, such as the location of each file on the hard drive. If a problem develops on an NTFS drive, Windows NT Server can probably correct the problem without losing any data. In contrast, FAT drives are prone to losing information.

Windows NT 4 Server

Windows NT Server 4 sports the same user interface as Windows 95, so if you already know your way around Windows 95, NT Server 4 will seem familiar. Unlike Windows 95, however, NT Server 4 includes a number of advanced networking features that make it suitable for use as a network server for small or large networks.

Windows NT Server 4 comes with a bunch of free Internet tools. These tools enable you to connect to the Internet and set up your own Internet Web site. In addition, you can use the Internet tools to set up an Intranet, which is simply a Web site that can be accessed only from the computers that are on your LAN.

Here's a summary of the more pertinent features of NT:

✔ The server processor must be at least a 486, with at least 16MB of memory. Yeah, right. I wouldn't use it on anything smaller than a 200MHz Pentium with 64MB of RAM.

✔ Some of the file-system limits are

- Max number of users: unlimited

- Number of disk volumes: 25

- Max size of a volume: 17,000GB

- Max hard drive space for server: 408,000GB

- Largest file: 17 billion GB (Wow! That's more than the maximum hard drive space for a server, which is impossible!)

- Max amount of RAM in server: 4GB

- Max number of open files: unlimited

Windows 2000 Server

The most current server operating system from Microsoft is Windows 2000 Server. Windows 2000 Server builds on the strengths of Windows NT Server 4, adding new features that make Windows 2000 Server faster, easier to manage, more reliable, and easier to use for large and small networks alike.

The most significant new feature of Windows 2000 Server is called *Active Directory,* which provides a single directory of all network resources and enables program developers to incorporate the directory into their programs. Active Directory integrates various directory services, such as Novell's NDS and NT's own directory services, and enables you to manage all the directory information on your network using a single interface that resembles the Internet's World Wide Web.

Windows 2000 Server comes in three versions:

✔ **Windows 2000 Server** is the basic server, designed for small- to medium-sized networks. It includes all the basic server features, including file and print sharing, and acts as an Internet Web and e-mail server.

✔ **Windows 2000 Advanced Server** is the next step up, designed for larger networks. Advanced Server can support server computers that have up to 8GB of memory (not hard drive — RAM!) and four integrated processors instead of the single processor that desktop computers and most server computers have.

✔ **Windows 2000 Datacenter Server** is Microsoft's most ambitious operating system yet. It can support servers that have as many as 32 processors with up to 64GB of RAM and is specially designed for large database applications. (As this book went to press, Windows 2000 Datacenter Server was not yet released but was expected within a few months.)

What's ahead for Windows .NET Server

As this book went to press, Microsoft was nearing the final stages of development for a new breed of Windows servers, dubbed Windows .NET Server (.NET is pronounced *dot-net*.) Windows .NET Server will build on Windows 2000 Server, with the following added features:

✔ A new and improved version of Active Directory with tighter security, an easier to use interface, and better performance.

✔ A major change in the way Windows programs operate, known as the .NET Framework.

✔ Support for ever-larger clusters of computers. A *cluster* is a set of computers that work together as if they were a single server. Previous versions supported clusters of four servers; Windows .NET Server will support clusters of eight servers. (Obviously, this is a benefit only for very large networks. The rest of us should just grin and say, "Cool!")

✔ An enhanced Distributed File System that lets you combine drives on several servers to create one shared volume.

✔ A built-in Internet firewall to secure your Internet connection.

For small networks with 50 or fewer computers, Microsoft offers a special bundle called the Small Business Server, which includes the following components for one low, low price:

✔ Windows 2000 Server, the operating system for your network server.

✔ Exchange Server 2000, for e-mail and messaging.

✔ Internet Security and Acceleration Server 2000, which provides improved security and performance for your Web applications

✔ SQL Server 2000, a database server

✔ FrontPage 2000, for building Web sites

✔ Outlook 2000, for reading e-mail

Novell NetWare

NetWare is one of the most popular network operating systems, especially for large networks. NetWare has an excellent reputation for reliability. In fact, some network administrators swear they have NetWare servers on their networks that have been running continuously, without a single reboot, since Teddy Roosevelt was president.

Novell currently sells two versions of NetWare: 5.1 and 6. NetWare 6, the latest and greatest version, is naturally the better and more expensive of the two. It sports a number of advanced features that make it suitable for larger networks. NetWare 5.1 is suitable for smaller networks but can also be used in larger networks.

What's so great about NetWare?

Throughout this book, I pound NetWare a bit for being overly complicated. However, a lot can be said in favor of NetWare. NetWare can be complicated to set up and administer, but it's still the most popular network operating system in use. There must be something good to say about it! So here goes:

- When Novell set out to design NetWare way back in the 1980s, the company recognized that the old DOS operating system just didn't cut it for networking. Rather than live with the limitations of DOS, Novell decided to bypass DOS altogether. NetWare file servers don't run DOS or Windows; instead, NetWare itself is the operating system for the file server. This frees NetWare from the many built-in limitations of DOS and Windows.

- Because NetWare servers don't run DOS or Windows, NetWare servers must be dedicated servers. In other words, you can't have a NetWare server double as a user's workstation. This setup costs more because you must purchase a separate server computer. However, the arrangement is more efficient because the server computer can concentrate on servicing the network.

- Clients on a NetWare network can include computers running DOS, Windows, OS/2, or the Mac OS. If you have a mix of PCs and Macintoshes, NetWare may be your best choice.

- The NetWare file server uses a more efficient structure for organizing files and directories than DOS or Windows.

- All versions of NetWare provide features for System Fault Tolerance (SFT), which keeps the network running even if a hardware failure occurs.

- NetWare is very reliable and stable. Although NetWare can be difficult to set up, after you get a NetWare server up and running and configured the way you want, the server will pretty much take care of itself with little maintenance.

NetWare 5.1

Although not the latest version, Novell still sells NetWare 5.1 for use on smaller networks. Here are just a few of the key features of NetWare 5.1:

- ✔ Web-based administration, which means you can administer your NetWare server from any computer on the network.
- ✔ Excellent support for TCP/IP, the networking protocol used for the Internet.
- ✔ Advanced operating system features, such as memory protection, virtual memory, and better multiprocessor support — up to 32 processors in a single server. (If you don't know what any of that means, count your blessings.)
- ✔ Files can be as large as 8 terabytes (that's 8,000GB), and NetWare 5 can support billions of files on a single hard drive.

A NetWare 5.1 server requires at least a Pentium processor, 128MB of RAM, and 1.3MB of free hard drive space. You probably want an even more powerful computer than that for your NetWare 5.1 server. Here's a recommended minimum configuration:

- ✔ 500MHz Pentium II processor
- ✔ 256MB RAM
- ✔ 10GB free hard drive space

Note that the 10GB disk space recommendation is just to hold the operating system. You'll need considerably more disk space for your users to store their files.

I don't get a penny for promoting *Networking With NetWare For Dummies*

If you think NetWare is the networking system for you, be sure to get a copy of *Networking With NetWare For Dummies*, 4th Edition, by Ed Tittel, James E. Gaskin, and Earl Follis (Wiley Publishing Inc.). This is a great book that shows you how to install, use, and manage your network and keep your sanity.

I thought I should get, like, a two percent commission or something for promoting *Networking With NetWare For Dummies*, 4th Edition, here, but no such luck. Bummer. Get the book anyway.

Do you have the savvy to install NetWare?

How do you know if you have what it takes to contend with NetWare? Try this little self-test. If you know all (or most) of the answers to these questions, you probably have enough computer savvy to figure out NetWare. If you don't, don't feel bad. As the Good Book says (sort of), "Some are prophets, some are evangelists, some are teachers, some are NetWare administrators, some are computer Dummies. . . ."

1. What command would you use to copy all the files, including files in subdirectories, from drive A to the current directory?

   A.   FDISK

   B.   DELETE A:*.*

   C.   FORMAT C:

   D.   XCOPY A:*.* /S

2. Which of these files is processed every time you start your computer?

   A.   LETSGETGOING.BAT

   B.   GETUPYOULITTLESLEEPYHEAD.COM

   C.   COMEBACKTOMORROW.BAT

   D.   AUTOEXEC.BAT

3. Which of the following bribes are appropriate when enlisting the help of a computer guru?

   A.   Cheetos

   B.   Doritos

   C.   Doughnuts

   D.   All of the above

4. Who is the most dangerous man in all of France?

   A.   Jacques Cousteau

   B.   Marcel Marceau

   C.   Big Bird

   D.   Chief Inspector Jacques Clouseau

If you answered D to three or more of these questions, you probably have the savvy to install NetWare yourself, unless the question you missed was #3, in which case you don't have a prayer.

NetWare 6

The latest and greatest version of NetWare is version 6. NetWare 6 is designed for larger networks than NetWare 5.1. Although you could use it for a small networks, it provides far more networking features than you'd probably need.

Here are a few of the most important new features of NetWare 6:

✔ An improved disk management system called Novell Storage Services that can manage billions of files on a single volume. Whether storing billions of files on a single volume is a good idea is a separate question; if you decide to do it, NetWare 6 will let you.

✔ Web-based access to network folders and printers.

✔ Built-in support for Windows, Linux, Unix, and Macintosh file systems so you can access data on the server from these operating systems without installing special client software.

✔ Folder, a cool feature that automatically keeps your files synchronized between your work computer and your home computer or a traveling laptop computer.

NetWare 6 is also available in a special Small Business edition, which includes the basic NetWare 6 operating system plus a collection of goodies designed to make networking easier for small businesses. Among the extras you get with NetWare for Small Business are the following:

✔ GroupWise 6, an e-mail and group scheduling program that is similar to Microsoft Outlook and Exchange.

✔ ZENWorks, a tool for managing software and hardware on your network.

✔ BorderManager, a suite of security programs for safeguarding your network's Internet access

✔ A basketful of programs for accessing the Internet and creating a Web server

Other Server Operating Systems

Although NetWare and Windows NT/2000 Server are the most popular choices for network operating systems, they're not the only available choices. The following sections briefly describe two other server choices: Linux and the Macintosh OS/X Server.

Linux

Perhaps the most interesting operating system available today is Linux. Linux is a free operating system that is based on UNIX, a powerful network operating system often used on large networks. Linux was started by Linus Torvalds, who thought it would be fun to write a version of UNIX in his free time — as a hobby. He enlisted help from hundreds of programmers throughout the world, who volunteered their time and efforts via the Internet. Today, Linux is a full-featured version of UNIX; its users consider it to be as good or better than Windows. In fact, almost as many people now use Linux as use Macintosh computers.

Linux offers the same networking benefits of UNIX and can be an excellent choice as a server operating system. For more information, see Chapter 25.

Apple Mac OS X Server

All the other server operating systems I describe in this chapter run on Intel-based PCs with Pentium or Pentium-compatible processors. But what about Macintosh computers? After all, Macintosh users need networks, too. For Macintosh networks, Apple offers a special network server operating system known as Mac OS X server. Mac OS X Server has all the features you'd expect in a server operating system: file and printer sharing, Internet features, e-mail, and so on. For more information, refer to Chapter 24.

Peer-to-Peer Networking with Windows

If you're not up to the complexity of NetWare or Windows 2000, you may want to opt for a simple peer-to-peer network based on Windows.

Advantages of peer-to-peer networks

The main advantage of a peer-to-peer network is that it is easier to set up and use than a NetWare or NT/2000 network, mainly because peer-to-peer relies on the networking features that are built into Windows. After you install Windows on a computer, all you have to do is adjust a few configuration settings to get your network up and running.

Another advantage of peer-to-peer networks is that they can be less expensive than server-based networks. Here are some of the reasons that peer-to-peer networks are inexpensive:

✔ Peer-to-peer networks don't require you to use a dedicated server computer. Any computer on the network can function as both a network server and a user's workstation. (However, you can configure a computer as a dedicated server if you want to. Doing so results in better performance but negates the cost benefit of not having a dedicated server computer.)

✔ Peer-to-peer networks are easier to set up and use, which means that you can spend less time figuring out how to make the network work and keep it working. And, as Einstein proved, time is money (hence his famous equation, $E=M\$^2$).

✔ Then there's the cost of the server operating system itself. Both NetWare and Windows 2000 Server can cost as much as $200 per user. And the total cost increases as your network grows larger, although the cost per user drops. For a peer-to-peer Windows server, you pay for Windows once. There are no additional charges based on the number of users on your network.

Drawbacks of peer-to-peer networks

Yes, peer-to-peer networks are easier to install and manage than NetWare or NT, but they do have their drawbacks:

✔ Because peer-to-peer networks are Windows-based, they're subject to the inherent limitations of Windows. Windows is designed primarily to be an operating system for a single-user, desktop computer rather than function as part of a network, so Windows can't manage a file or printer server as efficiently as a real network operating system.

✔ If you don't set up a dedicated network server, someone (hopefully, not you) may have to live with the inconvenience of sharing his or her computer with the network. With NetWare or NT/2000 Server, the server computers are dedicated to network use so that no one has to put up with this inconvenience.

✔ Although a peer-to-peer network may have a lower cost per computer for smaller networks, the cost difference between peer-to-peer networks and NetWare or NT/2000 is less significant in larger networks (say, 20 or more clients).

✔ Peer-to-peer networks do not work well when your network starts to grow. Peer-to-peer servers just don't have the security or performance features required for a growing network.

Windows XP

Windows XP is the latest and greatest version of Windows. Windows XP comes in two flavors: Home Edition and Professional Edition. As its name suggests, the Home Edition is designed for home users. It includes great multimedia features such as a home movie editor called Windows Movie Maker and built-in support for CD-ROM burners, scanners, video cameras, and many other features. Windows XP Professional Edition is designed for users with more demanding network needs.

The best thing about Windows XP is that it uses what techno-gurus like to call the 32-bit Windows NT/2000 code base rather than the old 16-bit Windows 95 code base. As a result, Windows XP is faster and more reliable than Windows 95, 98, or Me. If you ask me, I wouldn't give two bits for a 16-bit operating system.

Windows 2000 Professional

Windows 2000 also comes in a desktop version, known as Windows 2000 Professional. Windows 2000 Pro incorporates the Windows 98 User Interface, so it's even easier to use than Windows NT 4 Workstation.

One of the main advantages of using Windows 2000 Professional as a peer-to-peer network server is the Windows 2000 security system. Windows 2000 Pro lets you implement user-based security rather than share-based security. In other words, with Windows 2000 Pro, you can set up user accounts that require users to log on to access the network. (Windows XP also lets you use the Windows 2000 security system.)

Chapter 9

Planning Your Servers

*O*ne of the key decisions you must make when networking your computers is how you make use of server computers. Even if you use a peer-to-peer network system, such as Windows XP, you must still deal with the question of servers.

This chapter helps you to make the best use of your network server, first by convincing you to use a dedicated server if possible and then by suggesting ways to use the server efficiently.

To Dedicate or Not to Dedicate

In case you haven't noticed, I'm a big believer in dedicated server computers, even if you use a peer-to-peer network. Yes, one of the strengths of a simple Windows peer-to-peer network is that you can use any computer on the network as both a server computer and a user's workstation. Does that mean you should make every computer a server? No way.

You give up a lot when your desktop computer doubles as a network server:

✔ Every time someone accesses data on your hard drive, your own work is temporarily suspended. If the data on your hard drive is popular, you become annoyed with the frequent delays.

✔ You lose the sense of privacy that comes with having your own computer. Remember that nasty memo about your boss? You'd better not leave it lying around on your hard drive . . . someone else may lift it off the network.

TIP

You can set up your hard drive so that you have some private space where other users can't snoop about. But make sure that you set it up right and remember to store confidential files in private space. And make sure that you know more about the networking software than anyone else in the office. Someone who knows more about networking than you do can probably figure out a way to thwart your security measures.

✔ You lose the independence of having your own computer. You have to leave your computer on all day even when you're not using it because someone else may be. Do you want to turn off your computer because the noise it makes interrupts your afternoon nap? You can't. Do you want to delete some unnecessary files to free up some hard drive space? You can't — at least, not if the files don't belong to you.

✔ Your computer isn't immune to damage caused by other network users. What if someone accidentally deletes an important file on your hard drive? What if someone copies a 100MB file onto your hard drive while you aren't looking, so that no free space is available when you try saving the spreadsheet that you've been working on all afternoon? Or what if someone infects your hard drive with a virus?

I hope that you're convinced. If you can at all afford it, set aside a computer for use as a dedicated server. Beg, borrow, or steal a computer if you must.

Here are a few other thoughts to consider about using dedicated servers:

✔ Peer-to-peer networks enable you to adjust certain configuration options for network servers. If you use a computer as both a server and a client, you must balance these options so that they provide reasonable performance for both server and client functions. But if you dedicate the computer as a server, you can skew these options in favor of the server functions. In other words, you're free to tweak the server's configuration for peak network performance. You can find details for doing this in Chapter 14.

✔ As a general rule, try to limit the number of servers on your network. Having one server sharing a 80GB drive is better than two servers each sharing a 40GB drive. The fewer servers you have on your network, the less time you have to spend administering them.

✔ In a larger network, you may want to use two dedicated server computers: one as a file server and the other as a print server. This improves the performance for file operations and network printing. (As an alternative, you can use a network-ready printer so that you don't have to tie up a server computer for printing.)

✔ If you're the greedy type, offer to donate your old 200MHz Pentium II computer as the network server if the company will purchase a new 2GHz Pentium 4 computer for your desktop.

Actually, this idea has merit: The file server doesn't have to be the fastest computer on the block, especially if it's mostly used to store and retrieve word processing, spreadsheet, and other types of files instead of being used for intensive database processing.

How Much Disk Space Do You Need?

The general rule for a network is that you can never have enough disk space. No matter how much you have, you eventually run out. Don't delude yourself into thinking that 80GB is twice as much space as you may ever need. Make that space available to the network, and it fills up in no time.

The good news is that disk drives keep getting bigger and cheaper. This is now the sixth edition of this book, and every time I've revised it, I've had to increase the size of the disk drive cited in the preceding paragraph. In the first edition, which I wrote in 1994, I wrote that you might think 200MB was twice as much disk space as you'd need. Reminds me of that scene in *Austin Powers* where Dr. Evil threatens to hold the world hostage for one *million* dollars!

What then? Should you just keep adding a new hard drive to your file server every time you run out of space? Certainly not. The key to managing network disk space is just that — managing it. Someone has to sign on the dotted line that he or she promises to keep tabs on the network disk and let everyone know when it's about to burst its seams. And every network user must realize that disk storage on the server is a precious resource — to be used judiciously and not squandered.

Here are a few additional tips that can help you make the best use of your server disk space:

✔ If you use Windows 98 for the server computer, consider activating the Windows DriveSpace feature on the shared network drive. To set up DriveSpace properly, you must first quote from *Wayne's World:* Say "Ex-squeeze me," and DriveSpace politely compresses the data on your hard drive so that its capacity is effectively doubled. The only trouble with compressing your data is that it slows down the server a bit. For the best server performance, you're better off purchasing a larger hard drive and not compressing it.

Both Windows 2000 and NetWare also allow you to use compression to extend disk space on your servers.

✔ Encourage all network users to remember that their computers have local hard drives in addition to the network drives. Just because you have a network doesn't mean that everything has to be stored on a network drive!

✔ If you use Windows 2000 or NetWare for your file server, you can set up quotas to limit the amount of disk space each network user can use.

✔ Several years ago, some network administrators went on a cost-cutting binge by using *diskless clients,* client computers that have no local drives at all. For this to work, a special chip was required in the network interface card so that the computer could boot without a hard drive. Diskless clients were cheaper, but they forced the user to store everything on the network. In addition, they bogged down the network because routine disk accesses, such as locating program files, had to travel across the network cable. Fortunately, diskless clients are pretty much a thing of the past.

What to Put on a File Server

Of course, the only way to predict how much network disk space that you need is to plan what files you're going to store on the server. You need enough space to accommodate the network itself, shared data files, private data files, and shared application programs.

The network itself

You can't make all the space on the network server's hard drive available to network users; you have to reserve some of it for the network operating system itself. Setting aside a few gigabytes of drive space for the network operating system, print spool files, sealing wax, and other fancy stuff is not unreasonable.

A network can take up an amazing amount of drive space. Check out these numbers:

✔ NetWare 5.1 consumes about 1.3GB.

✔ NetWare 6 requires about 2GB.

✔ Windows NT Server needs about 125MB.

✔ Windows 2000 Server swallows about 1GB.

✔ Both Windows 98 and Windows Me chew up about 200MB.

✔ Windows XP requires a whopping 1.5GB of hard disk space!

Shared data files

Allow sufficient space on the file server for the data files that network users share. One large database file, or hundreds, or even thousands of small word processing or spreadsheet files may take up most of this space. Either way, don't skimp on space here.

Estimate the amount of space that you need for shared files. The only way you can estimate this is to add up the size of the files that must be shared. Now, double the result. If you can afford to, double it again.

Private data files

Every user wants access to network disk space for private file storage — perhaps because their own drives are getting full, they want the security of knowing that their files are backed up regularly, or they just want to try out the network.

You have two approaches to providing this private space:

✔ Create a folder for each network user on a shared network drive. For example, the Cleavers set up the following folders for private storage:

- Ward   \WARD
- June   \JUNE
- Wally   \WALLY
- Beaver   \BEAVER

Now, just tell each network user to store private files in his or her own folder. The problem with this setup is that these folders aren't really private; nothing keeps Beaver from looking at the files in Wally's directory.

To make these directories more secure, you can password-protect them by using the security features in your network operating system.

✔ Create a separate network drive mapping for each private folder. For example, you can map drive P to each network user's private directory. Then you can tell each user to store private files on his or her P drive. For Wally, the P drive refers to the \WALLY folder, but for Beaver, the P drive refers to \BEAVER. This setup keeps Beaver out of Wally's files.

The net effect (groan, sorry) of this setup is that each user seems to have a separate P drive on the server. In reality, these drives are merely folders on the server drive.

Estimating the disk space required for private file storage is more difficult than estimating space for shared file storage. After your users figure out that they have seemingly unlimited private storage on the network server, they start filling it up. That's why it's a good idea to set up user disk quotas on NetWare and Windows 2000 servers.

Shared programs

If several users use the same application program, consider purchasing a network version of the program and storing the program file on the network server. The advantage of sharing the program rather than storing a separate copy of the program on each user's local drive is that you have to manage only one copy of the software. For example, if a new version of the software comes out, you have to update just the copy on the server rather than separate copies on each workstation.

The network version of most programs enables each network user to set the program's options according to his or her preferences. Thus, one user may run the program using the default setup with boring colors, while another user may prefer to change the screen colors so that the program displays magenta text on a cyan background. Stalin probably would have outlawed network versions.

Many application programs create temporary files that you're not aware of and don't normally need to worry about. When you use these programs on a network, be sure to configure them so that the temporary files are created on a local drive rather than on a network drive. This configuration not only gives you better performance, but also ensures that one user's temporary files don't interfere with another's.

Planning Your Network Drive Mapping

If you plan to use mapped drive letters to access network drives, you should scope out which drive letters you will use. Here are some general rules to follow:

✔ Be consistent. If a network drive is accessed as drive Q from one workstation, map it as drive Q from all workstations that access the same drive. Don't have one user referring to a network drive as drive Q and another using the same drive but with a different letter.

✔ Use drive letters that are high enough to avoid conflicts with drive letters that are used by local drives. For example, suppose that one of your computers has three disk partitions, a CD-ROM drive, and a CD-RW drive. This computer would already have drive letters C through G assigned. I usually start network drive assignments with drive M and continue with N, O, P, and so on.

Novell NetWare usually begins drive assignments at drive F.

✔ If you use DriveSpace on a Windows 98 server computer, be aware that DriveSpace uses up drive letters, which can affect your network drive letter assignments. To protect yourself, start your network before you install DriveSpace so that DriveSpace can find its way around your network drive assignments. And always wear a helmet and safety goggles when using DriveSpace.

✔ For Windows client computers, keep in mind that drive letter mapping isn't a requirement. Users can access any shared network drive via the Network Neighborhood icon that appears on the Windows desktop. But setting up a mapped drive makes it easier to access the shared data via My Computer.

Sharing CD or DVD Drives

CD drives have become standard equipment on desktop computers, and many newer computers come with DVD drives, which have even higher capacity and let you watch *Star Wars* movies from the comfort of your office chair. If your computer is the only one in the office with a DVD drive, you may have users waiting in line to borrow time on your computer so that they can use it.

Fortunately, all the network operating systems described in this book enable you to set up a CD or DVD drive as a shared network drive so that users throughout the network can access it. In fact, sharing a CD or DVD drive is no different than sharing a regular disk drive.

But an annoying problem crops up when you share a desktop computer's CD or DVD drive with other network users. Imagine that you're using your DVD drive for important work, such as watching *Harry Potter and the Sorcerer's Stone,* when some clown down in sales wants to access the master price list on DVD that just arrived from corporate headquarters. You get an annoying message that says something like `Please Insert the Master Price List disk in Drive D`. And that won't be the last of it, either. You're going to be pestered by annoying interruptions like this all day long.

If you're going to share a CD or DVD drive, make sure that it's located on a dedicated server computer and the disk you need to share is dedicated to a particular drive. For example, if corporate headquarters really does send you a DVD containing the master price list and the network users need to access this disk frequently, dedicate an entire DVD drive just for this disk. Then you won't have to contend with annoying messages about changing the disks.

If you have more than one CD or DVD to be shared, just install more than one drive in the server computer. With the cost of CD and DVD drives being so low — a basic CD drive is about $50 these days — this solution isn't unrealistic. If you share more than a few disks, you can even buy special *towers* with stacks of CD or DVD drives built in. These towers are self-contained servers with network software built in, so you can connect them directly to your network.

An alternative to a tower is a *jukebox*. A jukebox is a single CD or DVD drive that can hold several discs and automatically swaps discs as they are accessed. Jukeboxes are less expensive than towers, but they're slower; whenever a user accesses a disc that isn't currently in the drive, the jukebox must switch discs. If two users simultaneously access two discs, the jukebox spends a lot of time shuttling discs back and forth. (To avoid this problem, you can get jukeboxes that have more than one CD or DVD reader built in — for more money, of course.)

If you don't want to fuss with shared CD or DVD drives, towers, or jukeboxes, you can always just copy the entire contents of your most popular disks to the server's hard drive.

Using a Separate Print Server

If you have a larger network (say, a dozen or more computers) and shared printing is one of the main reasons that you're networking, you may want to consider using two dedicated server computers — one as a file server and the other as a print server. By using separate server computers for file and print sharing, you improve the overall performance of your network.

Here are some thoughts to keep in mind when you use a separate print server:

> ✔ If the printer is used exclusively for text output, the print server can be the slowest computer on the network and you still won't notice any performance delay. If you do a lot of graphics printing on a high-quality laser printer, however, don't use a dog computer for the print server. I've seen ten-minute print jobs slowed to an hour or more by a cheap print server.

✔ As an alternative to dedicating a separate computer to use as a print server, you can connect most printers directly to the network via an inexpensive print server device. The most commonly used device of this type is called the *HP JetDirect,* made by Hewlett-Packard (the same folks who make all those great printers). An external HP JetDirect is a small box that contains an Ethernet port (RJ-45 for twisted-pair, BNC for thinnet, or both) and a parallel port to which you can attach a printer. Internal HP JetDirect cards are designed to be installed in Hewlett-Packard printers, enabling you to connect the printer directly to the network. You can get a single-printer external HP JetDirect for about $150.

Buying a Server Computer

If you have a spare computer lying around that you can use as a server, great. Most of us don't have spare computers in the closet, though. If you plan to buy a new computer to use as a network server, here are some tips for configuring it properly:

✔ A network server computer doesn't need to have the latest in large-screen color monitors and supercharged graphics cards. An ordinary 15-inch monitor with an inexpensive video card will do.

✔ On the other hand, don't scrimp on the processor and memory. Buy the fastest Pentium 4 processor that you can afford and equip it with at least 512MB; 1GB is better. Every last byte of extra memory can be put to good use on a server.

✔ Buy the biggest hard drive that you can afford. The price of hard drive storage has dropped so much in recent years that you can easily outfit a server computer with at least 100GB of hard drive storage. I've seen 60GB drives advertised for under $80, and you can get a 160GB drive for about $250.

✔ While you're at it, buy SCSI drives instead of IDE drives. SCSI offers much better performance for network servers, where several users are accessing the drive simultaneously. SCSI is more expensive than IDE, but the performance benefit is worth the increased cost, especially for Web servers, which tend to process lots of files. For more information about the benefits of SCSI over IDE, see Chapter 14.

✔ Have the computer built in a tower-style case that has plenty of room for expansion — several free bays for additional hard drives and a more-than-adequate power supply. You want to make sure that you can expand the server when you realize that you didn't buy enough drive space.

Keeping the Power On

One feature that people often overlook when setting up a network server is the power. You can simply plug the server computer into the wall, or you can plug it into a surge protector to smooth out power spikes before they damage your computer. Using a surge protector is a good idea, but an even better idea is to connect your server computer to a device called an *uninterruptible power supply,* or UPS.

Inside the UPS box is a battery that is constantly charged and some electronics that monitor the condition of the power coming from the wall outlet. If a power failure occurs, the battery keeps the computer running. The battery can't run the computer forever, but it can keep your computer running long enough — anywhere from ten minutes to more than an hour, depending on how much you paid for the UPS — to shut things down in familiar Presbyterian fashion (decently and in order). For most small networks, a UPS that keeps you going for ten minutes is enough. You just want to make sure that any disk in progress (I/O) has time to finish. A decent UPS that is capable of protecting a single server computer can be had for about $150.

Here are a few additional thoughts about UPS:

✔ Using a UPS can prevent you from losing data when a power outage occurs. Without a UPS, your server computer can be shut down at the worst of times, such as while your computer is updating the directory information that tracks the location of your files. With a UPS, the computer can stay on long enough for such meticulous operations to be completed safely.

✔ In a true UPS, power is always supplied to the computer from the battery; the current from the wall outlet is used only to keep the battery charged. Most inexpensive UPS devices are actually *stand-by power supplies* (*SPSs*). An SPS runs the computer from the wall-outlet current but switches to battery within a few gazillionths of a second if a power failure occurs. With a true UPS, you have no delay between the power failure and the battery takeover, so a true UPS does a better job than an SPS of protecting your computer against power outages, brownouts, and other minor power glitches. SPSs are less expensive than UPSs, though, so they're more commonly used.

✔ The ultimate power-failure protection is to attach a UPS to every computer on the network. That gets a bit expensive, though. At the very least, you should protect the server.

✔ If a power outage occurs and your server is protected by a UPS, get to the server as quickly as you can, log everyone off, and shut down the server. You should also go to each computer and turn off the power switch. Then, when power is restored, you can restart the server, restart each workstation, and assess the damage.

✔ Better yet, get a UPS that can be connected to the server computer through a serial port, a USB port, or a network port. Then configure the UPS to automatically power down the server should the power fail.

Location, Location, and Location

The final network server consideration that I need to address in this chapter is where to put the server. In the old days, you put the network server in a room with glass windows all around, paid a full-time lab technician in a white coat to tend to its every need, and gave it a name like ARDVARC or SHADRAC.

Nowadays, the most likely location for a file server is in the closet. Nothing says that the server has to be in a central location; it can be in the closet down at the end of the hall, atop the filing cabinets in the storage room, or in the corner office. The server can be almost anywhere, as long as it's near an electrical outlet and a network cable can be routed to it.

Of course, a print server is different. Ideally, the print server should be near the printer, which should be in an accessible location with storage space for paper and toner (for laser printers), a place to leave printouts that belong to other users, and a box to drop waste paper so that it can be recycled.

Some bad locations for the server:

✔ In the attic. Too dusty.

✔ In the bathroom. Too much moisture.

✔ In the kitchen. Your computer gurus raid your refrigerator every time you call them. They start showing up spontaneously "just to check."

✔ In your boss's office. You don't want him or her to think of you every time the server beeps.

The good news is that you still get to name your server computer. You can call it something boring like SERVER1, or you can give it an interesting name like BERTHA or SPOCK.

Chapter 10

Oh, What a Tangled Web We Weave: Cables, Adapters, and Other Stuff

- -

- -

Cable is the plumbing of your network. In fact, working with network cable is a lot like working with pipe: You have to use the right kind of pipe (cable), the right valves and connectors (hubs and switches), and the right fixtures (network interface cards).

Network cables have one compelling advantage over pipes: You don't get wet when they leak.

This chapter tells you far more about network cables than you probably need to know. I introduce you to *Ethernet,* the most common system of network cabling for small networks. Then you find out how to work with the cables used to wire an Ethernet network. You also find out how to select the right network interface cards, which enable you to connect the cables to your computers.

What Is Ethernet?

Ethernet is a standardized way of connecting computers to create a network. You can think of Ethernet as a kind of municipal building code for networks: It specifies what kind of cables to use, how to connect the cables together, how long the cables can be, how computers transmit data to one another using the cables, and more.

Historical Footnote Warning: Although Ethernet is today the overwhelming choice for networking, that wasn't always the case. Many moons ago, Ethernet had competition from two other network cabling standards: Token Ring and ARCnet. Token Ring is an IBM standard for networking that is still used in some organizations, especially where older IBM mainframe or midrange systems are

TECHNICAL STUFF

Worthless filler about network topology

A networking book wouldn't be complete without the usual textbook description of the three basic *network topologies.* The first type of network topology is called a *bus,* in which network nodes (that is, computers) are strung together in a line, like this:

A bus is the simplest type of topology but it has some drawbacks. If the cable breaks somewhere in the middle, the break splits the network into two.

The second type of topology is called a *ring:*

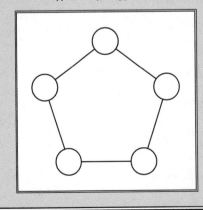

A ring is very much like a bus except with no end to the line: The last node on the line is connected to the first node, forming an endless loop.

The third type of topology is called a *star:*

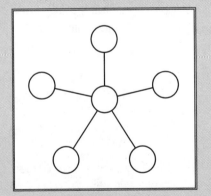

In a star network, all the nodes are connected to a central hub. In effect, each node has an independent connection to the network, so a break in one cable doesn't affect the others.

Ethernet networks are based on a bus design. However, fancy cabling tricks make an Ethernet network appear to be wired like a star when twisted-pair cable is used.

included in the network. ARCnet has all but vanished from the office networking scene but is still commonly used for industrial network applications, such as building automation and factory robot control.

Some people treat Ethernet, Token Ring, and ARCnet like religions that they're willing to die for. To a Lord of the Token Ring, Ethernet is like an evil troll. Ethernet fanatics often claim that you can hear evil messages if you send data backward through a Token Ring network. Ethernet and Token Ring fanatics both treat ARCnet users as if they were a cult — possibly due to reports of ARCnet disciples giving away flowers at airports. Don't engage an Ethernet, Token Ring, or ARCnet Pharisee in a discussion about the merits of his or her network beliefs over the opponents' beliefs. It's futile.

Without regard to the technical merits of Ethernet, Token Ring, or ARCnet, the fact is that the vast majority of business networks use Ethernet. You can purchase inexpensive Ethernet components at just about any computer store, and you can even purchase Ethernet cable and connectors at many hardware warehouse stores. Because Ethernet is inexpensive and readily available, it is really the only choice for new networks — small as well as large.

Here are a few interesting tidbits about Ethernet standards:

✔ Ethernet is a set of standards for the infrastructure on which a network is built. All the network operating systems that I discuss in this book — including all versions of Windows, NetWare, Linux, and Macintosh OS/X — can operate on an Ethernet network. If you build your network on a solid Ethernet base, you can change network operating systems later.

✔ Ethernet is often referred to by network gurus as 802.3 (pronounced *eight-oh-two-dot-three*), which is the official designation used by the *IEEE* (pronounced *eye-triple-e*), a group of electrical engineers who wear bow ties and have nothing better to do than argue about inductance all day long. This situation is a good thing, though, because if not for them, you wouldn't be able to mix and match Ethernet components made by different companies.

✔ Standard old-fashioned Ethernet transmits data at a rate of 10 million bits per second, or 10 Mbps. (*Mbps* is usually pronounced *megabit*.) Because 8 bits are in a byte, that translates into roughly 1.2 million bytes per second. In practice, Ethernet can't move information that fast because data must be transmitted in packages of no more than 1,500 bytes, called *packets*. So 150KB of information has to be split into 100 packets.

Ethernet's transmission speed has nothing to do with how fast electrical signals move on the cable. The electrical signals themselves travel at about 70 percent of the speed of light, or as Captain Picard would say, "Warp factor point-seven-oh. Engage."

Stop me before I tell you about Token Ring!

Just in case you do get into an argument about Ethernet with a Token Ring fanatic, let me tell you where he or she is coming from. Ethernet can get bogged down if the network gets really busy and messages start colliding like crazy. Token Ring uses a more orderly approach to sending packets through the network. Instead of sending a message whenever it wants to, a computer on a Token Ring network must wait its turn. In a Token Ring network, a special packet called the *token* is constantly passed through the network from computer to computer. A computer can send a packet of data only when it has the token. In this way, Token Ring ensures that collisions won't happen.

Sometimes, a computer with a defective network interface card accidentally swallows the token. If the token disappears for too long, the network assumes that the token has been swallowed, and the network burps to generate a new token.

Two versions of Token Ring are in use. The older version runs at 4 Mbps. The newer version runs at 16 Mbps, plus it allows two tokens to exist at once, which makes the network even faster.

Oh, in case you're wondering, ARCnet uses a similar token-passing scheme.

- The newer version of Ethernet, called *Fast Ethernet* or *100 Mbps Ethernet,* moves data ten times as fast as normal Ethernet. Because Fast Ethernet moves data at a whopping 100Mbps and uses twisted-pair cabling, it's often called *100BaseT* (and sometimes *100BaseTx*).

- Most networking components you can buy these days support both 10 Mbps and 100Mbps Ethernet. These components are often referred to as *10/100 Mbps components* because they support both speeds.

- An even faster version of Ethernet, known as *Gigabit Ethernet,* is also available. Gigabit Ethernet components are expensive, though, so they are usually used to create a high-speed network backbone.

Two Types of Ethernet Cable

You can construct a 10/100 Mbps Ethernet network by using one of two different types of cable: *coaxial cable,* which resembles TV cable, or *twisted pair cable,* which looks like phone cable. Twisted-pair cable is sometimes called *UTP,* or *10baseT cable,* for reasons I try hard not to explain later (in the section "Twisted-pair cable").

TECHNICAL STUFF

Who cares what CSMA/CD stands for?

Besides specifying the mechanical and electrical characteristics of network cables, Ethernet specifies the techniques used to control the flow of information over the network cables. The technique that Ethernet uses is called *CSMA/CD,* which stands for "carrier sense multiple access with collision detection." This phrase is a mouthful, but if you take it apart piece by piece, you get an idea of how Ethernet works (as if you want to know).

Carrier sense means that whenever a computer wants to send a message on the network cable, it first listens to the cable to see whether anyone else is already sending a message. If it doesn't hear any other messages on the cable, the computer assumes that it's free to send one.

Multiple access means that nothing prevents two or more computers from trying to send a message at the same time. Sure, each computer listens before sending. But suppose that

two computers listen, hear nothing, and then proceed to send their messages? Picture what happens when you and someone else arrive at a four-way stop sign at the same time. You wave the other driver on, he or she waves you on, you wave, he or she waves, you all wave, and then you both end up going at the same time.

Collision detection means that after a computer sends a message on the network, it listens carefully to see whether the message crashed into another message. Kind of like listening for the screeching of brakes at the four-way stop. If the computer hears the screeching of brakes, it waits for a random period of time and tries to send the message again. Because the delay is random, two messages that collide are sent again after different delay periods, so a second collision is unlikely.

Now, wasn't that a waste of time?

You may encounter other types of cable in an existing network: thick yellow cable that used to be the only type of cable used for Ethernet, fiber-optic cables that span long distances at high speeds, or thick twisted-pair bundles that carry multiple sets of twisted pair cable between wiring closets in a large building. For all but the largest networks, the choice is between coax cable and twisted-pair cable.

Coax cable

One type of cable you can use for Ethernet networks is coaxial cable, usually called *thinnet* or sometimes *BNC cable* because of the type of connectors used on each end of the cable. Figure 10-1 shows a typical coax cable.

Figure 10-1:
A coax
cable with a
BNC
connector.

Here are some salient points about coaxial cable:

✔ You attach thinnet to the network interface card by using a goofy twist-on connector called a *BNC connector*. You can purchase pre-assembled cables with BNC connectors already attached in lengths of 25 or 50 feet, or you can buy bulk cable on a big spool and attach the connectors yourself by using a special tool. (I suggest buying pre-assembled cables. Attaching connectors to bulk cable can be tricky.)

✔ With coax cables, you connect your computers point-to-point, as shown in Figure 10-2. At each computer, a T connector is used to connect two cables to the network interface card. Figure 10-2 shows a typical thinnet arrangement. One length of thinnet connects Ward's computer to June's, a second length of cable connects June's computer to Wally's, and a third length of cable connects Wally's computer to Beaver's.

✔ A special plug called a *terminator* is required at each end of a series of thinnet cables. In Figure 10-2, terminators are required at Ward's computer and at Beaver's computer. The terminator prevents data from spilling out the end of the cable and staining the carpet.

✔ The cables strung end-to-end from one terminator to the other are collectively called a *segment*. The maximum length of a thinnet segment is about 200 yards (actually, 185 meters). You can connect as many as 30 computers on one segment. To span a distance greater than 185 meters or to connect more than 30 computers, you must use two or more segments with a funky device called a *repeater* to connect each segment.

✔ Although Ethernet coax cable resembles TV coax cable, the two types of cable are not interchangeable. Don't try to cut costs by wiring your network with cheap TV cable.

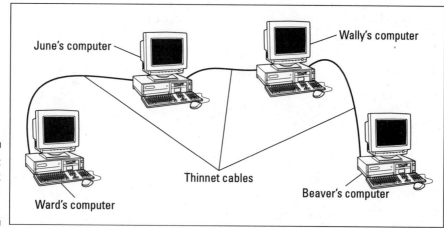

Figure 10-2:
A network
wired with
coax cable.

June's computer

Wally's computer

Thinnet cables

Ward's computer

Beaver's computer

Twisted-pair cable

A popular alternative to thinnet cable is *twisted-pair cable,* or *UTP.* (The U
stands for *Unshielded,* but no one says *unshielded twisted pair.* Just *twisted
pair* will do.) UTP cable is even cheaper than thin coaxial cable, and best of
all, many modern buildings are already wired with twisted-pair cable because
this type of wiring is often used with modern phone systems. Figure 10-3
shows a twisted-pair cable.

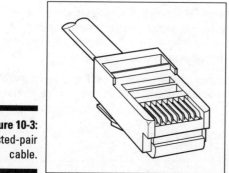

Figure 10-3:
Twisted-pair
cable.

When you use UTP cable to construct an Ethernet network, you connect the
computers in a star arrangement, as Figure 10-4 illustrates. In the center of
this star is a device called a *hub.* Depending on the model, Ethernet hubs
enable you to connect from 4 to 24 computers using twisted-pair cable.

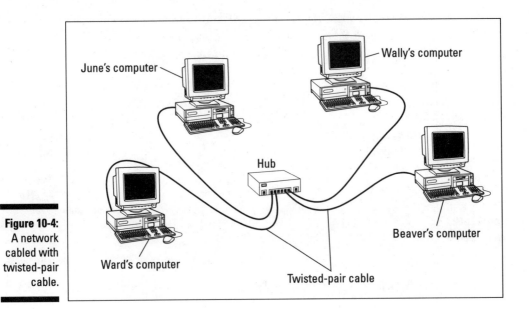

Figure 10-4:
A network
cabled with
twisted-pair
cable.

June's computer

Wally's computer

Hub

Ward's computer

Beaver's computer

Twisted-pair cable

An advantage of UTP's star arrangement is that if one cable goes bad, only the computer attached to that cable is affected; the rest of the network continues to chug along. With coax, a bad cable affects the entire network, not just the computer that the bad cable is connected to.

Here are a few other details that you should know about twisted-pair cabling:

- ✔ UTP cable consists of pairs of thin wire twisted around each other; several such pairs are gathered up inside an outer insulating jacket. Ethernet uses two pairs of wires, or four wires all together. The number of pairs in a UTP cable varies, but it is often more than two.

- ✔ UTP cable comes in various grades called Categories. Don't use anything less than Category 5 cable for your network. Although cheaper, it may not be able to support faster networks.

  Although higher Category cables are more expensive than lower Category cables, the real cost of installing Ethernet cabling is the labor required to actually pull the cables through the walls. As a result, I recommend that you always spend the extra money to buy Category 5 cable.

- ✔ If you want to sound like you know what you're talking about, say "Cat 5" instead of "Category 5."

- ✔ Although Category 5 cable is fine for 100 Mbps networks, the newer 1000 Mbps networks require an even better cable. Category 5e cable (the *e* stands for *enhanced*) is a slightly improved type of cable that will work for Fast Ethernet networks. And new standards for Category 6 and even Category 7 cables are expected soon.

✔ UTP cable connectors look like modular phone connectors but are a bit larger. UTP connectors are officially called *RJ-45 connectors*.

✔ Like thinnet cable, UTP cable is also sold in prefabricated lengths. However, RJ-45 connectors are much easier to attach to bulk UTP cable than BNC cables are to attach to bulk coaxial cable. As a result, I suggest that you buy bulk cable and connectors unless your network consists of just two or three computers. A basic crimp tool to attach the RJ-45 connectors costs about $50.

✔ The maximum allowable cable length between the hub and the computer is 100 meters (about 328 feet).

Hubs and Switches

The biggest difference between using coax cable and twisted-pair cable is that when you use twisted-pair cable, you also must use a separate device called a *hub*. Years ago, hubs were expensive devices — expensive enough that most do-it-yourself networkers who were building small networks opted for thinnet cable to avoid the expense and hassle of using hubs.

Nowadays, the cost of hubs has dropped so much that the advantages of twisted-pair cabling outweigh the hassle and cost of using hubs. With twisted-pair cabling, you can more easily add new computers to the network, move computers, find and correct cable problems, and service the computers that you need to remove from the network temporarily.

Chubby hubs and switch hitters

Both hubs and switches let you connect four or more computers to a twisted-pair network. Switches are more efficient than hubs, but not just because they are faster. If you really want to know, here's the actual difference between a hub and a switch:

✔ In a hub, every packet that arrives at the hub on any of its ports is automatically sent out on every other port. The hub has to do this because it doesn't keep track of which computer is connected to each port. For example, suppose Wally's computer is connected to port 1 on an 8-port hub, and Ward's computer is connected to port 5. If Ward's computer sends a packet of information

to Wally's computer, the hub receives the packet on port 1 and then sends it out on ports 2-8. All the computers connected to the hub get to see the packet so they can determine whether or not the packet was intended for them.

✔ A switch does keep track of which computer is connected to each port. So if Wally's computer on port 1 sends a packet to Ward's computer on port 5, the switch receives the packed on port 1 and then sends the packet out only on port 5. This is not only faster, but also improves the security of the system because other computers don't see packets that aren't meant for them.

TECHNICAL STUFF

Ten base what?

The IEEE, in its infinite wisdom, has decreed that the following names shall be used to designate the various types of cable used with 802.3 networks (in other words, with Ethernet):

✔ 10base5 is old-fashioned thick coaxial cable (the yellow stuff).

✔ 10base2 is thin coaxial cable (thinnet).

✔ 10baseT is unshielded twisted-pair cable (UTP).

In each moniker, the number *10* means that the cable operates at 10 Mbps, and *base* means that the cable is used for baseband networks as opposed to broadband networks (don't ask). The number *5* in 10base5 is the maximum length of a yellow cable segment: 500 meters. The number *2* in 10base2 stands for 200 meters, which is about the 185-meter maximum segment length for thinnet cable. (For a group of engineers, the IEEE is odd; I didn't know that the word *about* can be part of an engineer's vocabulary.) And the letter *T* in 10baseT stands for *twisted.*

Of these three official monikers, 10baseT is the only one used frequently; 10base5 and 10base2 are usually just called *thick* and *thin*, respectively.

Also, Fast Ethernet running over 10baseT cabling uses the designation 100baseT.

A *switch* is simply a more sophisticated type of hub. Because the cost of switches has come down dramatically in the past few years, most new networks are built with switches rather than hubs. If you have an older network that uses hubs and seems to run slowly, you may be able to improve the network's speed by replacing the older hubs with newer switches. (For more information, see the sidebar, "Chubby hubs and switch hitters.")

If you use twisted-pair cabling, you need to know some of the ins and outs of using hubs:

✔ Because you must run a cable from each computer to the hub or switch, find a central location for the hub or switch to which you can easily route the cables.

✔ The hub or switch requires electrical power, so make sure that an electrical outlet is handy.

✔ When you purchase a hub or switch, purchase one with at least twice as many connections as you need. Don't buy a four-port hub or switch if you want to network four computers; when (not *if*) you add the fifth computer, you have to buy another hub or switch.

✔ You can connect hubs or switches to one another as shown in Figure 10-5; this is called *daisy-chaining.* When you daisy-chain hubs or switches, you connect a cable to a standard port on one of the hubs or switches and the daisy-chain port on the other hub or switch. Be sure to read the instructions that come with the hub or switch to make sure that you daisy-chain them properly.

✔ You can daisy-chain no more than three hubs or switches together. If you have more computers than three hubs can accommodate, don't panic. For a small additional cost, you can purchase hubs that have a BNC connection on the back. Then, you can string the hubs together using thinnet cable. The three-hub limit doesn't apply when you use thinnet cable to connect the hubs. You can also get stackable hubs or switches that have high-speed direct connections that enable two or more hubs or switches to be counted as a single hub or switch.

✔ When you shop for network hubs, you may notice that the expensive ones have network-management features that support something called *SNMP*. These hubs are called *managed hubs*. Unless your network is very large and you know what SNMP is, don't bother with the more expensive managed hubs. You'd be paying for a feature that you may never use.

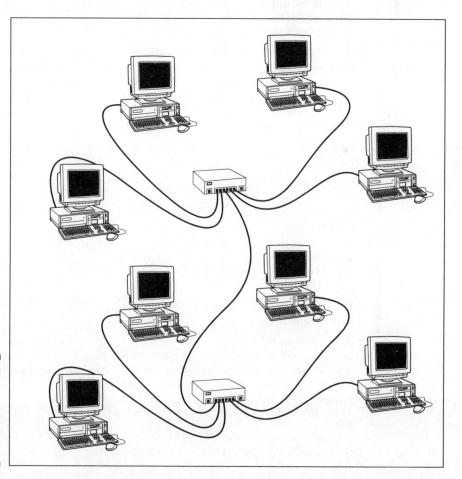

Figure 10-5:
You can daisy-chain hubs or switches together.

Network Interface Cards

Now that you know far more about network cable than you really need to, I want to point out a few things about network interface cards that you should consider before you buy:

- The network interface cards that you use must have a connector that matches the type of cable that you use. If you plan on wiring your network with thinnet cable, make sure that the network cards have a BNC connector. For twisted-pair wiring, make sure that the cards have an RJ-45 connector.

- Some network cards provide two or three connectors. I see them in every combination: BNC and AUI, RJ-45 and AUI, BNC and RJ-45, and all three. Selecting a card that has both BNC and RJ-45 connectors isn't a bad idea. That way, you can switch from thinnet cable to twisted-pair cable or vice versa without buying new network cards. You can get both types of connectors for a cost of only $5 to $10 more per card. Don't worry about the AUI connector, though. You'll probably never need it.

- You can get 10 Mbps cards, 100 Mbps cards, or 10/100 Mbps cards, which automatically determine whether your network is running at 10 Mbps or 100 Mbps and switch accordingly. I suggest that you always purchase 10/100 Mbps auto-sensing cards. They are a few dollars more, but well worth the additional cost. Even if you don't need a 100 Mbps network now, you may eventually.

- Long ago and far away, Novell manufactured a network interface card known as the *NE2000*. The NE2000 card is no longer made, but NE2000 remains a standard of compatibility for network interface cards. If a card is NE2000-compatible, you can use it with just about any network. If you buy a card that is not NE2000-compatible, make sure that the card is compatible with the network operating system that you intend to use.

- When you purchase a network card, make sure that you get one that's compatible with your computer. Many older computers can accommodate cards designed for the standard 16-bit ISA bus. Newer computers can accommodate cards with that use the PCI bus. If your computer supports PCI, you should purchase a PCI card. Not only are PCI cards faster than ISA cards, they are also easier to configure. So you should use ISA cards only for older computers that can't accommodate PCI cards.

- If at all possible, purchase a PCI card rather than an older ISA card. But first, make sure your computer has at least one available PCI slot inside. For example, suppose your computer has two ISA bus slots and three PCI bus slots, but all three of the PCI slots are already in use, while both of the ISA slots are available. In this case, get an ISA card.

✓ Make sure that the card is compatible with Plug and Play. This feature enables Windows to automatically configure the card so that you don't have to go through a bunch of tedious configuration gyrations just to get the card working.

✓ Network cards can be a bit tricky to set up — even Plug and Play cards. Each different card has its own nuances. You can simplify your life a bit if you use the same card for every computer in your network. Try not to mix and match network cards.

✓ If you see Ethernet cards advertised on late-night television for an unbelievably low price (like for $2.95, or free with Proof of Purchase seals from three cereal boxes), make sure that the card is a PCI card. You won't be satisfied with the slow performance and configuration problems that are inherent with bargain-basement ISA cards unless your computer is also of the bargain-basement variety.

✓ Some computers come with network ports built in. In that case, you don't have to worry about adding a network card.

Network Starter Kits

Often, the easiest way to buy the equipment that you need to build a network is to purchase a network starter kit. A typical network starter kit includes everything that you need to network two computers. To add additional computers, you purchase add-on kits that include everything that you need to add one computer to the network.

For example, suppose you want to network three computers in a small office. You could start with a two-computer network starter kit, which would include the following items:

✓ Two 10/100 Mbps auto-switching PCI Ethernet cards

✓ One 4-port Ethernet 100 Mbps switch

✓ Two 25-foot-long 10baseT twisted-pair cables

✓ Software for the cards

✓ Instructions

This kit, which should set you back about $100, connects two of the three computers. To connect the third computer, purchase an add-on kit that includes a 10/100 auto-switching PCI Ethernet card, another 25-foot-long twisted-pair cable, software, and instructions — all for about $40.

Installing Network Cable

The hardest part about working with network cable is attaching the cable connectors. That's why the easiest way to wire a network is to buy prefabricated cables, with the connectors already attached. Thinnet cable is commonly sold in prefabricated lengths of 25, 50, or 100 feet. You can buy prefabricated twisted-pair cable, or you can attach the connectors yourself (it isn't hard to do).

Before I show you how to attach cable connectors, here are a few general tips for working with cable:

- Always use more cable than you need, especially if you're running cable through walls. Leave plenty of slack.

- When running cable, avoid sources of interference like fluorescent lights, big motors, and so on. The most common source of interference for cables run behind fake ceiling panels are fluorescent lights; be sure to give light fixtures a wide berth as you run your cable. Three feet should do it.

- If you must run cable across the floor where people walk, cover the cable so that no one trips over it. Inexpensive cable protectors are available from most hardware stores.

- When running cables through walls, label each cable at both ends. Most electrical supply stores carry pads of cable labels that are perfect for the job. These pads contain 50 sheets or so of precut labels with letters and numbers. They look much more professional than wrapping a loop of masking tape around the cable and writing on the tape with a marker.

  Or, if you want to scrimp, you can just buy a permanent marker and write directly on the cable.

- When several cables come together, tie them with plastic cable ties. Avoid masking tape if you can; the tape doesn't last, but the sticky glue stuff does. It's a mess a year later. Cable ties are available from electrical supply stores.

- Cable ties have all sorts of useful purposes. On my last backpacking trip, I used a pair of cable ties to attach an unsuspecting buddy's hat to a high tree limb. He wasn't impressed with my innovative use of the cable ties, but my other hiking companions were.

- When you run cable above acoustic ceiling panels, use cable ties, hooks, or clamps to secure the cable to the actual ceiling or to the metal frame that supports the ceiling tiles. Don't just lay the cable on top of the tiles.

Getting the tools that you need

Of course, to do a job right, you must have the right tools.

Start with a basic set of computer tools, which you can get for about $15 from any computer store or large office-supply store. These kits include the right screwdrivers and socket wrenches to open up your computers and insert adapter cards. (If you don't have a computer tool kit, make sure that you have several flat-head and Phillips screwdrivers of various sizes.)

If all your computers are in the same room, and you're going to run the cables along the floor, and you're using prefabricated cables, the computer tool kit should contain everything that you need.

If you're using bulk cable and plan on attaching your own connectors, you need the following tools in addition to the tools that come with the basic computer tool kit:

- **Wire cutters.** Big ones for thinnet cable; smaller ones are okay for 10baseT cable. If you're using yellow cable, you need the Jaws of Life.

- **A crimp tool that is appropriate for your cable type.** You need the crimp tool to attach the connectors to the cable.

- **Wire stripper.** You need this only if the crimp tool doesn't include a wire stripper. For thinnet cable, a special wire-stripper-doohickey is required because the cable's inner conductor, outer conductor, and outer insulation must be cut at precise lengths.

If you plan on running cables through walls, you need these additional tools:

- **A hammer.**
- **A bell.**
- **A song to sing.** Just kidding about these last two.
- **A keyhole saw.** This is useful if you plan on cutting holes through walls to route your cable.
- **A flashlight.**
- **A ladder.**
- **Someone to hold the ladder.**

✔ **Possibly a *fish tape*.** A fish tape is a coiled-up length of stiff metal tape. To use it, you feed the tape into one wall opening and fish it toward the other opening, where a partner is ready to grab it when the tape arrives. Next, your partner attaches the cable to the fish tape and yells something like "Let 'er rip!" or "Bombs away!" Then you reel in the fish tape and the cable along with it. (You can find fish tape in the electrical section of most well-stocked hardware stores.)

If you plan on routing cable through a concrete sub-floor, you need to rent a jackhammer and a backhoe and hire someone to hold a yellow flag while you work.

Attaching a BNC connector to coax cable

Properly connecting a BNC connector to coax cable is an acquired skill. You need two tools — a wire stripper that can cut through the various layers of the coaxial cable at just the right location, and a crimping tool that crimps the connector tightly to the cable after you get the connector into position. BNC connectors have three separate pieces, as shown in Figure 10-6.

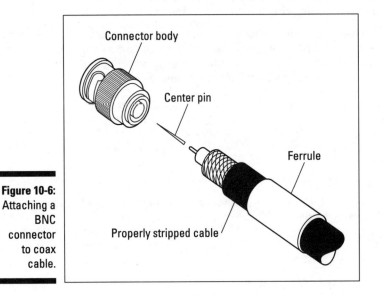

Connector body

Center pin

Ferrule

Properly stripped cable

Figure 10-6:
Attaching a
BNC
connector
to coax
cable.

Here's the procedure, in case you ignore my advice and try to attach the connectors yourself:

1. **Slide the hollow tube portion of the connector (lovingly called the *ferrule*) over the cable.**

   Let it slide back a few feet to get it out of the way.

2. **Cut the end of the cable off cleanly.**

3. **Use the stripping tool to strip the cable.**

   Strip the outer jacket back ½ inch from the end of the cable, strip the braided shield back ¼ inch from the end, and strip the inner insulation back ³⁄₁₆ inch from the end.

4. **Insert the solid center conductor into the center pin.**

   Slide the center pin down until it seats against the inner insulation.

5. **Use the crimping tool to crimp the center pin.**

6. **Slide the connector body over the center pin and inner insulation but under the braided shield.**

   After you push the body back far enough, the center pin clicks into place.

7. **Now slide the ferrule forward until it touches the connector body.**

   Crimp it with the crimping tool.

Don't get sucked into the trap of trying to use easy "screw-on" connectors. They aren't very reliable.

Attaching an RJ-45 connector to UTP cable

RJ-45 connectors for UTP wiring are much easier to connect than thinnet connectors. The only trick is making sure that you attach each wire to the correct pin. Each pair of wires in a UTP cable has complementary colors. One pair consists of one white wire with an orange stripe and an orange wire with a white stripe, and the other pair has a white wire with a green stripe and a green wire with a white stripe.

Here are the proper pin connections:

Pin Number	Proper Connection
Pin 1	White/orange wire
Pin 2	Orange/white wire
Pin 3	White/green wire
Pin 6	Green/white wire

One type of 100 Mbps network, known as 100baseT4, requires that you use cable with four pairs of wires rather than two pairs and that all eight wires be connected. If you're wiring a 100baseT4 network, connect the wires like this:

Pin Number	Proper Connection
Pin 1	White/orange wire
Pin 2	Orange/white wire
Pin 3	White/green wire
Pin 4	White/blue wire
Pin 5	Blue/white wire
Pin 6	Green/white wire
Pin 7	White/brown wire
Pin 8	Brown/white wire

Figure 10-7 shows an RJ-45 plug properly connected.

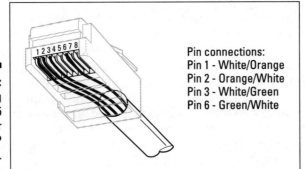

Figure 10-7:
Attaching
an RJ-45
connector
to UTP
cable.

Pin connections:
Pin 1 - White/Orange
Pin 2 - Orange/White
Pin 3 - White/Green
Pin 6 - Green/White

Here's the procedure for attaching an RJ-45 connector:

1. **Cut the end of the cable to the desired length.**

   Make sure that you make a square cut — not a diagonal cut.

2. **Insert the cable into the stripper portion of the crimp tool so that the end of the cable is against the stop.**

   Squeeze the handles and slowly pull the cable out, keeping it square. This strips off the correct length of outer insulation without puncturing the insulation on the inner wires.

3. **Arrange the wires so that they lay flat in the following sequence from left to right: white/orange, orange/white, white/green, green/white.**

   Pull the green/white wire a bit to the right and then insert the cable into the back of the plug so that each wire slides into the channel for the correct pin.

4. **Make sure that the wires are in the correct pin channels; especially make sure that the green/white cable is in the channel for pin 6.**

5. **Insert the plug and wire into the crimping portion of the tool and then squeeze the handles to crimp the plug.**

   Remove the plug from the tool and double-check the connection.

Here are a few other points to remember when dealing with RJ-45 connectors and twisted-pair cable:

✔ The pins on the RJ-45 connectors are not numbered, but you can tell which is Pin 1 by holding the connector so that the metal conductors are facing up, as shown in Figure 10-7. Pin 1 is on the left.

✔ Some people wire 10baseT cable differently — using the green and white pair for Pins 1 and 2 and the orange and white pair for Pins 3 and 6. This doesn't affect the operation of the network (the network is color-blind), *as long as the connectors on both ends of the cable are wired the same!*

✔ Yes, I know that any normal person would have set up the RJ-45 connectors using Pins 1 through 4, and not Pins 1, 2, 3, and 6. But remember, computer people aren't normal in any particularly relevant sense, so why would you expect the fourth wire to connect to the fourth pin? That's pretty naive, don't you think?

✔ If you're installing cable for a Fast Ethernet system, you should be extra careful to follow the rules of Category-5 cabling. That means, among other things, make sure that you use Category-5 components throughout. The cable and all the connectors must be up to Category-5 specs.

When you attach the connectors, do not untwist more than ½ inch of cable. And do not try to stretch the cable runs beyond the 100-meter maximum. When in doubt, have cable for a 100 Mbps Ethernet system professionally installed.

Professional Touches

If most of the stuff that I discuss in this chapter makes sense to you, and if you want to impress your friends, consider adding the following extra touches to your network installation. These extra touches make the job look professionally done. (If you find this chapter to be hopelessly confusing, you should probably concentrate on just getting your network up and running. Worry about making it look pretty later.)

Figure 10-8 shows some of the following professional touches:

- Use 10baseT wiring — that's what most network pros are doing these days.

- Run the wiring through the ceiling and walls instead of along the floor, and mount a wall jack near each computer. Then plug each computer into the wall jack by using a short (10 foot or so) patch cable. Be sure to use top-quality Category-5 jacks and make sure that each pair of wires inside the cable is twisted right up to the point where the wires attach to the jack. In other words, don't untwist the wires any more than absolutely necessary to make them easier to work with.

- When you run the wiring through the walls and ceiling, take special care to avoid power cords, fluorescent lamps, and other electrical devices that may interfere with the signals traveling inside the network cable. And don't kink the cable: Curve it gently around corners. Inside false ceilings, hang the cable from the metal ceiling supports using cable ties, hooks, or cable clamps.

- To really do it right, run 10baseT cable to every possible computer location in your office, even if you don't yet have a computer there. That way, when you do decide to move a computer to this location, the hard wiring (up in the ceiling and through the wall) is already done. All you have to do then is attach the computer to the wall jack with a patch cord.

✔ Designate a corner of a closet or storeroom to be your wiring closet. Bundle all the cables together and attach them to a patch panel, which is nothing more than a series of RJ-45 jacks arranged neatly in a row.

✔ Connect the appropriate jacks in the patch panel to your network hub with short patch cables. The whole thing looks a bit like a rat's nest, but you can easily reconfigure the network at a moment's notice. If someone changes locations, all you have to do is adjust the patch cables in the wiring closet accordingly.

✔ Be careful about making your network look too good. People may assume that you're a network geek and start offering you Cheetos to solve their problems.

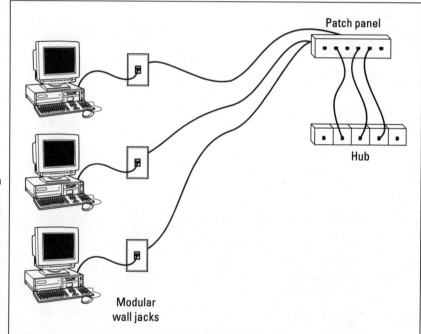

Figure 10-8: Professional touches can create the appearance that you know what you're doing.

Going Wireless

If all the talk about network cables, hubs and switches, and patch panels causes you to break out in a cold sweat, you may want to consider creating a wireless network instead. For a wireless network, you need two basic components:

- ✔ Wireless networking cards, which add a set of antennas to your computer so it can communicate with other wireless computers.

- ✔ A *wireless access point*, or *WAP,* which connects your wireless computers to the rest of your network. You need this device only if some of your computers are cabled in the normal fashion and others are wireless. If all the computers are wireless, you don't need a WAP.

For more information about wireless networking, see Chapter 20.

Chapter 11

Configuring Your Network Computers

. . . .

In This Chapter

▶ Installing a network card

▶ Installing a server operating system

▶ Configuring a Windows computer to access the network

▶ Checking out your installation

. . . .

*A*fter the cable is all strung, the fun part begins: You actually get to connect your computers to your network and configure them so that your network runs properly. Get ready to roll up your sleeves and dig into the bowels of your computers. Make sure that you scrub thoroughly first.

Installing a Network Interface Card

You have to install a network interface card into each computer before you can connect the computers to the network cables. Installing a network card is a manageable task, but you have to be willing to roll up your sleeves.

If you've installed one adapter card, you've installed them all. In other words, installing a network card is just like installing a modem, a new video controller card, a sound card, or any other type of card. If you've ever installed one of these cards, you can probably install a network card blindfolded.

If you haven't installed a card, here's a step-by-step procedure:

1. **Shut down Windows and then turn the computer off and unplug it.**

   Never work in your computer's insides with the power on or the power cord plugged in!

2. **Remove the cover from your computer.**

Figure 11-1 shows the screws that you must typically remove to open the cover. Put the screws someplace where they won't wander off.

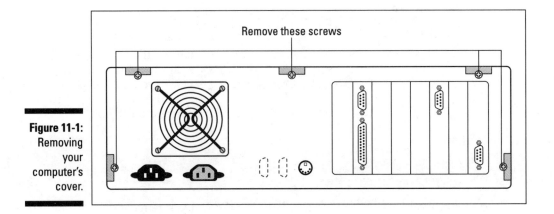

Remove these screws

Figure 11-1:
Removing
your
computer's
cover.

3. **Find an unused expansion slot inside the computer.**

The expansion slots are lined up in a neat row near the back of the computer; you can't miss 'em. Most newer computers have at least two or three slots known as *PCI slots.*

Many computers, especially those that are a year or more old, also have several slots known as *ISA slots.* You can distinguish ISA slots from PCI slots by noting the size of the slots. PCI slots are smaller than ISA slots, so you can't accidentally insert a PCI card in an ISA slot or vice versa.

Some computers also have other types of slots — mainly VESA and EISA slots. Standard ISA or PCI networking cards won't fit into these types of slots, so don't try to force them.

4. **When you find the right type of slot that doesn't have a card in it, remove the metal slot protector from the back of the computer's chassis.**

If a small retaining screw holds the slot protector in place, remove the screw and keep it in a safe place. Then, pull the slot protector out, and put the slot protector in a box with all your other old slot protectors. (After a while, you collect a whole bunch of slot protectors. Keep them as souvenirs.)

5. **Insert the network card into the slot.**

Line up the connectors on the bottom of the card with the connectors in the expansion slot, and then press the card straight down. Sometimes you have to press uncomfortably hard to get the card to slide into the slot.

6. **Secure the network card with the screw that you removed in Step 4.**

7. **Put the computer's case back together.**

Watch out for the loose cables inside the computer; you don't want to pinch them with the case as you slide it back on. Secure the case with the screws that you removed in Step 2.

8. **Turn the computer back on.**

If you're using a Plug and Play card with Windows, the card is automatically configured after you start the computer again. If you're working with an older computer or an older network card, you may need to run an additional software installation program. See the installation instructions that come with the network interface card for details.

Installing a Server Operating System

After you install the network cards and cable, all that remains is to install the network software. The procedures for doing this task vary considerably, depending on the network that you use, so you need to consult your network software's manual for the details. Here, I describe some general things to keep in mind when you install software on a server computer.

Installing NetWare

If you're using NetWare, installing the server software is the most difficult part of setting up the network. Read the manual carefully, place it ceremoniously on your highest bookshelf, and pick up a copy of *Networking With NetWare For Dummies,* 4th Edition, by Ed Tittel, James E. Gaskin, and Earl Follis (Wiley Publishing, Inc.).

The tricky part about installing NetWare is that you must first completely remove any operating system that is already installed on your computer. Then, you use the DOS 7 floppy disk that comes with NetWare to boot your computer and create a 50MB DOS partition on the server's hard drive. You can then install NetWare from the distribution CD-ROM. After the installation program starts, you can simply follow the instructions that appear on the screen to complete the installation. (Installing NetWare is easier if the computer has a bootable CD-ROM drive.)

During the NetWare installation, the installation program asks you for a lot of detailed information about how you want the NetWare server to be set up. For example, if you are installing NetWare 5.1, you are asked to supply the following information:

✔ The version of NDS that you want to use (Version 7 or Version 8). Choose NDS 7 only if you are installing the server in an existing network and you have not already upgraded the network to NDS 8.

✔ The Server ID number. The installation program creates a default server ID for you, but you can provide your own number if you want to use some type of numbering scheme to identify your servers.

✔ The amount of hard drive space to allocate to the NetWare partition and the SYS volume.

✔ The name to use for the server.

✔ The name and size of any additional volumes that you want to create in the NetWare partition.

✔ The networking protocols that you want to enable. You can enable IP, IPX, or both. *IP* is the protocol used for the Internet, and *IPX* is the original NetWare protocol. For most networks, you should enable just IP. Use IPX if all your servers are NetWare.

In most cases, you can simply choose the default options to create a functional server.

Installing Windows 2000 Server

Installing Windows 2000 Server is relatively straightforward. However, you should make a few decisions before you start the Setup process — in particular:

✔ The partitions arrangement for the server's disk. You can set the entire disk up as a single partition, or you can subdivide the disk into several smaller partitions that are easier to manage.

✔ The file system to use for each Windows 2000 volume. Windows 2000 Server supports three file systems: NTSF, FAT, and FAT32. In most cases, you should create NTSF volumes.

✔ The name of the domain that the server belongs to and whether the server is a domain controller. (A *domain* is a group of network computers that are managed together.)

✔ The server's computer name.

✔ The password for the administrator account.

After you start the Setup program, you simply follow the instructions that appear on the screen and provide any information that the Setup program requests. In most cases, the Setup program gives you default choices that allow you to create a functioning server.

Configuring Windows 9x/Me/XP for file and printer sharing

If your server computer runs Windows 95, 98, Millennium Edition, or XP, you must adjust the Windows settings to allow for file and printer sharing. For information about doing this, refer to Chapter 4.

Configuring Client Computers

Before your network setup is complete, you must configure the network's client computers. In particular, you have to configure each client's network interface card so that it works properly, and you have to install the right protocols so that the clients can communicate with other computers on the network.

Fortunately, configuring client computers for the network is child's play with Windows. For starters, Windows automatically recognizes your network interface card when you start up your computer. All that remains to connect to the network in Windows is to make sure that Windows installed the network protocols and client software properly. Here's how to do it with Windows 98 or Me:

1. **Choose the Start⊅Settings⊅Control Panel command to summon the Control Panel. Then double-click the Network icon.**

   The Network dialog box appears, as shown in Figure 11-2.

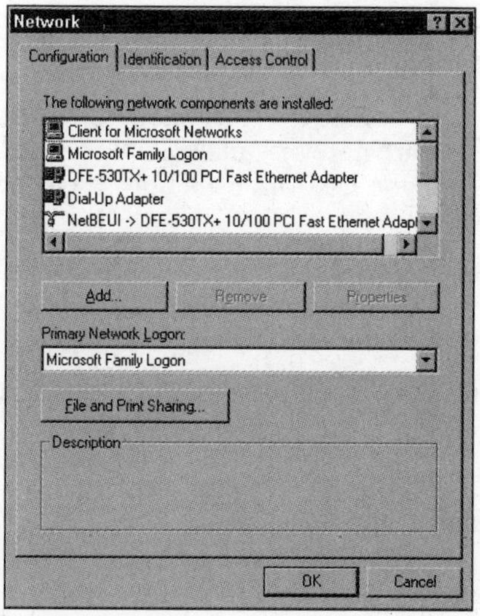

Figure 11-2:
The
Network
control
panel.

2. **Make sure that the network protocol that you're using appears in the list of network resources.**

   If you're creating a Windows-based network, make sure that you have the NETBEUI protocol listed. For a NetWare network, make sure that the IPX/SPX-compatible Protocol is listed. To enable access to the Internet or an intranet server, also make sure that TCP/IP is listed.

   If you wish, you can just enable TCP/IP and use it for Internet access as well as Windows and NetWare file and printer sharing. In many cases, this can simplify your network administration.

3. **If a protocol that you need isn't listed, click the A̲dd button to add the protocol that you need.**

   A dialog box appears asking if you want to add a network client, adapter, protocol, or service, as shown in Figure 11-3. Click Protocol and then click Add. A list of available protocols appears. Select the one that you want to add and then click OK. (You may be asked to insert a disk or the Windows CD-ROM.)

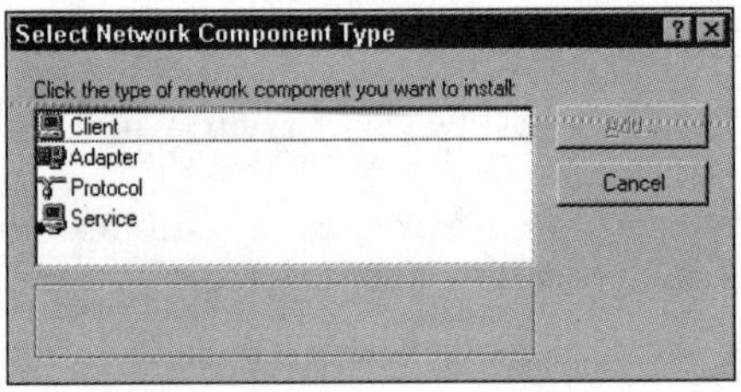

Figure 11-3:
Adding a
network
component.

Select Network Component Type	? ✕
Click the type of network component you want to install:	
Client	Add
Adapter	
Protocol	Cancel
Service	

4. **Make sure that the network client that you want to use appears in the list of network resources.**

   For a Windows-based network, make sure that Client for Microsoft Networks is listed. For a NetWare network, make sure that Client for NetWare Networks appears. If you network uses both types of servers, you can choose both clients.

   If you have NetWare servers, use the NetWare client software that comes with NetWare rather than the client supplied by Microsoft with Windows.

5. **If the client that you need isn't listed, click the A̲dd button to add the client that you need.**

   The dialog box in Figure 11-3 appears again. This time, click Client and then click Add. Select the network client that you want to add and then click OK.

6. **Click the client you just added and then click Properties.**

This summons a properties dialog box, whose appearance varies slightly depending on which client you selected.

7. Fill in the logon information and then click OK.

For the Microsoft Networks client, you can specify the name of the Windows NT or 2000 domain you want to log on to. For NetWare clients, you can type the name of the preferred server and a drive letter for the network drive. For a peer-to-peer Windows network without a dedicated server, you need to specify the name of the Windows workgroup.

8. Click OK to dismiss the Network dialog box.

You're done! Your computer reboots itself to enable the new network features that you just installed.

Configuring a Windows XP computer for networking is even easier because of the new Network Setup Wizard. Start it by clicking Start, then choosing All Programs⇨Accessories⇨Communications⇨Network Setup Wizard. Then answer the questions and smile while the Wizard configures your network for you.

Testing Your Network Installation

Your network isn't finished until you test it to make sure that it works. Hold your breath as you fire up your computers, starting with the server and then proceeding to the clients. Watch for error messages as each computer starts up. Then log on to the network to see whether it works. If it doesn't, the following paragraphs should help you find the problem:

- ✔ If you have a problem, the first culprit to suspect is your network cable. Check all your connections, especially any connections you crimped yourself. If you're using thinnet, make sure that the terminators are attached properly. If you're using UTP, make sure that the hub is plugged in and turned on.

- ✔ If you're using UTP, you can find a bad cable by checking the light on the back of each network card and each hub connection. The light should be glowing steadily. If it's not glowing at all or if it's glowing intermittently, replace the cable or reattach the connector.

- ✔ Make sure that your network card's resource settings are set correctly by choosing System from the Control Panel (Start⇨Settings⇨Control Panel) and clicking the Device Manager tab. If the card is configured incorrectly, an exclamation mark appears next to the icon for the network card.

- ✔ Call up the Network Control Panel program and carefully review all the network settings. Make sure that you have bound the necessary protocols — NetBEUI, IPX/SPX, or TCP/IP — to your network card.

✔ If the network doesn't work, you may benefit from running the Windows built-in Networking Troubleshooter, as shown in Figure 11-4. To access the Networking Troubleshooter, click the Start button, and then choose the Help command. When the Help window appears, click Troubleshooting, and then locate the troubleshooter that you want to run.

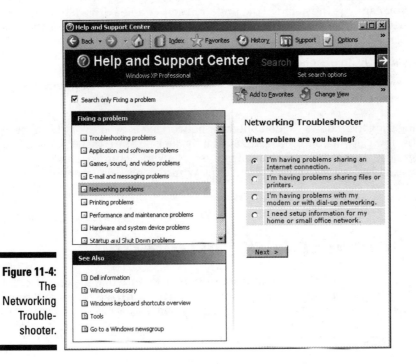

Figure 11-4:
The
Networking
Trouble-
shooter.

Part III
The Dummies Guide to Network Management

The 5th Wave   By Rich Tennant

"This part of the test tells us whether you're personally suited to the job of network administrator."

In this part . . .

You discover that there's more to networking than installing the hardware and software. After you get the network up and running, you have to keep it up and running. That's called network management.

The chapters in this section show you how to set up your network's security system, how to improve its performance, and how to protect your network from disaster. I include a bit of technical stuff here, but no one said life was easy.

Chapter 12

Help Wanted: A Network Manager's Job Description

*H*elp wanted. Network manager to help small business get control of a network run amok. Must have sound organizational and management skills.
Only moderate computer experience required. Part-time only.

Does this sound like an ad that your company should run? Every network
needs a network manager, whether the network has 2 computers or 200. Of
course, managing a 200-computer network is a full-time job, whereas managing a 2-computer network isn't. At least, it shouldn't be.

This chapter introduces you to the boring job of network management.
Oops . . . you're probably reading this chapter because you've been elected to
be the network manager, so I'd better rephrase that: This chapter introduces
you to the wonderful, exciting world of network management! Oh boy! This is
going to be fun!

Identifying the Network Manager: A Closet Computer Geek

Most small companies can't afford and don't need a full-time computer geek.
So the network manager is usually just a part-time computer geek. The ideal
network manager is a *closet computer geek:* someone who has a secret interest
in computers but doesn't like to admit it.

The job of managing a network requires some computer skills, but it isn't entirely a technical job. Much of the work that is done by the network manager is routine housework. Basically, the network administrator dusts, vacuums, and mops the network periodically to keep it from becoming a mess.

Here are some additional ideas about picking a network administrator:

- ✔ The network manager needs to be an organized person. Conduct a surprise office inspection and place the person with the neatest desk in charge of the network. (Don't warn them in advance, or everyone may mess up their desks intentionally the night before the inspection.)

- ✔ Allow enough time for network management. For a small network (say, no more than a dozen computers), an hour or two each week is enough. More time is needed up-front as the network manager settles into the job and finds out about the ins and outs of the network. But after an initial settling-in period, network management for a small office network doesn't take more than an hour or two per week. (Of course, larger networks take more time to manage.)

- ✔ Make sure that everyone knows who the network manager is and that the network manager has the authority to make decisions about the network, such as what access rights each user has, what files can and cannot be stored on the server, how often backups are done, and so on.

- ✔ Pick someone who is assertive and willing to irritate people. A good network manager should make sure backups are working *before* a disk fails and make sure everyone is following good anti-virus practices *before* a virus wipes out the entire network. People will be irritated by this, but it's for their own good.

- ✔ In most cases, the person who installs the network is also the network manager. That's appropriate because no one understands the network better than the person who designs and installs it.

- ✔ The network manager needs an understudy — someone who knows almost as much about the network, is eager to make a mark, and smiles when the worst network jobs are "delegated."

- ✔ The network manager has some sort of official title, such as Network Boss, Network Czar, Vice President in Charge of Network Operations, or Dr. Network. A badge, a personalized pocket protector, or a set of Spock ears helps, too.

Going by the Book

One of the network manager's main jobs is to keep the network book up-to-date. In Chapter 7, I suggest that you keep all the important information about your network in a ¼-inch binder. Give this binder a clever name, such as *The Network Bible* or *My Network and Welcome to It*. Here are some things that it should include:

✔ An up-to-date diagram of the network. This diagram can be a detailed floor plan, showing the actual location of each computer, or something more abstract and Picasso-like. Any time that you change the network layout, update the diagram. And include a detailed description of the change, the date that the change was made, and the reason for the change.

Microsoft sells a program called *Visio* that is specially designed for creating network diagrams. Figure 12-1 shows an example of a network diagram created with Visio.

✔ A detailed inventory of your computer equipment. Here is a sample form that you can use to keep track of your computer equipment:

Computer Equipment Checklist

Computer location:

User:

Manufacturer:

Model number:

Serial number:

Date purchased:

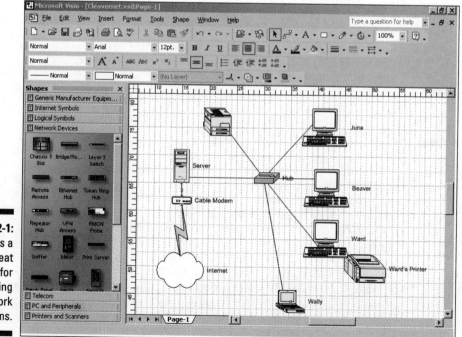

Figure 12-1:
Visio is a great program for scratching out network diagrams.

CPU type and speed:

Memory:

Hard drive size:

Video type:

Printer type:

Other equipment:

Operating system version:

Application software & version:

Network card type:

Connector (BNC/RJ-45):

✔ A printout from Microsoft System Information for each computer. (For more information about Microsoft System Information, refer to Chapter 7.)

✔ A detailed list of network resources and drive assignments.

✔ Any other information that you think may be useful, such as details about how you must configure a particular application program to work with the network, and copies of every network component's original invoice — in case something breaks and you need to seek warranty service.

✔ Backup schedules.

✔ Do not put passwords in the binder!

You may want to keep track of the information in your network binder using a spreadsheet or a database program. However, make sure you keep a printed copy of the information on hand.

Managing the Network

The most obvious duty of the network manager is to manage the network itself. The network's hardware — the cables, network adapter cards, hubs, and so on — needs oversight, as does the network operating system. On a big network, these responsibilities can become a full-time job. Large networks tend to be volatile: Users come and go, equipment fails, cables break, and life in general seems to be one crisis after another.

Smaller networks are much more stable. After you get your network up and running, you probably won't have to spend much time managing its hardware and software. An occasional problem may pop up, but with only a few computers on the network, problems should be few and far between.

Regardless of the network's size, all network administrators must attend to several common chores:

- The network manager should be involved in every decision to purchase new computers, printers, or other equipment. In particular, the network manager should be prepared to lobby for the most network-friendly equipment possible, such as new computers that already have network cards installed and configured and printers that are network-ready.

- The network manager must put on the pocket protector whenever a new computer is added to the network. The network manager's job includes considering what changes to make to the cabling configuration, what computer name and user ID to assign to the new user, what security rights to grant the user, and so on.

- Every once in a while, your trusty operating system vendor (in other words, Microsoft and Novell) releases a new version of your network operating system. The network manager's job is to read about the new version and decide whether its new features are beneficial enough to warrant an upgrade. In most cases, the hardest part of upgrading to a new version of your network operating system is determining the *migration path* — that is, how to upgrade your entire network to the new version while disrupting the network or its users as little as possible. Upgrading to a new network operating system version is a bit of a chore, so you need to carefully consider the advantages that the new version can bring.

- In between upgrades, Microsoft and Novell have a nasty habit of releasing patches and service packs that fix minor problems with their server operating systems. For more information, see the section "Patching Things Up" later in this chapter.

- One of the easiest traps that you can get sucked into is the quest for network speed. The network is never fast enough, and users always blame the hapless network manager. So the manager spends hours and hours tuning and tweaking the network to squeeze out that last 2 percent of performance. You don't want to get caught in this trap, but in case you do, Chapter 14 can help. It clues you in to the basics of tuning your network for best performance.

Doing the Routine Stuff That You Hate to Do

Much of the network manager's job is routine stuff — the equivalent of vacuuming, dusting, and mopping. Yes, it's boring, but it has to be done.

✔ The network manager needs to make sure that the network is properly backed up. If something goes wrong and the network isn't backed up, guess who gets the blame? On the other hand, if disaster strikes, yet you're able to recover everything from yesterday's backup with only a small amount of work lost, guess who gets the pat on the back, the fat bonus, and the vacation in the Bahamas? Chapter 15 describes the options for network backups. You'd better read it soon.

✔ Chapter 15 also describes another routine network chore — checking for computer viruses. If you don't know what a virus is, read Chapter 15 to find out.

✔ Users think that the network server is like the attic: They want to throw files up there and leave them there forever. The network manager gets the fun job of cleaning up the attic once in a while. Oh, joy. The best advice I can offer is to constantly complain about how messy it is up there and warn your users that spring-cleaning is coming up.

Managing Network Users

Managing network technology is the easiest part of network management. Computer technology can be confusing at first, but computers are not nearly as confusing as people. The real challenge of managing a network is managing the network's users.

The difference between managing technology and managing users is obvious: You can figure out computers, but you can never really figure out people. The people who use the network are much less predictable than the network itself. Here are some tips for dealing with users:

✔ Training is a key part of the network manager's job. Make sure that everyone who uses the network understands it and knows how to use it. If the network users don't understand the network, they may do all kinds of weird things to it without meaning to.

✔ Never treat your network users like they are idiots. If they don't under-stand the network, it's not their fault. Explain it to them. Offer a class. Buy them each a copy of this book and tell them to read the first six chapters. Hold their hands. But don't treat them like idiots.

✔ Make up a network cheat sheet that contains everything that the users need to know about using the network on one page. Make sure that everyone gets a copy.

✔ Be as responsive as possible when a network user complains of a net-work problem. If you don't fix the problem soon, the user may try to fix it. You probably don't want that.

Patching Things Up

One of the annoyances that every network manager faces is applying software patches to keep your operating system and other software up-to-date. A software *patch* is a minor update that fixes small glitches that crop up from time to time, such as minor security or performance issues. These glitches are not significant enough to merit a new version of the software, but they are important enough that they need to be fixed. Most of the patches correct security flaws that computer hackers have uncovered in their relentless attempts to prove that they are smarter than the security programmers at Microsoft or Novell.

Periodically, all the recently-released patches are combined into a *service pack*. Although the most diligent network administrators apply all patches as they are released, many administrators just wait for the service packs.

For all versions of Windows, you can use the Windows Update Web site to apply patches to keep your operating system and other Microsoft software up-to-date. In Windows XP, you can access Windows Update from the Help and Support Center (Start⇨Help and Support). In previous versions of Windows, you can find Windows Update in the Start menu. If all else fails, just fire up Internet Explorer and go to `windowsupdate.microsoft.com`. Windows Update automatically scans your computer's software and creates a list of software patches and other components that you can download and install. You can also configure Windows Update to automatically notify you of updates so that you don't have to remember to check for new patches.

Novell periodically posts patches and updates to NetWare on its product support Web site (`support.novell.com`). You can subscribe to an e-mail notification service that automatically sends you e-mail to let you know of new patches and updates.

Getting the Tools of a Network Manager

Network managers need certain tools to get their jobs done. Managers of big, complicated, and expensive networks need big, complicated, and expensive tools. Managers of small networks need small tools.

Some of the tools that the manager needs are hardware tools like screwdrivers, cable crimpers, and hammers. But the tools that I'm talking about here are software tools.

✔ Many of the software tools that you need to manage a network come with the network itself. As the network manager, you should read through the manuals that come with your network software to see what management tools are available. For example, Windows includes a `net diag` command that you can use to make sure that all the computers on a network can communicate with one another. (You can run `net diag` from an MS-DOS prompt.) For TCP/IP networks, you can run the `winipcfg` command from an MS-DOS prompt to verify a computer's TCP/IP configuration.

✔ The Microsoft System Information program that comes with Windows is a useful utility for network managers.

✔ Another handy tool you can get from Microsoft is the Hotfix Checker, which scans your computers to see what patches need to be applied. You can download the Hotfix Checker free of charge from Microsoft's web site. Just go to `www.microsoft.com` and search for `hfnetchk.exe`.

✔ I suggest that you get one of those 100-in-1 utility programs, such as Symantec's Norton Utilities. Norton Utilities includes invaluable utilities for repairing damaged disk drives, rearranging the directory structure of your disk, gathering information about your computer and its equipment, and so on.

Never use a disk repair program that was not designed to work with the operating system version that your computer uses. Any time that you upgrade to a newer version of your operating system, you should also upgrade your disk repair programs to a version that supports the new operating system version.

✔ More software tools exist for NetWare and Windows NT/2000 networks than for peer-to-peer networks — not only because NetWare and Windows NT are more popular than peer-to-peer networks, but also because NetWare and Windows NT networks tend to be larger and more in need of software management tools than peer-to-peer networks.

Chapter 13

Who Are You? (Or, Big Brother's Guide to Network Security)

*B*efore you had a network, computer security was easy. You just locked your door when you left work for the day. You could rest easy, secure in the knowledge that the bad guys would have to break down the door to get to your computer.

The network changes all of that. Now, anyone with access to any computer on the network can break into the network and steal *your* files. Not only do you have to lock your door, but you also have to make sure that everyone else locks their doors, too.

Fortunately, network operating systems have built-in provisions for network security. This situation makes it difficult for someone to steal your files even if they do break down the door. All modern network operating systems have security features that are more than adequate for all but the most paranoid users.

And when I say *more* than adequate, I mean it. Most networks have security features that would make even Maxwell Smart happy. Using all these security features is kind of like Smart insisting that the Chief lower the "Cone of Silence." The Cone of Silence worked so well that Max and the Chief couldn't hear each other! Don't make your system so secure that even the good guys can't get their work done.

If any of the computers on your network are connected to the Internet, then you have a whole new world of security issues to contend with. For more information about Internet security, refer to Chapter 17. Also, if your network supports wireless devices, you have to contend with wireless security issues. For more information about security for wireless networks, see Chapter 20.

Do You Need Security?

Most small networks are in small businesses or departments where everyone knows and trusts everyone else. They don't lock up their desks when they take a coffee break, and although everyone knows where the petty cash box is, money never disappears.

Network security isn't necessary in an idyllic setting like this one, is it? You bet it is. Here's why any network should be set up with at least some minimal concern for security:

- Even in the friendliest office environment, some information is and should be confidential. If this information is stored on the network, you want to store it in a directory that's only available to authorized users.

- Not all security breaches are malicious. A network user may be routinely scanning through his or her files and discover a filename that isn't familiar. The user may then call up the file, only to discover that it contains confidential personnel information, juicy office gossip, or your resume. Curiosity, rather than malice, is often the source of security breaches.

- Sure, everyone at the office is trustworthy now. But what if someone becomes disgruntled, a screw pops loose, and he or she decides to trash the network files before jumping out the window? Or what if that same person decides to print a few $1,000 checks before packing off to Tahiti?

- Sometimes the mere opportunity for fraud or theft can be too much for some people to resist. Give people free access to the payroll files, and they may decide to vote themselves a raise when no one is looking.

- Finally, remember that not everyone on the network knows enough about how Windows and the network work to be trusted with full access to your network disks. One careless mouse click can wipe out an entire directory of network files. One of the best reasons for activating your network's security features is to protect the network from mistakes made by users who don't know what they're doing.

Two Approaches to Security

When you plan how you to implement security on your network, you should first consider which of two basic approaches to security you will take:

✔ An open-door type of security, in which you grant everyone access to everything by default, and then place restrictions just on those resources you want to limit access to.

✔ A closed-door type of security, in which you begin by denying access to everything, and then grant specific users access to the specific resources they need.

In most cases, the open-door policy is easier to implement. After all, typically only a small portion of the data on a network really needs security, such as confidential employee records or secrets like the Coke recipe. The rest of the information on a network can be safely made available to everyone who can access the network.

If you choose the closed-door approach, you set up each user so that he or she has access to nothing. Then, you grant each user access only to those specific files or folders that he or she needs.

The closed-door approach results in tighter security, but leads to the Cone of Silence Syndrome: like Max and the Chief who can't hear each other talk while they're under the Cone of Silence, your network users will constantly complain that they can't access the information they need. As a result, you'll find yourself frequently adjusting users' access rights. Choose the closed-door approach only if your network contains a lot of information that is very sensitive, and only if you are willing to invest time administrating your network's security policy.

Mastering Your Domain

A *domain* is a group of related computers that are managed together. Most smaller networks consist of a single domain, but larger networks can be partitioned into two or more domains to simplify the task of administration. That feature is why the login dialog box for a Windows network requires that you enter a domain name to access the network.

A company with offices in separate locations is likely to create a separate domain for each location. For example, the San Francisco and Los Angeles offices may have separate domains. Or different departments may have separate domains: The accounting and marketing departments may have their own domains.

Domains can be connected by *trust relationships*. For example, the marketing department domain can be set up so that it trusts the accounting department domain — the marketing domain recognizes users in the accounting department domain.

As you can imagine, managing domains and trust relationships for a large network is the stuff of pocket protectors and propeller caps. If your network is large enough to require more than one domain, you need more help than this gentle introduction to network security can offer. I suggest that you consult *Windows NT Networking For Dummies,* by Ed Tittel, Mary Madden, and Earl Follis (Wiley Publishing, Inc.).

Every domain must have one server designated as the *Primary Domain Controller* (also known as the *PDC*), which is responsible for managing the directory information for the domain. Large networks with several servers can also have one or more *Backup Domain Controllers,* which reduces the workload of the Primary Domain Controller and can take over in case the PDC server fails.

Windows 2000 partially alleviates the pain of managing large multi-domain networks with its new Active Directory. *Active Directory* provides a single directory database to cover the entire network, no matter how many different servers or users you have and regardless of whether your network is contained within a single room or spread across the entire planet.

In Active Directory, domain names are hierarchical and resemble Internet names. For example, the root domain for a company might be *cleaver.com.* This domain can be partitioned into child domains such as *marketing.cleaver.com* and *research.cleaver.com.*

Domains are an important part of your security plan because many of the details of network security are managed by domains. For example, domains are used to manage user accounts that allow users to access the network. After a user has logged on to a domain, he or she can access the network resources that are shared by that domain.

User Accounts

The first level of network security is the use of *user accounts* to allow only authorized users access to the network. Without an account, a computer user can't log in and therefore can't use the network.

Every user account is associated with a *user ID,* which the user must enter when logging in to the network. Each account also has other network information associated with it, such as the user's password, the user's full name, user rights that tell the network what the user can and cannot do on the network, and file system rights that determine which drives, folders, and files the user can access.

Besides simply identifying network users, user accounts provide additional controls as well:

> ✔ Both NetWare and Windows NT/2000 Server enable you to specify that certain users can log in only during certain times of the day. This feature enables you to restrict your users to normal working hours, so that they

can't sneak in at 2 a.m. to do unauthorized work. The feature also discourages your users from working overtime because they can't access the network after hours, so use it judiciously.

✔ Both NetWare and Windows NT/2000 Server enable you to create *group accounts* that you can use to set up several accounts with identical access rights. When you use a group account, each user still has an individual account with a user ID and password. In addition, the user accounts indicate which group or groups the user belongs to. All user accounts that belong to a particular group "inherit" the group account's access rights.

✔ Group accounts are the key to managing your user accounts. Set up group accounts for each different type of network user that your network has. For example, you may create one type of group account for the accounting department and another for the sales department. Then you can easily configure the group accounts so that the accounting users can't mess with the sales users' files and vice versa.

✔ A user can belong to more than one group, in which case the user inherits the rights of each group. For example, suppose you have groups set up for Accounting, Sales, Marketing, and Finance. A user who needs to access both Accounting and Finance information can be made a member of both the Accounting and Finance groups. And a user who needs access to both Sales and Marketing information can be made a member of both the Sales and Marketing groups.

✔ Only real server operating systems such as NetWare and Windows NT/2000 Server have actual user accounts that prevent users who do not have accounts from accessing the network. Peer-to-peer networks that use Windows 9x, Me, or XP for their servers do not use user accounts. Instead, they merely allow you to password-protect shared resources, such as hard drives and printers. Any user who knows the correct password can access a shared resource. That is why you should always use NetWare, Windows NT/2000, or a similar server operating system (such as Unix or Linux) if security is a concern.

✔ Windows XP has a new file-sharing feature called Simple File Sharing, which does away with password protection for shared files and folders. If you need password protection for your shared files and folders, use Windows XP Professional Edition, which lets you disable Simple File Sharing.

Passwords

One of the most important aspects of network security is the use of passwords. User IDs are not usually considered secret. In fact, network users often need to know one another's user IDs. For example, if you use your network for e-mail, you have to know your colleagues' user IDs in order to address your e-mail properly.

Passwords, on the other hand, are top secret. Your network password is the one thing that keeps an impostor from logging on to the network using your user ID and therefore receiving the same access rights that you ordinarily have. *Guard your password with your life.*

Here are some tips for creating good passwords:

✔ Don't use obvious passwords, such as your last name, your kid's name, or your dog's name. Don't pick passwords based on your hobbies, either. A friend of mine is into boating, and his password is the name of his boat. Anyone who knows him can guess his password after a few tries. Five lashes for naming your password after your boat.

✔ Store your password in your head, not on paper. Especially bad: Writing your password down on a stick-on note and sticking it on your computer's monitor. Ten lashes for that. (If you must write your password down, write it on digestible paper that you can swallow after you've memorized the password.)

✔ Most network operating systems enable you to set an expiration time for passwords. For example, you can specify that passwords expire after 30 days. When a user's password expires, the user must change it. Your users may consider this process a hassle, but it helps limit the risk of someone swiping a password and then trying to break into your computer system later.

✔ You can also configure user accounts so that when they change passwords, they cannot specify a password that they've used recently. For example, you can specify that the new password cannot be identical to any of the user's past three passwords.

✔ Some network managers opt against passwords altogether because they feel that security is not an issue on their network. Or short of that, they choose obvious passwords, assign every user the same password, or print the passwords on giant posters and hang them throughout the building. In my opinion, ignoring basic password security is rarely a good idea, even in small networks. You should consider not using passwords only if your network is very small (say, two or three computers), if you do not keep sensitive data on a file server, or if the main reason for the network is to share access to a printer rather than sharing files. (Even if you don't use passwords, imposing basic security precautions like limiting certain users' access to certain network directories is still possible. Just remember that if passwords aren't used, nothing prevents a user from signing on using someone else's user ID.)

Generating Passwords For Dummies

How do you come up with passwords that no one can guess but that you can remember? Most security experts say that the best passwords don't correspond to any words in the English language but consist of a random sequence of letters, numbers, and special characters. But how in the heck are you supposed to memorize a password like DKS4%DJ2? Especially when you have to change it three weeks later to something like 3PQ&X(D8.

Here's a compromise solution that enables you to create passwords that consist of two four-letter words back to back. Take your favorite book (if it's this one, you need to get a life) and turn to any page at random. Find the first four-letter word on the page. Suppose that word is When. Then repeat the process to find another four-letter word; say you pick the word Most the second time. Now combine the words to make your password: WhenMost. I think you agree that WhenMost is easier to remember than 3PQ&X(D8 and is probably just about as hard to guess. I probably wouldn't want the folks at the Los Alamos Nuclear Laboratory using this scheme, but it's good enough for most of us.

Here are some additional thoughts on concocting passwords from your favorite book:

- ✔ If the words end up being the same, pick another word. And pick different words if the combination seems too commonplace, such as WestWind or FootBall.

- ✔ For an interesting variation, pick one four-letter word and one three-letter word and randomly pick one of the keyboard's special characters (like *, &, or >) to separate the words. You end up with passwords like Into#Cat, Ball$And, or Tree>Dip.

- ✔ If you want to use longer passwords, just use longer words. For example, if your passwords can be ten characters long, use a five-letter word, a four-letter word, and a separator, as in Right)Door, Horse!Gone, or Crime^Mark. Or, combine three four-letter words, such as WordGoodHard or WithThatYour.

- ✔ To further confuse your friends and enemies, use medieval passwords by picking words from Chaucer's *Canterbury Tales*. Chaucer is a great source for passwords because he lived before the days of word processors with spell-checkers. He wrote *seyd* instead of *said, gret* instead of *great, welk* instead of *walked, litel* instead of *little*. And he used lots of seven-letter and eight-letter words suitable for passwords, such as *glotenye* (gluttony), *benygne* (benign), and *opynyoun* (opinion).

- ✔ If you use any of these password schemes and someone breaks into your network, don't blame me. You're the one who's too lazy to memorize D#SC$H4@.

- ✔ If you do decide to go with passwords such as KdI22UR3xdkL, you can find random password generators on the Internet. Just go to a search service such as Google (www.google.com) and search for Password Generator. You'll find Web pages that generate random passwords based on criteria you specify, such as how long the password should be, whether it should include letters, numbers, punctuation, upper- and lowercase letters, and so on.

User Rights

User accounts and passwords are only the front line of defense in the game of network security. After a user gains access to the network by typing a valid user ID and password, the second line of security defense comes into play — rights.

In the harsh realities of network life, all users are created equal, but some users are more equal than others. The Preamble to the Declaration of Network Independence contains the statement, "We hold these truths to be self-evident, that *some* users are endowed by the network administrator with certain inalienable rights. . . ."

The specific rights that you can assign to network users depend on which network operating system you use. Here is a partial list of the user rights that are possible with Windows NT/2000 Server:

- ✔ **Log on locally:** The user can log on to the server computer directly from the server's keyboard.
- ✔ **Change system time:** The user can change the time and date registered by the server.
- ✔ **Shut down the system:** The user can perform an orderly shutdown of the server.
- ✔ **Back up files and directories:** The user can perform a backup of files and directories on the server.
- ✔ **Restore files and directories:** The user can restore backed-up files.
- ✔ **Take ownership of files and other objects:** The user can take over files and other network resources that belong to other users.

NetWare has a similar set of user rights.

Network rights that we'd like to see

The network rights allowed by most network operating systems are pretty boring. Here are a few rights I wish would be allowed:

- ✔ **Cheat:** Provides a special option that enables you to see what cards the other players are holding when you're playing Hearts.
- ✔ **Complain:** Automatically sends e-mail messages to other users that explain how busy, tired, or upset you are.

- ✔ **Set Pay:** Grants you special access to the payroll system so that you can give yourself a pay raise.
- ✔ **Sue:** In America, everyone has the right to sue. So this right should be automatically granted to all users.

File System Rights (Who Gets What)

User rights control what a user can do on a network-wide basis. File system rights enable you to fine-tune your network security by controlling specific file operations for specific users. For example, you can set up file system rights to allow users into the accounting department to access files in the server's \ACCTG directory. File system rights can also enable some users to read certain files but not modify or delete them.

Each network operating system manages file system rights in a different way. Whatever the details, the effect is that you can give permission to each user to access certain files, folders, or drives in certain ways.

Any file system rights that you specify for a folder apply automatically to any of that folder's subfolders, unless you explicitly specify a different set of rights for the subfolder.

In Novell's NetWare, file system rights are referred to as *trustee rights*. NetWare has eight different trustee rights, listed in Table 13-1. For every file or directory on a server, you can assign any combination of these eight rights to any individual user or group.

Table 13-1	NetWare Trustee Rights	
Trustee Right	**Abbreviation**	**What the User Can Do**
Read	R	The user can open and read the file.
Write	W	The user can open and write to the file.
Create	C	The user can create new files or directories.
Modify	M	The user can change the name or other properties of the file or directory.
File Scan	F	The user can list the contents of the directory.
Erase	E	The user can delete the file or directory.
Access Control	A	The user can set the permissions for the file or directory.
Supervisor	S	The user has all rights to the file.

Windows NT/2000 Server refers to file system rights as *permissions*. Windows NT/2000 Server has six basic permissions, listed in Table 13-2. As with NetWare trustee rights, you can assign any combination of Windows NT/2000 Server permissions to a user or group for a given file or folder.

Table 13-2	Windows NT/2000 Server Basic Permissions	
Permission	*Abbreviation*	*What the User Can Do*
Read	R	The user can open and read the file.
Write	W	The user can open and write to the file.
Execute	X	The user can run the file.
Delete	D	The user can delete the file.
Change	P	The user can change the permissions for the file.
Take Ownership	O	The user can take ownership of the file.

Note the last permission listed In Table 13-2: Take Ownership. In Windows NT/2000 Server, the concept of file or folder ownership is important. Every file or folder on a Windows NT/2000 Server system has an owner. The *owner* is usually the user who creates the file or folder. However, ownership can be transferred from one user to another. So why the *Take Ownership* permission? This permission prevents someone from creating a bogus file and giving ownership of it to you without your permission. Windows NT/2000 Server does not allow you to give ownership of a file to another user. Instead, you can give another user the right to take ownership of the file. That user must then explicitly take ownership of the file.

You can use Windows NT/2000 Server permissions only for files or folders that are created on drives formatted as NTFS volumes. If you insist on using FAT or FAT32 for your Windows NT/2000 Server shared drives, you can't protect individual files or folders on the drives. This is one of the main reasons for using NTFS for your Windows NT/2000 Server drives.

It's Good to Be the Administrator

It stands to reason that at least one network user must have the authority to use the network without any of the restrictions imposed on other users. This user is called the *administrator*. The administrator is responsible for setting up the network's security system. To do that, the administrator must be exempt from all security restrictions.

Many networks automatically create an administrator user account when you install the network software. The user ID and password for this initial administrator are published in the network's documentation and are the same for all networks that use the same network operating system. One of the first things that you must do after getting your network up and running is to change the password for this standard administrator account. Otherwise, all your elaborate security precautions are a farce; anyone who knows the default administrator user ID and password can access your system with full administrator rights and privileges, bypassing the security restrictions that you so carefully set up.

✔ Most network administrators use a boring user ID for the supervisor account, such as `Admin`, `Manager`, or `Super`. Some network administrators like to pretend that they're creative by using a clever user ID for the supervisor account. Here are some suitable user IDs for your supervisor account:

Matrix	Yoda
Chosen1	OB1
Aladdin	Picard
Genie	Data
Titan	Borg
Zeus	Barney
Skipper	HAL
Gilligan	M5

✔ ***Don't forget the password for the supervisor account!*** If a network user forgets his or her password, you can log in as the supervisor and change that user's password. But if you forget the supervisor's password, you're stuck.

User Profiles

User profiles are a Windows feature that keeps track of an individual user's preferences for his or her Windows configuration. For a non-networked computer, profiles enable two or more users to use the same computer, each with his or her own desktop settings, such as wallpaper, colors, Start menu options, and so on.

The real benefit of user profiles becomes apparent when profiles are used on a network. A user's profile can be stored on a server computer and accessed whenever that user logs on to the network from any Windows computer on the network.

The following are some of the elements of Windows that are governed by settings in the user profile:

- ✔ Desktop settings from the Display Properties dialog box, including wallpaper, screen savers, and color schemes.

- ✔ Start menu programs and Windows toolbar options.

- ✔ Favorites, which provide easy access to the files and folders that the user accesses frequently.

- ✔ Network settings, including drive mappings, network printers, and recently visited network locations.

- ✔ Application settings, such as option settings for Microsoft Word.

- ✔ The My Documents folder.

Chapter 14

If I Could Save Time in a Bottleneck: Optimizing Your Network's Performance

*T*he adage that there's no such thing as a free lunch really is true. When you network your computers, you reap the benefits of being able to share information and resources such as disk drives and printers. But you also have many costs. You have the cost of purchasing network cards, cable, and software, plus the cost of the time required to install the network, find out how to use it, and keep it running.

Another cost of networking exists that you may not have considered yet: the performance cost. No matter how hard you try, you can't hide the ugly truth that putting a computer on a network slows down the computer. Retrieving a word processing document from a network disk takes a bit longer than retrieving the same document from your local disk drive. Sorting that big database file takes a bit longer. And printing a 300-page report also takes a bit longer.

Notice that I use the word *bit* three times in the preceding paragraph. Lest my editor chide me for Overuse of a Three-Letter Word (OTLW), I better point out that I use the word three times to make a point. The network inevitably slows things down, but only a bit. If your network has slowed things down to a snail's pace — so that your users are routinely taking coffee breaks whenever they save a file — you have a performance problem that you can probably solve.

What Exactly Is a Bottleneck?

The term *bottleneck* does not in any way refer to the physique of your typical computer geek. (Well, I guess it *could,* in some cases.) Rather, computer geeks coined the phrase when they discovered that the tapered shape of a bottle of Jolt Cola limited the rate at which they could consume the beverage. "Hey," a computer geek said one day, "the gently tapered narrowness of this bottle's neck imposes a distinct limiting effect upon the rate at which I can consume the tasty caffeine-laden beverage contained within. This draws to mind a hitherto undiscovered yet obvious analogy to the limiting effect that a single slow component of a computer system can have upon the performance of the system as a whole."

"Fascinating," replied all the other computer geeks who were fortunate enough to be present at that historic moment.

The phrase stuck and is used to this day to draw attention to the simple fact that a computer system is only as fast as its slowest component. It's the computer equivalent of the old truism that a chain is only as strong as its weakest link.

For a simple demonstration of this concept, consider what happens when you print a word processing document on a slow printer. Your word processing program reads the data from disk and sends it to the printer. Then you sit and wait while the printer prints the document.

Would buying a faster CPU or adding more memory make the document print faster? No. The CPU is already much faster than the printer, and your computer already has more than enough memory to print the document. The printer itself is the bottleneck, so the only way to print the document faster is to replace the slow printer with a faster one.

Here are some other random thoughts about bottlenecks:

> ✔ **A computer system always has a bottleneck.** For example, suppose you've decided that the bottleneck on your file server is a slow IDE disk drive, so you replace it with the fastest SCSI drive money can buy. Now, the disk drive is no longer the bottleneck: The drive can process information faster than the controller card the disk is connected to. That doesn't mean you have eliminated the bottleneck; it just means that the disk controller is now the bottleneck instead of the disk drive. No matter what you do, the computer will always have some component that limits the overall performance of the system.

✔ **One way to limit the effect of a bottleneck is to avoid waiting for the bottleneck.** For example, print spooling lets you avoid waiting for a slow printer. Spooling doesn't speed up the printer, but it does free you up to do other work while the printer chugs along. Similarly, disk caching lets you avoid waiting for a slow hard drive.

✔ **One of the reasons computer geeks are switching from Jolt Cola to Snapple is that Snapple bottles have wider necks.**

The Eight Most Common Network Bottlenecks

Here are the eight most common network bottlenecks, in no particular order:

✔ **CPU in the file server:** If the file server is used extensively, it should have a powerful CPU. If you use NetWare or Windows NT or 2000 Server, look into getting a server computer that can house two or more processors for even better performance. This is especially true for servers that do more than simply serve up files, such as databases or Web servers.

✔ **The amount and type of memory in the file server:** You can never have too much memory in the server. With the cost of memory so cheap these days, why not upgrade to 512MB or even 1GB? Also, make sure that you get the fastest type of RAM your computer's motherboard will support. Don't try to save a few dollars by using cheap, slow RAM.

✔ **The file server computer's bus:** Oops . . . this is kind of technical, so I put the details in a sidebar that you can skip. The nontechnical version is this: Make sure that your server computer has plenty of PCI slots and use only PCI network cards and disk controllers.

✔ **The network card:** Cheap $19.95 network cards are fine for small business or home networks, but don't use one in a file server that supports 50 users and expect to be happy with the server's performance. Remember that the server computer uses the network a lot more than any of the clients. So equip your servers with good network cards.

✔ **The file server's disk drives:** Get the fastest drives that you can find. If possible, use SCSI drives. Sorry! I went technical on you again. Time for another sidebar.

✔ **The file server's disk controller card:** All disks must connect to the computer via a controller card, and sometimes the bottleneck isn't the disk itself but the controller card. A beefed-up controller card can do wonders for performance. Also, if possible, it's best to give each drive its own controller card.

✔ **The server's configuration options:** All network operating systems have options that you can configure. Some of these options can make the difference between a pokey network and a zippy network. Unfortunately, no hard-and-fast rules exist for setting these options. Otherwise, you wouldn't have options.

✔ **The network itself:** If you have too many users, the network can become bogged down. Many ways exist to improve the performance of the network itself. One is to upgrade from 10 Mbps to 100 Mbps. Another is to use fast 100 Mbps switches instead of ordinary hubs. Still another is to segment the network into two or more smaller networks with a cool little device called a *bridge*.

The hardest part about improving the performance of a network is determining what the bottlenecks are. With sophisticated test equipment and years of experience, network gurus can make pretty good educated guesses. Without the equipment and experience, you can still make pretty good uneducated guesses. I'll give you some pointers on how to discover your computer's bottlenecks and improve your computer's performance in the remaining sections in this chapter.

Warning! Reading this may be hazardous to your sanity

Every computer has a *bus,* which is basically a row of slots into which you can plug expansion cards, such as disk controllers, modems, video controllers, and network adapter cards. New computers today come with two types of buses:

✔ **ISA:** ISA stands for Industry Standard Architecture. ISA bus is the most common type of expansion bus. It was designed many years ago when IBM introduced its first computers based on the 80286 processor. The ISA bus sends data between the CPU and the expansion cards at 8 or 16 bits at a time, depending on whether you use it with 8- or 16-bit adapter cards. The ISA bus runs at 8 MHz.

✔ **PCI:** Modern computers include a high-speed bus called a PCI bus, which overcomes the speed limitation inherent in the ISA bus design. Most new computers have several PCI slots and just one or two ISA slots. Some new computers have PCI slots exclusively, without even one ISA slot.

The original PCI slots, which came out with the first batch of Pentium computers, have PCI buses that work in 32-bit mode and operate at up to 33 MHz. Newer computers have faster 64-bit PCI slots (sometimes called PCI-X slots) that operate at up to 100 MHz.

If your network server uses disk drives or networking cards that are connected to the ISA bus, don't bother with any other efforts to improve network performance until you upgrade your server to use faster PCI disk controllers and network cards.

TECHNICAL STUFF

Just say no to technical stuff about drive interfaces

Disk drives come in several varieties, and not all of them are made equal. Here are the two basic types of drives used today:

✔ **IDE:** IDE, which stands for Integrated Drive Electronics (as if that matters), is the most common drive type used today. Don't embarrass yourself by trying to pronounce this term in any way other than spelling out the letters. The newest form of IDE, which allows larger drives and faster performance, is called by various names, including EIDE, ATA, ATA-2, Fast ATA, Ultra IDE, DMA, and probably others.

✔ **SCSI:** SCSI stands for Small Computer System Interface but is pronounced *Scuzzy*. SCSI drives have several advantages over IDE drives but are also a bit more expensive. SCSI also wins the prize for Best Computer

Acronym, hands down. Two newer, faster forms of SCSI are now available. Fast SCSI is twice as fast as basic SCSI, and fast-wide SCSI is twice as fast as fast SCSI, making it four times as fast as basic SCSI.

Performance zealots assure us that SCSI's network performance and reliability are vastly superior to IDE's. Unfortunately, SCSI drives are also more expensive than IDE, which is why IDE remains so popular. In computers, as in everything else, you get what you pay for. If you want top-notch file server performance, use only SCSI drives. And whether you use IDE or SCSI drives, make sure that you use PCI controller cards rather than older ISA controller cards. And finally, remember the old you-get-what-you-pay-for adage. A top-quality SCSI card may be more expensive than a cheap SCSI card but will probably perform better.

Tuning Your Network the Compulsive Way

You have two ways to tune your network. The first is to think about it a bit, take a guess at what may improve performance, try it, and see whether the network seems to run faster. This approach is the way most people go about tuning the network.

Then you have the compulsive way, which is suitable for people who organize their sock drawers by color and their food cupboards alphabetically by food groups. The compulsive approach to tuning a network goes something like this:

1. **Establish a method for objectively testing the performance of some aspect of the network.**

   This method is called a *benchmark*. For example, if you want to improve the performance of network printing, use a stopwatch to time how long printing a fairly large document takes.

2. **Change one variable of your network configuration and rerun the test.**

   For example, if you think that increasing the size of the disk cache can improve performance, change the cache size, restart the server, and run the benchmark test. Note whether the performance improves, stays the same, or becomes worse.

3. **Repeat Step 2 for each variable you want to test.**

Here are some salient points to keep in mind if you decide to tune your network the compulsive way:

- ✔ If possible, test each variable separately — in other words, reverse the changes you've made to other network variables before proceeding.

- ✔ Write down the results of each test so that you have an accurate record of the impact that each change has on your network's performance.

- ✔ Be sure to change only one aspect of the network each time you run the benchmark. If you make several changes, you won't know which one caused the change. Or one change may improve performance, but the other change may worsen performance so that the changes cancel each other out — kind of like offsetting penalties in a football game.

- ✔ If possible, make sure that no one else uses the network when you conduct the test; otherwise, the unpredictable activities of other network users can spoil the test.

- ✔ To establish your baseline performance, run your benchmark test two or three times to make sure that the results are repeatable. If the print job takes one minute the first time, three minutes the second time, and 22 seconds the third time, something is wrong with the test. A variation of just a few seconds is acceptable, though.

Tuning a Windows 95/98 or Millennium Edition Server

When you use Windows 95/98 or Me as a server, you have several options available that you can fiddle around with to improve the performance. Taking the time to set these options is worthwhile, because all network users notice the effect of a more efficient server computer.

Setting the File System performance option

Windows has a handy tuning feature that enables you to configure server options with a single click of the mouse. Here's how to tune a Windows server computer:

1. **Choose Start➪Settings➪Control Panel and then double-click the System icon.**

   The System Properties dialog box appears.

2. **Click the Performance tab.**

   The performance settings for your computer appear, as shown in Figure 14-1.

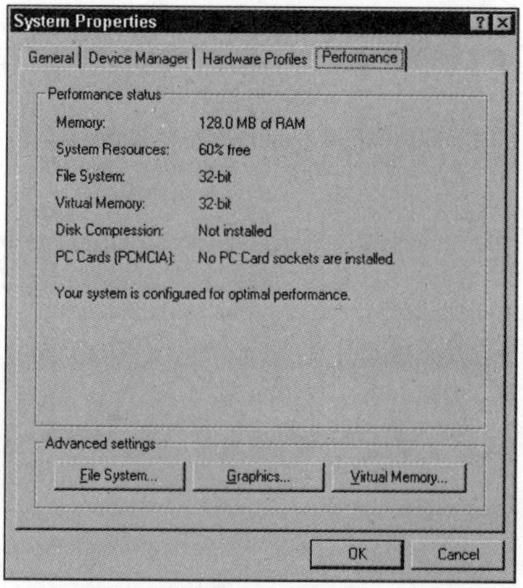

Figure 14-1:
Performance options for a Windows server.

3. **Click the File System button.**

   The File System Properties dialog box, shown in Figure 14-2, appears.

4. **Set the drop-down list box, which is labeled Typical Role of This Computer, to Network Server.**

   Your computer is now tuned as a network server.

5. **Click OK to dismiss the File System Properties dialog box.**

   You return to the System Properties dialog box.

6. **Click OK to dismiss the System Properties dialog box.**

That's all there is to it.

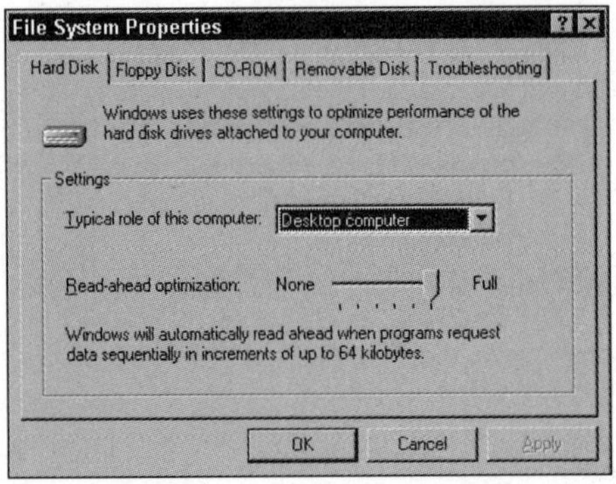

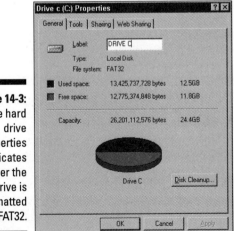

Figure 14-2:
Tuning the file system of a Windows server.

Using the FAT32 file system

FAT32, which was first introduced with Windows 98, is an improved method of storing data on your computer's hard drive. Formatting your disk drive with FAT32 slightly increases the amount of data you can store on the disk. Plus, it enables your computer to retrieve data from the disk faster, resulting in improved network performance.

The hard drives on most newer computers are already formatted with FAT32. To find out if yours is, double-click the My Computer icon on your desktop. Then, right-click the icon for the C drive and choose Properties from the menu that appears. That summons the Properties dialog box for the drive, as shown in Figure 14-3. The File System line, right below the disk drive's label, tells you whether the drive is formatted with FAT32.

Figure 14-3:
The hard drive Properties indicates whether the drive is formatted with FAT32.

If your hard drive is not already formatted with FAT32, you can convert the drive to FAT32 by choosing Start⇨Programs⇨Accessories⇨System Tools⇨ FAT32 Converter. The conversion takes a long time — perhaps an hour or more. You can't use your computer during the conversion, so just before lunch may be a good time to start.

Unfortunately, FAT32 imposes some limitations on you:

- ✔ If you convert a drive to FAT32, you can't use Microsoft's disk compression program DriveSpace to compress the data on the drive.
- ✔ After you convert a drive to FAT32, you have no easy way to convert it back to the old format.

In spite of these limitations, I recommend that you always use FAT32 for Windows 9x computers.

Tuning up Windows 9x

To help you tweak the performance of your Windows 9x computers, Windows 98 and Windows Me include a performance-tuning feature called Windows Tune-Up. Windows Tune-Up enables you to run several programs that optimize the performance of Windows, including ScanDisk (which corrects errors on your disk drive); Disk Defragmenter (which juggles your disk data so that it's arranged efficiently on the disk); and a program called Disk Cleanup (which removes unnecessary files from your computer).

The best thing about Windows Tune-Up is that it enables you to set up a schedule so that the tune-up programs run automatically on a periodic basis. For example, you can use Windows Tune-Up to specify that Disk Defragmenter and ScanDisk run every night at midnight and that Disk Cleanup runs every Friday at noon. This feature can help ensure that you always maintain your Windows 9x server computer at peak efficiency.

You can find Windows Tune-Up buried in the Start menu, under Programs⇨ Accessories⇨System Tools.

Tuning Windows XP

Windows XP Professional has several settings that can help improve performance for a computer that's used as a server. (These settings aren't available for Windows XP Home Edition because the Home Edition is not designed to operate as a server.) The most important settings are reached by opening the Control Panel, double-clicking the System icon, then choosing the Advanced tab and clicking the Performance Settings button. This brings up Performance Options dialog box. The Advanced tab of this dialog box, shown in Figure 14-4, sports the following performance options:

- ✔ **Processor Scheduling:** This option affects whether Windows should give preference to programs that are run by a user or programs run as background services. Because server features such as disk and printer sharing are background services, you should set this option to background services for a computer that's used as a dedicated server.

- ✔ **Memory Usage:** This option affects whether Windows gives more memory to programs run by users or reserves more memory for use as system cache. System cache memory is used by network services, so a dedicated server will run more efficiently if you select the System cache option.

- ✔ **Virtual Memory:** This option allows you to devote more disk space to a special file called the *paging file*. A larger paging file can support more network users, so if an XP server is performing poorly, increasing the size of the paging file may help. I recommend you set the minimum paging size to 1.5 times the amount of actual memory and the maximum size to twice the minimum. For example, if your computer has 256MB of RAM, set the paging file minimum to 384MB and the maximum to 768MB.

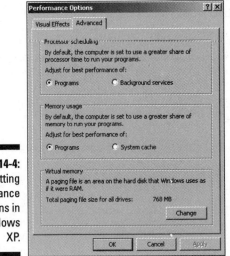

Figure 14-4:
Setting
Performance
Options in
Windows
XP.

Tuning a Windows NT/2000 Server

Tuning a Windows NT/2000 Server computer is more difficult than tuning a Windows 9*x* computer. A Windows NT/2000 Server includes dozens of options that can affect server performance. You can spend hours tweaking these options to squeeze optimum performance out of NT/2000. Plus, NT/2000 supports advanced hardware features such as multiple processors and RAID disk arrays, which can boost network performance.

The good news is that NT/2000 tends to be somewhat self-tuning. After NT/2000 runs for a few days, it soon adjusts itself to the pattern of usage it sees on your network and is purring like a kitten. You only need to trouble yourself with tuning Windows NT/2000 if something appears drastically wrong with the network's performance — for instance, if users complain that opening a two-page document on the network server takes ten minutes or that the print job they sent to the printer last Tuesday still hasn't printed.

To help monitor performance so that you can determine exactly where a performance problem lies, NT/2000 comes with a program called Performance Monitor. Performance Monitor gathers statistics about all kinds of activities on your server computer, such as disk I/O, program execution, network traffic, and so on. By analyzing these statistics, you can determine the source of a network performance problem. Depending on the problem, adjusting one of NT/2000's configuration settings may solve it, or you may need to purchase additional hardware to correct the problem.

Using Performance Monitor is simple. But interpreting the statistics it gathers isn't. Unless you're really into counting cache hits and average disk seek times, you probably want to steer clear of Performance Monitor if you possibly can.

Tuning a NetWare Server

Like Windows NT/2000 Server, NetWare is also a self-tuning system. Let it run for a few days to adjust to the usage patterns of your network, and it runs just fine. If you have a problem, you can always play with the server settings to try to improve performance.

Many NetWare configuration options are controlled with SET commands that you place in the AUTOEXEC.NCF file or the STARTUP.NCF file. For example, SET enables you to specify the amount of memory to use for file caching, the size of each cache buffer, the size of packet-receive buffers, and a whole bunch of other stuff that's way too low-level and detailed to go into in a proud book such as this one.

Chapter 15

Things That Go Bump in the Night: How to Protect Your Network Data

*I*f you're the hapless network manager, the safety of the data on your network is your responsibility. You get paid to lie awake at night worrying about your data. Will it be there tomorrow? If it's not, will *you* be able to get it back? And — most importantly — if you can't get it back, will *you* be there tomorrow?

This chapter covers the ins and outs of being a good, responsible, trustworthy network manager. They don't give out merit badges for this stuff, but they should.

Planning for Disaster

On April Fool's Day about 15 years ago, my colleagues and I discovered that some loser had broken into the office the night before and pounded our computer equipment to death with a crowbar. (I'm not making this up.)

Sitting on a shelf right next to the mangled piles of what used to be a Wang minicomputer system was an undisturbed disk pack that contained the only complete backup of all the information that was on the destroyed computer. The vandal didn't realize that one more swing of the crowbar would have escalated this major inconvenience into a complete catastrophe. Sure, we were up a creek until we could get the computer replaced. And in those days, you couldn't just walk into your local Computer Depot and buy a new computer off the shelf — this was a Wang minicomputer system that had to be specially ordered. But after we had the new computer, a simple restore from the backup disk brought us right back to where we were on March 31. Without that backup, getting back on track would have taken months.

I've been paranoid about disaster planning ever since. Before then, I thought that disaster planning meant doing good backups. That's a part of it, but I can never forget the day we came within one swing of the crowbar of losing everything. Vandals are probably much smarter now: They know to smash the backup disks as well as the computers themselves. There's more to being prepared for disasters than doing regular backups.

Don't think it can happen to you? A few years ago, wildfires in New Mexico came close to destroying the Los Alamos labs. How many computers do you think were lost to Hurricane Andrew? Not to mention the floods along the Mississippi in 1993 or the San Francisco earthquake in 1989? (I doubt that many computers were lost in the 1906 earthquake.) And I assume you saw *Armageddon.*

Most disasters are of the less spectacular variety. Make at least a rudimentary plan for how you can get your computer network back up and running should a major or minor disaster strike.

Here are a few additional things you can lay awake at night worrying about when it comes to disaster planning:

- ✔ The cornerstone of any disaster/recovery plan is a program of regular backups. I devote much of this chapter to helping you get a backup program started. Keep in mind, though, that your backups are only one swing of the crowbar from being useless. Don't leave your backup disks or tapes sitting on the shelf next to your computer: Store them in a fire-proof box or safe and store at least one set at another location.

- ✔ Your network binder is an irreplaceable source of information about your network. You should have more than one copy. I suggest that you take a copy home so that if the entire office burns to the ground, you still have a copy of your network documentation. Then you can decide quickly what equipment you need to purchase, and how you need to configure it to get your network back up and running again.

- ✔ After your computers are completely destroyed by fire, vandalism, or theft, how can you prove to your insurance adjuster that you really had all that equipment? A frequently overlooked part of planning for disaster is keeping a detailed record of what computer equipment you own. Keep copies of all invoices for computer equipment and software in a safe place. And consider making a videotape or photographic record of your equipment, too.

✔ Another aspect of disaster planning that's often overlooked is expertise. In many businesses, the one person who takes charge of all the computers is the only one who knows anything more than how to start Word and print a letter. What if that person becomes ill, decides to go work for the competition, or wins the lottery and retires to the Bahamas? Don't let any one person at the office form a computer dynasty that only he or she can run. As much as possible, spread the computer expertise around.

Backing Up Your Data

The main goal of backups is simple: Make sure that no matter what happens, you never lose more than one day's work. The stock market may crash, hanging chads may factor into another presidential election, and Jar Jar Binks may be in yet another *Star Wars* movie. But you never lose more than one day's work if you stay on top of your backups.

Now that we agree on the purpose of backups, we can get to the good stuff: how to do it.

Why you should buy a tape drive

If you plan on backing up the data on your network server's disk drives, you need something to back up the data to. You could copy the data onto diskettes, but a 20GB disk drive would need about 14,000 diskettes to do a full backup. That's a few more diskettes than most of us want to keep in the closet. Instead of diskettes, you want to back up your network data to tape. With an inexpensive tape drive, you can copy as much as 20GB of data onto a single tape.

The beauty of a tape drive is that you can start your backups and leave. You don't have to baby-sit your computer, feeding it disk after disk and reading a bad novel in between disk swaps. The labor savings can pay for the cost of the tape drive in the first week.

✔ The most popular style of tape backup for smallish networks is called *Travan drives*. Travan drives come in a variety of models with tape capacities ranging from 8GB to 20GB. You can purchase a 8GB drive for under $200 and a 20GB unit for about $300. (Travan drives used to be known as QIC drives.)

✔ For larger networks, you can get tape backup units that offer higher capacity and faster backup speed than Travan drives, for more money of course. DAT (Digital Audio Tape) units can back up as much as 40GB on a single tape, and DLT (Digital Linear Tape) drives can store up to 80GB on one tape. DAT and DLT drives can cost $1,000 or more, depending on the capacity.

✔ If you're really up the backup creek with hundreds of gigabytes to back up, you can get robotic tape backup units that automatically fetch and load tape cartridges from a library, so you can do complete backups without having to load tapes manually. Naturally, these units aren't cheap: The small ones, which have a library of 8 tapes and a total backup capacity of over 300GB, start at about $5,000.

✔ An alternative to tape drives for backups is removable disk drives — disk drives housed in cartridges that you can insert or remove like a giant floppy disk. The best known removable disk drives are made by Iomega. Iomega's Jaz Drive sells for about $350 and can back up 2GB of data on each cartridge.

✔ Another alternative to tape drives for backups is rewritable CD drives, known as *CD-RW* drives. A CD-RW drive can write about 600MB of data to each CD.

Backup programs

All versions of Windows come with a built-in backup program. In addition, most tape drives come with backup programs that are often faster or more flexible than the standard Windows backup. And you can purchase sophisticated backup programs that are specially designed for large networks, which have multiple servers with data that must be backed up.

For a simple Windows 9*x* server in a peer-to-peer network, the built-in backup program that comes with Windows is adequate for backing up the server. Figure 15-1 shows the Windows 98 backup program in action.

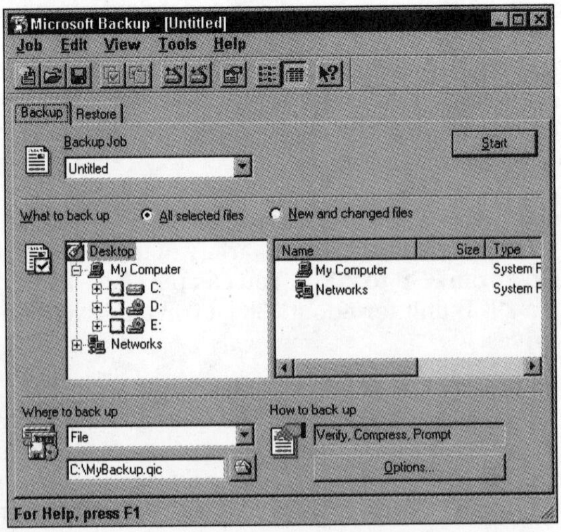

Figure 15-1: Windows Backup.

Backup programs do more than just copy data from your hard drive to tape. Backup programs use special compression techniques to squeeze your data so that you can cram more data onto fewer tapes. Compression factors of 2:1 are common, so you can usually squeeze 4GB of data onto a tape that would hold only 2GB of data without compression. (Tape drive manufacturers tend to state the capacity of their drives using compressed data, assuming a 2:1 compression ratio. So a 20GB tape has an uncompressed capacity of 10GB.)

Backup programs also help you keep track of which data has been backed up and which hasn't, and they offer options such as incremental or differential backups that can streamline the backup process, as described in the next section.

You don't have to back up every file every day

If you have a tape drive and all your network data can fit on one tape, the best approach to backups is to back up all your data every day. Backing up all of the data on a server is referred to as a *full* backup.

If you have more data than can fit on one tape, consider using *incremental* backups instead. An incremental backup backs up only the files that you've modified since the last time you did a backup. Incremental backups are a lot faster than full backups because you probably only modify a few files each day. And if a full backup takes three tapes, you can probably fit an entire week's worth of incremental backups on a single tape.

Stop me before I get carried away

The archive bit is not an old Abbott & Costello routine ("All right, I wanna know who modified the archive bit." "What." "Who?" "No, what." "Wait a minute . . . just tell me what's the name of the guy who modified the archive bit!" "Right.").

The archive bit is a little flag that's tucked into each file's directory entry, right next to the file name. Any time that a program modifies a file, Windows (or your server operating system) sets the file's archive bit to the ON position. Then after a backup program backs up the file, it sets the file's archive bit to the OFF position.

Because backup programs reset the archive bit after they back up a file, they can use the archive bit to select just the files that have been modified since the last backup. Clever, eh?

Differential backups work because they don't reset the archive bit. When you use differential backups, each differential backup backs up all the files that have been modified since the last full backup.

Here are some additional tips on using incremental backups:

- The easiest way to use incremental backups is to do a full backup every Monday and then do an incremental backup on Tuesday, Wednesday, Thursday, and Friday. (This assumes, of course, that you can do a full backup overnight on Monday. If your full backup takes more than 12 hours, you might want to do it on Friday instead so that it can run over the weekend.)

- When you use incremental backups, the complete backup consists of the full backup tapes and all the incremental backup tapes you've made since you did the full backup.

- A variation of the incremental backup idea is the *differential* backup. A differential backup backs up all the files that have been modified since the last time you did a *full* backup. When you use differential backups, the complete backup consists of the full backup disks plus the disks from your most recent differential backup.

Server versus client backups

When you back up network data, you have two basic approaches to running the backup software: You can run the backup software on the file server itself, or you can run the backups from one of the network's clients. If you run the backups from the file server, you'll tie up the server while the backup is running. Your users will complain that their access to the server has slowed to a snail's pace. On the other hand, if you run the backup over the network from a client computer, you'll flood the network with gigabytes of data being backed up. Your users will complain that the entire network has slowed to a snail's pace.

Network performance is one of the main reasons you should try to run your backups during off hours, when other users are not accessing the network. Another reason is so that you can perform a more thorough backup. If you run your backup while other users are accessing files, the backup program will skip over any files that are being accessed by users at the time the backup runs. As a result, your backup won't include those files. Ironically, the files most likely to get left out of the backup are often the files that need backing up the most because they're the files that are being used and probably modified.

Here are some extra thoughts on client and server backups:

- You may think that backing up directly from the server would be more efficient than backing up from a client because data doesn't have to travel over the network. Actually, this assumption isn't usually the case, because most networks are faster than most tape drives. The network probably won't slow down backups unless you back up during the busiest time of the day, when hordes of network users are storming the network gates.

✔ To improve network backup speed and to minimize the effect that network backups have on the rest of the network, consider using a 100 Mbps switch rather than a normal hub to connect the servers and the backup client. That way, network traffic between the server and the backup client won't bog down the rest of the network.

✔ Setting up a special user ID for the user who does backups is best. This user ID requires access to all the files on the server. If you're worried about security, take special precautions to guard the backup user's user ID and password. Anyone who knows it — and its password — can log in and bypass any security restrictions that you've placed on that user's normal user ID.

You can counter potential security problems by restricting the backup user ID to a certain client and a certain time of the day. If you're really clever (and paranoid), you can probably set up the backup user's account so that the only program it can run is the backup program.

✔ Any files that happen to be open while the backups are run won't get backed up. That's usually not a problem because backups are run at off hours when people have gone home for the day. However, if someone leaves their computer on with a Word document open, that Word document won't be backed up. One way to solve this problem is to set up the server so that it automatically logs everyone off the network before the backups begin.

Windows NT/2000 Server provides a special user group that you can use to create backup users.

How many sets of backups should you keep?

Don't try to cut costs by purchasing one backup tape and reusing it every day. What happens if you accidentally delete an important file on Tuesday and don't discover your mistake until Thursday? Because the file didn't exist on Wednesday, it won't be on Wednesday's backup tape. If you have only one tape that's reused every day, you're outta luck.

The safest scheme is to use a new backup tape every day and keep all your old tapes in a vault. Pretty soon, though, your tape vault can start looking like the warehouse where they stored the Ark of the Covenant at the end of *Raiders of the Lost Ark.*

As a compromise between these two extremes, most users purchase several tapes and rotate them. That way, you always have several backup tapes to fall back on in case the file you need isn't on the most recent backup tape. This technique is called *tape rotation,* and several variations are in common use:

- The simplest approach is to purchase three tapes and label them A, B, and C. You use the tapes on a daily basis in sequence: A the first day, B the second day, C the third day, then A the fourth day, B the fifth day, C the sixth day, and so on. On any given day, you have three *generations* of backups: today's, yesterday's, and the day-before-yesterday's. Computer geeks like to call these the *grandfather, father,* and *son* tapes.

- Another simple approach is to purchase five tapes and use one each day of the week.

- A variation of this scheme is to buy eight tapes. Take four of them and write *Monday* on one label, *Tuesday* on another, *Wednesday* on the third, and *Thursday* on the fourth label. On the other four tapes, write *Friday 1, Friday 2, Friday 3,* and *Friday 4.* Now, tack a calendar up on the wall near the computer and number all the Fridays in the year: 1, 2, 3, 4, 1, 2, 3, 4, and so on.

  On Monday through Thursday, you use the appropriate daily backup tape. When you do backups on Friday, you consult the calendar to decide which Friday tape to use. With this scheme, you always have four weeks' worth of Friday backup tapes, plus individual backup tapes for the past five days.

- If bookkeeping data lives on the network, making a backup copy of all your files (or at least all your accounting files) immediately before closing the books each month and retaining those backups for each month of the year is a good idea. Does that mean you should purchase 12 additional tapes? Not necessarily. If you back up just your accounting files, you probably can fit all 12 months on a single tape. Just make sure that you back up with the "append to tape" option rather than the "erase tape" option so that the previous contents of the tape aren't destroyed. And treat this accounting backup as completely separate from your normal daily backup routine.

You should also keep at least one recent full backup at another location. That way, if your office should fall victim to an errant Scud missile or a rogue asteroid, you can re-create your data from the backup copy you stored offsite.

A word about tape reliability

From experience, I've found that although tape drives are very reliable, once in a while they run amok. Problem is, they don't always tell you they're not working. A tape drive — especially the less expensive Travan type drives — can spin along for hours, pretending to back up your data, when in reality, your data isn't being written reliably to the tape. In other words, a tape drive can trick you into thinking that your backups are working just fine, but when disaster strikes and you need your backup tapes, you may just discover that the tapes are worthless.

Don't panic! You have a simple way to assure yourself that your tape drive is working. Just activate the "compare after backup" feature of your backup software. Then, as soon as your backup program finishes backing up your data, it rewinds the tape, reads each backed-up file, and compares it with the original version on disk. If all files compare, you know your backups are trustworthy.

Here are some additional thoughts about the reliability of tapes:

✔ The compare function doubles the time required to do a backup, but that doesn't matter if your entire backup fits on one tape. You can just run the backup after hours. Whether the backup and repair operation takes one hour or ten doesn't matter, as long as it's finished by the time you arrive at work the next morning.

✔ If your backups require more than one tape, you may not want to run the compare-after-backup option every day. But be sure to run it periodically to check that your tape drive is working.

✔ If your backup program reports errors, throw away the tape and use a new tape.

Changing the Oil Every 3,000 Miles

Like cars, disk drives need periodic maintenance. Fortunately, all versions of Windows as well as Netware come with programs that can do some of the necessary maintenance for you.

ScanDisk

Bad news: Windows sometimes has trouble keeping track of all the files you heap onto your computer's disk drives. In particular, if your dog steps on your computer's power cord while you're working on a file, Windows may lose track of exactly where the file is located on the disk. The same thing can happen if you simply turn your computer off without first choosing Shut Down from the Start menu and waiting for Windows to tell you it's okay to turn off your computer.

Good news: Windows comes with a program called ScanDisk, which can correct the type of file damage that occurs when your computer is turned off at the wrong moment. In fact, ScanDisk does such a good job of correcting this type of problem that Windows runs it automatically when you turn your computer back on after turning it off without first using the Start⇨Shut Down command.

ScanDisk does more than repair files damaged by premature shutdown. ScanDisk can also check the reliability of your computer's disk drives by trying to write something onto every sector of your disk and then reading it back to see whether it took. (Don't worry — ScanDisk does this without upsetting any of the existing data on your disk.) Figure 15-2 shows the Windows XP version of ScanDisk. (To access this program in Windows XP, open My Computer, right-click the icon for the disk you want to check, and then choose Properties. Click the Tools tab; then click the Check Now button.)

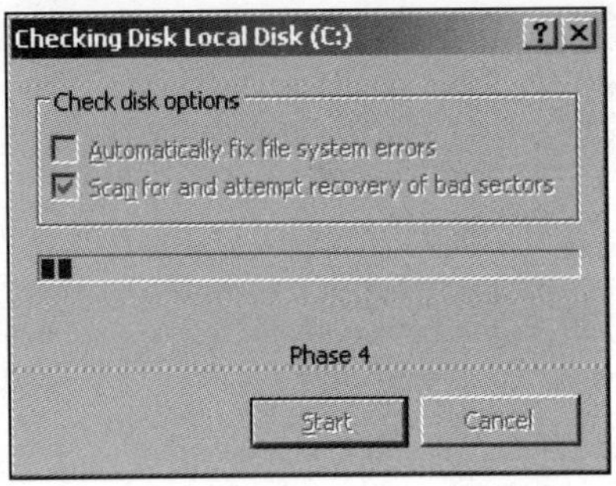

Figure 15-2:
ScanDisk.

ScanDisk can do a thorough check of your disk's recording surface to make sure that it can reliably read and write data. The check takes a while, but it's worth the wait.

If ScanDisk detects a problem, it displays a message that describes the problem and offers to fix it for you. Read the instructions on the screen and select the "More Info" function if you don't understand what's going on.

Windows NT includes its own version of ScanDisk built into the Disk Administrator program. To activate it, choose Start⇨Programs⇨Administrative Tools⇨Disk Administrator.

Disk defragmenting

Another routine type of service you should perform on your computer periodically is to defragment its disk drives. Defragmenting a drive rearranges all the data that's stored on the drive so that the data can be accessed efficiently. Because normal use causes the data on most drives to become scattered about, or fragmented, defragment your drives on a regular basis.

Windows includes a program that defragments your hard drives, named appropriately Disk Defragmenter. You can find it on the Start menu under Programs➪Accessories➪System Tools.

Guarding against Dreaded Computer Viruses

Viruses are one of the most misunderstood computer phenomena around these days. What is a virus? How does it work? How does it spread from computer to computer? I'm glad you asked.

What is a virus?

Make no mistake, viruses are real. Now that most of us are connected to the Internet, viruses have really taken off. Every computer user is susceptible to attacks by computer viruses, and using a network increases your vulnerability because it exposes all network users to the risk of being infect by a virus that lands on any one network user's computer.

Viruses don't just spontaneously appear out of nowhere. Viruses are computer programs that are created by malicious programmers who've lost a few screws and should be locked up.

What makes a virus a virus is its capability to make copies of itself that can be spread to other computers. These copies, in turn, make still more copies that spread to still more computers, and so on, ad nauseam.

Then, the virus patiently waits until something triggers it — perhaps when you type a particular command, press a certain key, or when a certain date arrives, depending on when the person who created the virus wants the virus to go off. What the virus does when it strikes also depends on what the virus creator wants the virus to do. Some viruses harmlessly display a "gotcha" message; others maliciously wipe out all the data on your hard drive. Ouch.

A few years back, viruses moved from one computer to another by latching themselves onto floppy disks. Whenever you borrowed a floppy disk from a buddy, you ran the risk of infecting your own computer with a virus that might have stowed away on the disk.

Nowadays, virus programmers have discovered that e-mail is a much more efficient method to spread their viruses. Typically, a virus masquerades as a useful or interesting e-mail attachment, such as instructions on how to make $1,000,000 in your spare time, pictures of naked celebrities, or a Valentine's Day greeting from your long lost sweetheart. When a curious but unsuspecting user double-clicks the attachment, the virus springs to life, copying itself onto the users computer and, in some cases, sending out copies of itself to all of the names in the user's address book.

Once the virus has worked its way onto a networked computer, the virus can then figure out how to spread itself to other computers on the network.

Here are some more tidbits about protecting your network from virus attacks:

- ✔ The term *virus* is often used to refer not only to true virus programs (which are able to replicate themselves) but also to any other type of program that's designed to harm your computer. These programs include so-called *Trojan horse* programs that usually look like games but are in reality hard-disk formatters.

- ✔ Computer virus experts have identified several thousand "strains" of viruses. Many of them have colorful names, such as the I Love You virus, the Stoned virus, and the Michelangelo virus.

- ✔ Antivirus programs can recognize known viruses and remove them from your system, and they can spot the telltale signs of unknown viruses. Unfortunately, the idiots who write viruses aren't idiots (in the intellectual sense), so they're constantly developing new techniques to evade detection by antivirus programs. New viruses are frequently discovered, and the antivirus programs are periodically updated to detect and remove them.

- ✔ A *worm* is similar to a virus, but doesn't actually infect other files. Instead, it just copies itself into other computers on a network. After a worm has copied itself onto your computer, there's no telling what it may do there. For example, a worm might scan your hard disk for interesting information such as passwords or credit card numbers and e-mail them to the worm's author. Yuk!

Antivirus programs

The best way to protect your network from virus infection is to use an antivirus program. These programs have a catalog of several thousand known viruses that they can detect and remove. In addition, they can spot the types of changes viruses typically make to your computer's files, decreasing the likelihood that some previously unknown virus will go undetected.

At one time, Microsoft got into the antivirus program business, bestowing its last and best version of MS-DOS with an antivirus program called MSAV. Unfortunately, neither Windows 9x nor Windows NT/2000 Server comes with antivirus protection, so you have to purchase a program on your own. The two best-known antivirus programs for Windows are Norton Antivirus by Symantec and McAfee's VirusScan.

The good folks who make antivirus programs maintain Internet sites that have updates that enable their programs to capture newly discovered viruses. Consult the documentation (ugh!) that came with your antivirus program to find out how you can obtain these updates.

Safe computing

Besides using an antivirus program, you have a few additional precautions that you can take to ensure virus-free computing. If you haven't talked to your kids about these safe-computing practices, you had better do so soon.

- ✔ Regularly back up your data. If you are hit by a virus and your anti-virus software can't repair the damage, you may need the backup to recover your data. Make sure that you restore from a backup that was created before you were infected by the virus!

- ✔ If you buy software from a store and discover that the seal has been broken on the disk package, take the software back. Don't try to install it on your computer. You don't hear about tainted software as often as you hear about tainted beef, but if you buy software that's been opened, it may well be laced with a virus infection.

- ✔ Use your antivirus software to scan your disk for virus infection after your computer has been to a repair shop or worked on by a consultant. These guys don't intend harm, but they occasionally spread viruses accidentally, simply because they work on so many strange computers.

- ✔ Do not open e-mail attachments from people you don't know or attachments you were not expecting. And don't let your users enable the HTML feature in their e-mail programs. It's all too easy to embed a virus in an HTML e-mail message. Such viruses can be activated simply by reading the message that contains them.

- ✔ Use your antivirus software to scan any floppy disk that doesn't belong to you before you access any of its files.

Beware of autorun viruses

A few years ago, a new kind of virus appeared on the virus scene. Once, you could safely assume that viruses were only transmitted via program files. In other words, you couldn't catch a virus from a document file such as a word processing document. Unfortunately, this assumption is no longer absolutely true. Most modern word processing and spreadsheet programs (including Word, WordPerfect, WordPro, Excel, and Lotus 1-2-3) have a feature called *autorun macros,* which enable you to attach small programs called *macros* to document files. These macros then automatically run whenever the document is opened.

Unfortunately, unscrupulous people have figured out how to exploit this seemingly innocent feature to infect document files with viruses. So catching a virus from a document file is now possible.

The best protection against this new virus threat is to make sure that you have the most recent version of a good antivirus program such as McAfee's VirusScan. The latest versions of these programs should be able to detect document-borne viruses.

Chapter 16

How to Stay on Top of Your Network and Keep the Users Off Your Back

---

Network managers really have a rotten deal. Users come to you whenever anything goes wrong, regardless of whether the problem has anything to do with the network. They knock on your door if they can't log in, if they've lost a file, or if they can't remember how to use the microwave. They probably even ask you to show them how to program their VCRs.

This chapter brushes over a few basic things you can do to simplify your life as a network manager.

Training Your Users

After you first get your network up and running, invite all the network users to Network Obedience School, so that you can teach them how to behave on the network. Show them the basics of accessing the network, make sure that they understand about sharing files, and explain the rules to them.

A great way to prepare your users for this session is to ask them to read the first six chapters of this book. Remember, I wrote those chapters with the network user in mind, so they explain the basic facts of network life. If your users read those chapters first, they are in a much better position to ask good questions during obedience school.

Here are some more ways to make the training process painless for you and your users:

- ✔ **Write up a summary of what your users need to know about the network, on one page if possible.** Include everyone's user ID, the names of the servers, network drive assignments and printers, and the procedure for logging in to the network. Make sure that everyone has a copy of this Network Cheat Sheet.

- ✔ **Emphasize the etiquette of network life.** Make sure that everyone understands that all the free space on the network drive isn't his or her own personal space. Explain the importance of treating other people's files with respect. Suggest that users check with their fellow users before sending a three-hour print job to the network printer.

- ✔ **Don't bluff your way through your role as network manager.** If you're not a computer genius, don't pretend to be one just because you know a little more than everyone else. Be up front with your users. Tell them that everyone is in this together, and you're going to do your best to try to solve any problems that may come up.

- ✔ **If you ask your users to read the first six chapters of this book, place special emphasis on Chapter 6, especially the part about bribes.** Subtly suggest which ones are your favorites.

Organizing a Library

One of the biggest bummers about being the network manager is that every network user expects you to be an expert at every computer program he or she uses. That's a manageable enough task when you have only two network users and the only program they use is Microsoft Word. But if you have a gaggle of users who use a bevy of programs, being an expert at all of them is next to impossible.

The only way around this dilemma is to set up a well-stocked computer library that has all the information you may need to solve problems that come up. When a user bugs you with some previously undiscovered bug, you can say with confidence, "I'll get back to you on that one."

Your library should include the following:

- ✔ **A copy of your network binder:** All the information you need about the configuration of your network should be in this binder. (Don't put the original copy of the network binder in the library. Keep the original under lock and key in your office.)

✔ **A copy of the manuals for every program used on the network:** Most users ignore the manuals, so they won't mind if you "borrow" them for the library. If a user won't part with a manual, at least make a note of the manual's location so that you know where to find it.

✔ **A copy of the *Windows Resource Kit* for every version of Windows in use on your network:** You can get the *Windows Resource Kit* at any bookstore that has a well-stocked section of computer books.

✔ **A copy of the network software manual or manuals.**

✔ **At least 20 copies of this book:** (Hey, I have bills to pay.) Seriously, your library should contain books appropriate to your level of expertise. Of course, *For Dummies* books are available on just about every major computer subject. Devoting an entire shelf to these yellow-and-black books isn't a bad idea.

Keeping Up with the Computer Industry

The computer business changes fast, and your users probably expect you to be abreast of all the latest trends and developments. "Hey, Ward," they ask, "what do you think about the new version of SkyWriter? Should we upgrade, or should we stick with Version 23?"

"Hey, Ward, we want to build an Intranet Web site. What's the best Web page editor for under $200?"

"Hey, Ward, my kid wants me to buy a sound card. Which one is better, the SoundSmacker Pro or the BlabberMouth 9000?"

The only way to give halfway intelligent answers to questions like these is to read about the industry. Visit your local newsstand and pick out a few computer magazines that appeal to you.

✔ Subscribe to at least one general-interest computer magazine and one magazine specifically written for network users. That way, you can keep abreast of general trends plus the specific stuff that applies just to networks.

✔ Subscribe to e-mail newsletters that have information about the systems you use.

✔ Look for magazines that have a mix of good how-to articles and reviews of new products.

✔ Don't overlook the value of the advertisements in many of the larger computer magazines. Some people (including me) subscribe to certain magazines to read the ads as much as to read the articles.

✔ Keep in mind that most computer magazines are very technical. Try to find magazines written to your level. You may discover that after a year or two, you outgrow one magazine and are ready to replace it with one that's more technical.

The Guru Needs a Guru, Too

No matter how much you know about computers, plenty of people know more than you do. This rule seems to apply at every rung of the ladder of computer experience. I'm sure that a top rung exists somewhere, occupied by the world's best computer guru. But I'm not sitting on that rung, and neither are you. (Not even Bill Gates is sitting on that rung. In fact, Bill Gates got to where he is today by hiring people on higher rungs.)

As the local computer guru, one of your most valuable assets can be a knowledgeable friend who's a notch or two above you on the geek scale. That way, when you run into a real stumper, you have a friend you can call for advice. Here are some tips for handling your own guru:

✔ In dealing with your own guru, don't forget the Computer Geek's Golden Rule: "Do unto your guru as you would have your own users do unto you." Don't pester your guru with simple stuff that you just haven't spent the time to think through. But if you have thought it through and can't come up with a solution, give your guru a call. Most computer experts welcome the opportunity to tackle an unusual computer problem. It's a genetic defect.

✔ If you don't already know someone who knows more about computers than you do, consider joining your local PC users' group. The group may even have a subgroup that specializes in your networking software or may be devoted entirely to local folks who use the same networking software you do. Odds are, you're sure to make a friend or two at a users' group meeting. And you can probably convince your boss to pay any fees required to join the group.

✔ If you can't find a real-life guru, try to find an online guru. Check out the various computing newsgroups on the Internet. And subscribe to online newsletters that are automatically delivered to you via e-mail. (You can find a good list of online newsletters by searching Yahoo's computer category for *Newsletter.*)

✔ Remember that you can use the bribes listed in Chapter 6 on your own guru. The whole point of these bribes is to make your guru feel loved and appreciated.

Helpful Bluffs and Excuses

As network manager, you sometimes just won't be able to solve a problem, at least not immediately. You can do two things in this situation. The first is to explain that the problem is particularly difficult and that you'll have a solution as soon as possible. The second is to lie. Here are some of my favorite excuses and phony explanations:

✔ Blame it on the version of whatever software you're using.

✔ Blame it on cheap, imported memory chips.

✔ Blame it on Democrats. Or Republicans. Or hanging chads. Whatever.

✔ Blame it on Enron executives.

✔ Hope that the problem wasn't caused by stray static electricity. Those types of problems are very difficult to track down. Tell your users that not properly discharging themselves before using their computers can cause all kinds of problems.

✔ You need more memory.

✔ You need a bigger disk.

✔ You need a Pentium 4 to do that.

✔ Blame it on Jar Jar Binks.

✔ You can't do that in Windows 2000.

✔ You can only do that in Windows 2000.

✔ You're not using Windows 2000, are you?

✔ You'll have to wait for Windows .NET Server.

✔ Could be a virus.

✔ Or sunspots.

✔ All work and no beer makes Homer something something something. . . .

Part IV
Webifying Your Network

"One of the first things you want to do before connecting our network to the Internet is fog the users to keep them calm during the procedure."

In this part . . .

You discover how to meld your network with the Internet. In these chapters, you'll learn how to connect your network to the Internet, how to set up a Web server, and how to create your very own Web pages. Happy surfing! And hey, be careful out there.

Chapter 17

Connecting Your Network to the Internet

In This Chapter

▶ Connecting your computers to the Internet

▶ Selecting a Web browser

▶ Making your Internet connection secure

So you've decided to connect your network to the Internet. All you have to do is run to the local computer discount store, buy a modem, and plug it in, right? Wrong. Unfortunately, connecting to the Internet involves more than just installing a modem. For starters, you have to make sure that a modem is the right way to connect — other methods are faster but more expensive. Then, you have to select and configure the software you use to access the Internet. And finally, you have to lie awake at night worrying that hackers are breaking into your network via its Internet connection.

Connecting to the Internet

Connecting to the Internet is not free. For starters, you have to purchase the computer equipment necessary to make the connection. Then, you have to obtain a connection from an *Internet Service Provider,* or *ISP.* The ISP charges you a monthly fee that depends on the speed and capacity of the connection.

The following sections describe the most commonly used methods of connecting network users to the Internet.

Connecting with modems

A *modem* is a device that enables your computer to connect to another computer via the telephone. When you want to access the Internet, the modem uses a telephone line to actually dial in to an Internet provider. For this reason, a modem connection is often called a *dial-up connection*.

Modems are the most common and least expensive way to connect to the Internet, but they're also the slowest. Modems are inexpensive — you can get cheap ones for as little as $20. The standard speed for modems is 56 Kbps, which means that the modem can send about 56,000 bits of information per second over a standard phone connection

To use a modem, you must also have a phone line with a phone jack located near the computer. The modem ties up the phone line whenever you're connected to the Internet, so you can't use the phone for a voice conversation and connect to the Internet at the same time. (If you have call-waiting on the phone line you use to connect to the Internet, be sure to disable the call-waiting feature before you connect.) If you need to use the phone and the Internet at the same time, you'll have to get separate voice and data lines.

If you're going to connect your network users to the Internet with modems, I suggest you provide each user his or her own modem and a phone line for the modem to use. That way, each user can access the Internet independently of the LAN. After you install the modems and phone lines, contact a local Internet service provider, and the folks there can help you set up your Internet accounts.

If several of your network users need only occasional access to the Internet, consider adding a modem to a server computer and then using the Windows Internet Connection Sharing feature to share the dial-up connection over your network. For information about sharing a dial-up connection, see the section "Sharing an Internet Connection" later in this chapter.

Frankly, modem connections to the Internet are rapidly becoming a thing of the past. They're quickly being replaced by high-speed connections such as cable or DSL. Just as I like to tell my kids about how we used to have "party lines" on our phones, which meant that we could use the phone only if our neighbors weren't already using it, my kids will someday tell their kids about the good old days when they had "modems" on their phones to connect to the Internet and they could actually hear the modem call the Internet, and how excited they would get when they heard the Internet answer with a screech and a buzz. Ah, those were the days . . . .

Connecting with cable or DSL

If your network users will use the Internet frequently, you may want to consider one of two popular high-speed methods of connecting to the Internet: cable and DSL. Cable and DSL connections are often called *broadband connections,* for technical reasons you don't really want to know.

Cable Internet access works over the same cable that brings 40 billion TV channels into your home, whereas DSL is a digital phone service that works over a standard phone line. Both offer three major advantages over normal dial-up connections:

✔ **Cable and DSL are much faster than dial-up connections.** A cable connection can be anywhere from 10 to 200 times faster than a dial-up connection, depending on the service you get. And the speed of a DSL line is comparable to cable. (Although DSL is a dedicated connection, cable connections are shared among several subscribers. The actual speed of a cable connection may slow down when several subscribers use the connection simultaneously.)

✔ **With cable and DSL, you are always connected to the Internet.** You don't have to connect and disconnect each time you want to go online. No more waiting for the modem to dial your service provider and listening to the annoying modem shriek as it attempts to establish a connection.

✔ **Cable and DSL do not tie up a phone line while you are online.** With cable, your Internet connection works over TV cables rather than phone cables. And with DSL, the phone company installs a separate phone line for the DSL service, so your regular phone line is not affected.

Unfortunately, there's no such thing as a free lunch, and the high-speed, always-on connections offered by cable and DSL do not come without a price. For starters, you can expect to pay a higher monthly access fee for cable or DSL. In most areas of the United States, cable runs about $50 per month for residential users; business users can expect to pay more, especially if more than one user will be connected to the Internet via the cable.

The cost for DSL service depends on the access speed you choose. In some areas, residential users can get a relatively slow DSL connection for as little as $30 per month. For higher access speeds or for business users, DSL can cost substantially more.

Cable and DSL access are not available everywhere. If you live in an area where cable or DSL is not available, you can still get high-speed Internet access via a satellite hookup. With satellite access, you still need a modem and a phone line to send data from your computer to the Internet. The satellite is used only to receive data from the Internet. Still, a satellite setup like this is much faster than a modem-only connection.

DSL stands for *Digital Subscriber Line,* but that won't be on the test.

What about ISDN?

ISDN, which stands for *Integrated Services Digital Network,* is a digital phone service that was popular a few years ago as an alternative to dial-up connections. ISDN allows data to be sent about twice as fast as a conventional phone line — up to 128Kbps (kilobits per second) rather than 56Kbps. As an added plus, a single ISDN line can be split into two separate channels, so you can carry on a voice conversation while your computer is connected to the Internet.

Sounds great — the only catch is that it's expensive. An ISDN connection doesn't require a modem. Instead, you use a special ISDN adapter, which sets you back at least $250. In addition, you have to pay the phone company anywhere from $50 to $200 to install the ISDN line, and you pay a monthly fee ranging from $25 to $50 in the United States (depending on your area). On top of that, you may be billed by the minute for usage. For example, in my area, an ISDN line costs $24.95 per month, plus usage fees of about a penny a minute.

With the spread of low-cost cable modem access in many areas and the cost of DSL access coming down, ISDN is fast becoming a thing of the past. It was a good idea for its time, but its time has passed.

Connecting with high-speed private lines: T1 and T3

If you're really serious about high-speed Internet connections, contact your local phone company (or companies) about installing a dedicated high-speed digital line. These lines can cost you plenty (on the order of hundreds of dollars per month), so they're best suited for large networks in which 20 or more users are accessing the Internet simultaneously.

A T1 line has a connection speed of up to 1.544Mbps. A T1 line can service as many as 24 users simultaneously. Each user has a 64Kbps connection to the Internet, roughly equivalent to the speed each user can achieve with a dedicated 56Kbps modem and phone line. However, the fewer the number of users, the faster each connection can be.

A T3 line is even faster than a T1 line. A T3 line transmits data at an amazing 44.184Mbps. Each T3 line can be divided into 28 T1 lines. Because each T1 line can handle 24 users at 64Kbps, a T3 line can handle 672 users ($24 \times 28 = 672$). Of course, T3 lines are also considerably more expensive than T1 lines.

If you don't have enough users to justify the expense of an entire T1 or T3 line, you can lease just a portion of the line. With a *fractional T1 line,* you can

TIP

Sh...

✔ ICS allows several network users to share an Int
taneously. As a result, multiple users can bro
e-mail, or play online games all at the same

✔ Unfortunately, ICS can share only one
work is large enough that a single I
speed cable or DSL connection
Internet demands, you have to
features of a Windows or Ne

✔ The gateway computer
to the Internet throu

✔ Windows XP sim
Sharing by co
Network Se

An alternati
network
examp
whi

TIP

...JL connection. The other computers on your network connect to the
Internet through the gateway computer.

Here are a some key points to keep in mind about Internet Connection
Sharing:

> ✔ ICS uses a technique called *Network Address Translation,* or *NAT,* to fool
> the Internet into thinking that your entire network is really just one com-
> puter with a single IP address. Whenever one of the computers on your
> network requests information from the Internet, ICS replaces that com-
> puter's IP address with the gateway computer's IP address before send-
> ing the request out to the Internet. Then, when the requested
> information returns from the Internet, ICS figures out which computer on
> your network actually requested the information and sends the informa-
> tion to the correct computer. In this way, all interaction with the Internet
> is funneled through the gateway computer.

ernet connection simul-
wse the Web, read their
e time.

nternet connection. If your net-
ernet connection — even a high-
is not enough to satisfy your users'
use the more advanced communication
tWare server instead of ICS.

must be on before other computers can connect
h ICS.

plifies the task of setting up Internet Connection
figuring it automatically for you when you run the
up Wizard. For more information, see Chapter 21.

ve to ICS is to use a special-purpose device that connects your
to the Internet via dial-up modems or a cable or DSL connection. For
le, Linksys makes a product called the EtherFast Cable/DSL Router,
ch you can purchase for about $200. As its name suggests, the EtherFast
Cable/DSL Router includes a router that creates a link between your LAN and
a Cable or DSL modem. In addition, the EtherFast Cable/DSL Router provides
a four-port 10/100Mbps Ethernet switch, which enables you to connect four
computers (or more if you cascade additional hubs or switches).

The EtherFast Cable/DSL Router provides Network Address Translation so
that anyone on the LAN can access the Internet through the cable or DSL connection and also acts as a firewall by preventing unauthorized users from
accessing your LAN via the Internet connection. (For more information about
firewalls, see the section "Setting up a firewall" later in this chapter.)

Figure 17-1 shows how a small network can use a cable/DSL router to share a
cable Internet connection among six network users. As you can see, the cable
modem, which is connected to the cable system via a coaxial cable, connects
to the cable/DSL router via a twisted-pair Ethernet cable. Two of the six computers on the network are connected directly to the cable/DSL router's
10/100Mbps switch. The other four computers are connected to the
cable/DLS router through an Ethernet hub.

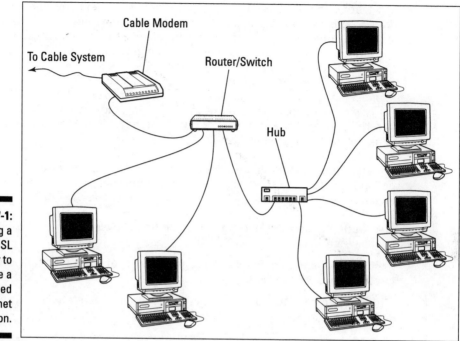

Figure 17-1:
Using a cable/DSL router to share a high-speed Internet connection.

Choosing a Web Browser

When you connect your LAN to the Internet, you must provide software known as a *Web browser* for your network's users to use when accessing the network. Although you have many different Web browsers to choose from, most people use Internet Explorer, the free Web browser that comes with Windows.

If you are using Windows XP, you already have the most current version of Internet Explorer (6). If not, you can download Internet Explorer 6 from Microsoft's Web site at www.microsoft.com/ie.

Internet Explorer isn't the only Web browser you can use to access the Internet. Many people prefer to use Netscape Navigator instead. In fact, some people have made the issue whether to use Navigator or Internet Explorer a type of Holy War, demonizing Internet Explorer and suggesting that it is nothing more than Microsoft chairman Bill Gates's most recent attempt at world domination.

The truth is that both Navigator and Internet Explorer are excellent programs. Both are so good, in fact, that recommending one over the other on any basis, other than personal preference, is difficult. I recommend that you use Internet Explorer, but I base my recommendation solely on the fact that I've written four books about Internet Explorer titled *Internet Explorer 4 For Windows For Dummies, Internet Explorer 5 For Windows For Dummies, Internet Explorer 5.5 For Windows For Dummies,* and *Internet Explorer 6 For Windows For Dummies.* (all published by Wiley Publishing, Inc., naturally). I would like to retire young. Choose whichever book matches the version of Internet Explorer that you're using.

Both Internet Explorer and Navigator come loaded with features that go beyond simple Web browsing. The complete Internet Explorer package includes a bunch of extra goodies, such as the following:

- **Outlook Express:** An e-mail program that can also handle Internet newsgroups
- **NetMeeting:** A conferencing program that enables you to conduct online meetings with other Internet users
- **MSN Messenger:** An online chatting program that lets you wile away the hours conversing with your online friends

Netscape distributes its Navigator program in a bundle of Internet products called Communicator. Besides Navigator, the Communicator package includes the following:

- **Netscape Messenger:** An e-mail and news reader program
- **Netscape Composer:** A tool for creating Web pages
- **Netscape Conference:** A feature, much like Microsoft's NetMeeting, that enables you to conduct online meetings with other users

The best news about Internet Explorer and Navigator is that both programs are free. You can go to www.microsoft.com/ie to download Internet Explorer from Microsoft's Web site, and you can go to www.netscape.com to download Communicator from Netscape's Web site.

Whichever browser you choose, you should standardize your entire network on one browser or the other. After all, when someone's Internet connection breaks, you're the one who's called in to fix it. If you standardize your Web browser, you become an expert in only one of them. If you don't standardize, you have to be an expert in both Navigator and Internet Explorer.

Understanding Internet Addresses

Just as every user of a LAN must have a user ID, everyone who uses the Internet must have an Internet address. Because the Internet has so many computers and so many users, a single user ID would not be sufficient. As a result, Internet addresses are constructed using a method called the *Domain Name System,* or *DNS*.

The term *domain,* when used in discussing Internet addresses, has nothing to do with Windows NT/2000 Server domains. Windows NT/2000 Server domains are used to segment large networks into smaller groups to simplify the task of managing user IDs and other network directory information. In contrast, Internet domains are simply a method of naming computers on the Internet.

The complete Internet address for a Web page is known as a URL, which stands for *Uniform Resource Locator.* A URL consists of three parts, written as follows:

```
protocol://host_address/resource_name
```

✔ For World Wide Web pages, the *protocol* portion of the URL is usually http (http stands for *Hypertext Transfer Protocol,* but you don't need to know that to use URLs). For secure Web sites, the protocol is https.

✔ The *host address* is the Internet address of the computer on which the Web page resides (for example, www.dummies.com).

✔ The final part, the *resource name,* is a name that the host computer assigns to a specific Web page or other file. In many cases, the resource name contains additional slashes that represent directories on the host system. Most of the time, you can omit the resource name completely if you simply want to display the home page for a company's Web site.

Here are some examples of complete URLs:

```
http://www.yahoo.com
```

```
http://www.cbs.com/network/tvshows/mini/lateshow
```

```
http://vol.com/~infidel/halloween/halloween.html
```

Notice that http:// must prefix all Web page addresses. However, Internet Explorer, Navigator, and other Web browsers cleverly add the http:// automatically, so you don't have to type it yourself.

Because the Web browser lets you omit the protocol part (http://), and because you can often omit the resource name, the only URL component you usually need to worry about is the host address. Host addresses themselves consist of three components separated from one another by periods, usually called *dots*.

✔ The first part of the Internet address is almost always www, to indicate that the address is for a page on the World Wide Web.

✔ The second part of the Internet address is usually a company or organization name, which is sometimes abbreviated if the full name is too long. Sometimes this second part actually consists of two or more parts in itself separated by periods. For example, in the address www.polis.iupui.edu, the second part is polis.iupui.

✔ The third and final part of an Internet address is a category that indicates the type of organization the name belongs to. The six most commonly used categories are summarized in Table 17-1. The category portion of an Internet address is also known as the *top-level domain*.

Table 17-1	Categories Used in Internet Addresses
Category	*Explanation*
edu	Education
mil	Military
gov	Government
com	Commercial
net	Network
org	Organizations that don't fit one of the other categories — usually nonprofit organizations

Besides the six top-level domains listed in Table 17-1, the top-level domain can also be a two-digit country code to indicate the country where the Web site resides, such as fr for France, ec for Ecuador, and la for Laos.

In addition, the people who govern the Internet recently adopted seven more top-level domains: .aero, .biz, .coop, .info, .museum, .name, and .pro. Although you may come across these top-level domains on occasion, they haven't really caught on so not many sites use them.

Putting these three address parts together, you get addresses such as www.microsoft.com, www.nasa.gov, and www.ucla.edu.

Occasionally, some Web addresses use a prefix other than www. Addresses get complicated when large organizations want to subdivide their networks into two or more groups. For example, a university may break its network down by department. Thus, the address of the history department at a university may be `history.gadolphin.edu`, whereas the track team may be located at `track.gadolphin.edu`.

Internet e-mail addresses are a bit different than Web page addresses. An e-mail address follows this format:

```
username@organization.category
```

As you can see, the address consists of a user name followed by an at-sign (@) and the organization and category portion of the domain name for the computer system which provides the user's e-mail account. For example, the e-mail address for a user named `Neil` who has an e-mail account at `nasa.gov` would be `neil@nasa.gov`.

When pronouncing an Internet address, the @ symbol is pronounced *at,* and the periods are pronounced *dot.* Thus, the address `neil@nasa.gov` would be pronounced *Neil at NASA dot gov.*

Coping with TCP/IP

TCP/IP — which stands for *Transmission Control Protocol/Internet Protocol* — is the low-level networking protocol that the Internet uses to send data back and forth between computers. Fortunately, you don't need to know many details about TCP/IP to work with the Internet, other than knowing that you have to make sure that TCP/IP is configured properly on each network computer if you want it to be able to access the Internet.

In network terms, a *protocol* is a set of rules that computers use to communicate with one another over a network. Unfortunately, the Internet uses different protocols than most local area networks use. To use the Internet successfully from a LAN, you have to convince your LAN's protocols and the Internet's protocols to coexist on the same network without stepping on one another's toes. Don't worry. . . you can do it. All modern network operating systems get along just fine with Internet protocols.

Here are a few other TCP/IP tidbits you should be aware of:

 ✔ TCP/IP is an open protocol, which means that it isn't tied to any one particular hardware or software vendor. Just about any vendor's hardware or software can work with TCP/IP. Earlier versions of both NetWare and Windows NT Server preferred to use their own protocols (IPX/SPX for

NetWare, NetBEUI for Windows NT). But nowadays, both NetWare and Windows NT/2000 Server can work as well with TCP/IP as with IPX/SPX or NetBEUI.

✔ TCP/IP isn't a cabling standard. TCP/IP works with whatever network cabling you already have installed. Thus, you can run TCP/IP on your existing Ethernet network cables.

✔ TCP/IP doesn't conflict with NetWare or Windows networking protocols. Thus, you can run the IPX/SPX, NetBEUI, and TCP/IP protocols together, over the same cables, at the same time.

✔ If you are able to access the Internet, TCP/IP is already up and running on your computer. If you are having trouble accessing the Internet, you can make sure TCP/IP is running by opening the Network Connections icon in the Control Panel and then opening the Properties dialog box for your local area network connection. TCP/IP should be listed as one of the protocols used by the connection. If it isn't, click the Add or Install button to add the TCP/IP protocol.

✔ TCP/IP is easy to configure. To add TCP/IP to your network, all you have to do is click the right buttons in the Network Control Panel.

What about IP addresses?

Friendly Internet addresses, such as microsoft.com and dummies.com, make surfing the Internet easy for us end users. But as you may imagine, computers don't deal directly with friendly addresses. Instead, TCP/IP uses special addresses called *IP addresses* to uniquely identify every computer in the world that's connected to the Internet.

An IP address is a 32-bit number that is usually written as a series of four decimal numbers separated by periods, like this: 130.32.15.3. Depending on the size of your network, the first two or three numbers in the address are assigned to your entire network. The rest of the address identifies an individual computer on your network.

If you connect your network to the Internet, every computer on your network that attempts to access the Internet needs its own IP address. Fortunately, you don't have to manually assign an IP address to each computer. Instead, a special server computer, which is called a *DHCP server,* can assign Internet addresses automatically. (Don't ask what *DHCP* stands for — you really don't need to know.) If you connect to the Internet via an Internet service provider (ISP), your ISP probably has its own DHCP Server that assigns IP addresses for you. If not, you can configure a Windows or NetWare server computer to operate as a DHCP server for your network. Or, you can manually assign an IP address to each of your computers.

Worrying about Security Issues

After any computer on your network connects to the Internet, a whole host of security issues arise. One of the most important security issues to worry about is that, unbeknownst to you, your Internet connection can function as a two-way street. Not only does it enable you to step outside the bounds of your network to access the Internet, but your Internet connection can also allow others to step in and access your network.

Securing your network

If any computer on your network is going to connect to the Internet via a modem, using proper security measures on the entire network is absolutely imperative. Here are some suggestions:

- ✔ **Never allow a computer attached to the Internet via a modem to enable file sharing for TCP/IP on its modem.** Doing so practically invites Internet hackers to explore your network. See the next section, "Disabling TCP/IP file sharing on a modem connection," for more information.

- ✔ **Make sure that every user must enter a password to access the system.** If you're using Windows NT/2000 Server or NetWare, require users to change passwords periodically and don't allow short passwords (fewer than seven or eight characters).

- ✔ **Make sure that all shared disk drives have restrictions so that only specific users or groups can access them.**

- ✔ **For Windows NT Server, use only NTFS volumes so that you can provide adequate security.**

Disabling TCP/IP file sharing on a modem connection

For a modem connection from a single Windows computer to the Internet, Windows allows you to enable file and printer sharing for TCP/IP connections over your modem. If you use that modem to connect to the Internet, you are inviting disaster. In Windows 98 and Me, you can follow these steps to make sure that file sharing is not enabled for TCP/IP via the modem:

1. **Choose Start⇨Settings⇨Control Panel and then double-click the Network icon.**

   This action brings up the Network control panel application, as shown in Figure 17-2.

2. **Click TCP/IP->Dial-Up Adapter in the list of network components.**

   You may have to scroll down this list to find it.

3. **Click the Properties button.**

   A dialog box appears, instructing you that this isn't the correct way to change the TCP/IP settings. Ignore it.

4. **Click OK to summon the TCP/IP Properties dialog box and then click the Bindings tab.**

   The dialog box shown in Figure 17-3 appears.

5. **Make sure that the File and Printer Sharing for Microsoft Networks option is *not* checked.**

   If this option is checked, click it to remove the check mark.

6. **Click OK to dismiss the TCP/IP Properties dialog box and then click OK again to dismiss the Network control panel.**

   Windows may pretend to look busy for a few moments and may even ask you to reboot your computer. If so, be patient.

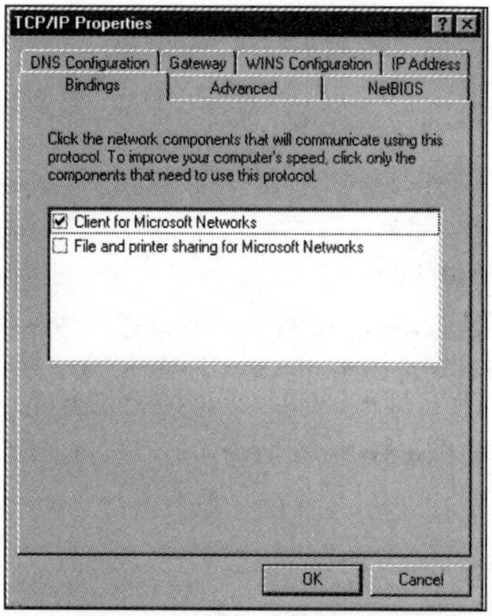

TCP/IP Properties

DNS Configuration | Gateway | WINS Configuration | IP Address
Bindings | Advanced | NetBIOS

Click the network components that will communicate using this protocol. To improve your computer's speed, click only the components that need to use this protocol.

☑ Client for Microsoft Networks
☐ File and printer sharing for Microsoft Networks

OK   Cancel

Figure 17-3:
Bindings for
TCP/IP on
the dial-up
adapter.

Setting up a firewall

A *firewall* is a security-conscious router that sits between the outside world and your network, in an effort to prevent *them* from getting to *us*. The firewall acts as a security guard between the Internet and your LAN. All network traffic into and out of the LAN must pass through the firewall, which prevents unauthorized users from accessing the LAN.

Some type of firewall is a must if you host a Web site on a server computer that's connected to your LAN. Without a firewall, anyone who visits your Web site can potentially break into your LAN and steal your top-secret files, read your private e-mail, or worse yet, reformat your hard drive.

Firewalls can also work the other way, preventing your network users from accessing Internet sites that you designate as off-limits.

There are several ways to set up a firewall. One is to purchase a hardware firewall, which is basically a router with built-in firewall features. Most hardware firewalls include a Web-based management program that enables you to connect to the firewall from any computer on your network using a Web browser. You can then customize the firewall settings to suit your needs.

Alternatively, you can set up a Windows NT/2000, NetWare, or UNIX/Linux server computer to function as a router and firewall. In fact, Chapter 25 offers some tips for creating a firewall using Linux.

If you are sharing an Internet connection via a Windows XP computer, you already have a built-in firewall. All you have to do is turn it on. Just follow these steps:

1. **Choose Start⇨Control Panel.**

   The control panel appears.

2. **Click the Network Connections link.**

   If Control Panel appears in Classic View rather than Category View, you won't see a Network Connections link. Instead, just double-click the Network Connections icon.

3. **Double-click the Local Area Connection icon.**

   A dialog box showing the connection's status appears.

4. **Click the Properties button.**

   The Connection Properties dialog box appears.

5. **Click the Advanced Tab, then check the Protect My Computer... option.**

   This option enables the firewall.

6. **Click OK.**

   That's all there is to it.

Considering other Internet security issues

Besides intruders breaking into your network via your Internet connection, you have other security concerns to worry about when your network users have Internet access. Here are some of the more important ones:

✔ **Sending information over the Internet.** Without the right security measures, sensitive information that users send out over the Internet can be intercepted and stolen. Sensitive information, such as passwords and credit card numbers, should always be transmitted over the Internet in an encrypted form.

✔ **Downloading programs over the Internet.** Programs that your users download to their computers may contain viruses that can infect your entire network. Virus protection is in order.

✔ **Viewing Web pages that do more than meets the eye.** Empowered by advanced programming tools, such as Java and ActiveX, and scripting languages, such as JavaScript and VBScript, a Web page can do more than display information: The page itself can act like a computer program. An unscrupulous Web programmer can set up a Web page that displays a smiley face while it secretly erases files on a user's hard disk or plants a virus that infects your network.

✔ **Opening unfriendly e-mail attachments.** One of the most common ways for viruses to spread themselves these days is via e-mail attachments. Be sure to provide adequate virus scanning for your mail server and instruct your users to never open attachments they are not expecting.

To guard against these threats, make sure that your Internet users use the built-in security features of their Web browsers. Fortunately, both Internet Explorer and Navigator have adequate security features to keep the bad guys at bay.

Chapter 18

Setting Up a Web Server

. . . .

. . . .

Sooner or later, you will discover that all your competitors have created their own home pages on the World Wide Web, and you will want to do likewise. Take a deep breath. Setting up your LAN so that your users can access the Internet is difficult enough. Creating your own Internet site is another matter altogether. I'm going to start by saying outright that this isn't something you should attempt on your own. Seek professional help.

If you choose to ignore my sage advice, read on. (Don't worry; I'm accustomed to being ignored. I have three teenaged daughters.)

The Web is one of the fastest changing fields in all of computerdom. As soon as you master one Web development tool, another one comes along to render the one you just learned obsolete. And every few months some hot new technology comes along that promises to revolutionize the way the Web works. Good luck and hang on!

Choosing a Hosting Service

The easiest way to set up a Web service is to set up an account with a Web hosting service. That way, you don't have to worry about setting up a server computer, configuring the Web server software, maintaining the server's Internet connection, and so on. You just pay a monthly fee for the privilege of setting up your Web site on someone else's Web server.

The best way to find a reliable Web hosting service is to ask people you know and trust and who have similar sites which service they use. You can also

search for "web host service" on a popular search engine such as Google
(www.google.com), but a recommendation from a trusted colleague is better
than a listing in a search engine.

Here are some pointers to keep in mind when choosing a Web host:

✔ Find out what software your Web host provides. Most provide either a
Microsoft Web server (Windows 2000 and IIS) or a Linux- or Unix-based
server such as Apache. Some also provide extra features such as a database server, support for Microsoft FrontPage, or a basic shopping-cart service that lets you sell your products directly from your Web site. These
services usually cost a bit more than the Web host's basic package.

✔ There is no such thing as unlimited bandwidth. Any company that claims
to offer unlimited bandwidth is lying. Reputable Web host services limit
the amount of data that can be transferred to or from your Web site,
either on a daily or monthly basis, and offer several different plans that
allow for varying amounts of traffic. For example, one company I've used
has several different plans, listed in Table 18-1.

Table 18-1	Typical Web Host Service Plans		
Plan Name	**Daily Allowance**	**Monthly Allowance**	**Monthly Fee**
Basic	100MB	3,000MB	$9.95
Advanced	300MB	9,000MB	$17.95
Webmaster	500MB	15,000MB	$27.95
Developer	600MB	18,000MB	$49.95
High-Volume	1,000MB	30,000MB	$129.95

✔ Web hosting plans also limit the amount of disk space available to you
on the server. Make sure your plan provides for enough disk space to
accommodate your site.

✔ Read the fine print before you sign a contract, especially the part about
how much extra you pay if you exceed the limits of your plan. And
review your bill each month to make sure you aren't being overcharged.

✔ If the Web hosting company offers to register your domain name for you,
make sure that they register it in your name, not theirs. If they register
your domain name in their own name, it may be difficult if not impossible for you to later move your site to another Web host. Better to register the name yourself. (For more information, see the section
"Registering Your Own Domain Name" later in this chapter.)

✔ If you use a Web hosting service, be sure to keep an up-to-date backup of
your Web site. Don't count on the hosting service to back up your site.

Setting Up Your Own Server

Another way to create your own home page is to set up your own Web server computer. The Web server computer is connected to the Internet via a high-speed connection, such as a DSL or a T1 or T3 line. The Internet server computer may run Windows NT or 2000 Server, NetWare, or a version of UNIX (including Linux). Most Internet servers run UNIX, although Windows NT/2000 is growing in popularity. In addition, you need special Internet server software.

Life gets more complicated if you want to connect the Internet server computer to your LAN. In that case, you must take special precautions to ensure that strangers can't use your Internet server as a back door into your LAN. Hackers love to break into computer systems this way, either to trash files, steal information, or just prove they can do it.

I definitely recommend against setting up your own server if you are building your first Web site. You have enough to worry about just creating your Web pages and keeping them up to date without having to worry about setting up and maintaining a Web server. If you insist on rolling your own, the following sections give you some pointers.

Selecting a Web server

To set up a Web site, you need to dedicate a separate computer to act as a Web server. All the information that's available via your Web site resides on this computer's disk, so plenty of disk storage is a must for your Web server. Plenty of RAM is a must also — consider 256MB to be the minimum. And get the biggest and fastest SCSI hard drives you can afford.

Selecting a Web-friendly operating system

For a Web-friendly network operating system, you have two basic choices: Windows NT or 2000 Server or UNIX. Because the Internet got its start in the UNIX world, more Web sites run UNIX than Windows NT. However, Windows NT is gaining ground, especially in intranets. If you're familiar with Windows but have never touched a UNIX computer, Windows NT Server is the way to go.

Oh, I know that Novell has recently endowed NetWare with Internet server tools. However, the vast majority of Web sites are hosted on Windows NT Server or UNIX. Stick with one of these options unless you're a NetWare zealot and want to be a renegade.

Selecting Web server software

In addition to a server operating system, you also need Web server software. The following sections briefly describe the three most popular Web server software choices.

Apache

By some estimates, two thirds or more of the Web servers on the Internet run Apache as their Web server software. Apache is available for several operating systems, including Windows NT/2000 and Mac OS Server, but most people who use Apache run the UNIX version.

Apache is popular for several reasons:

- ✔ **Apache is free.** You can download it from `www.apache.org`.
- ✔ **Apache is very reliable.** Apache is not the fastest Web server software available, but it is among the most bug-free.
- ✔ **Apache runs on just about any version of UNIX, including Linux.** In fact, just about all distributions of Linux come with Apache.
- ✔ **Apache is the direct descendant of the NCSA HTTPd server, which was the very first Web server.** Many of Apache's most ardent followers are Web old-timers, who started Web sites back when the Internet had only a few million users.

Microsoft Internet Information Server

A distant second in popularity behind Apache is Microsoft's Internet Information Server (IIS). IIS is a built-in part of Windows NT and Windows 2000 Server. IIS also comes with Windows XP Professional Edition. Because IIS runs well with Windows, IIS is the best Web server to use if you don't know or don't want to learn UNIX.

Sun ONE Web Server and other Web servers

Sun, the people who make high-power UNIX workstations and who invented Java, have their own Web server designed to compete with IIS and Apache, known as ONE Web Server. (Previous versions of ONE Web Server were known as iPlanet Web Server.) Unlike Apache and IIS, however, ONE Web Server gives you a choice of operating systems: You can run it on UNIX or Windows NT.

The bad news is that iPlanet Web Server isn't free. You must pay a license fee of $295–$1,495, depending on which edition you choose.

Besides IIS, Apache, and ONE Web Server, there are many other lesser-used servers out there to choose from. You can find them by using any search engine to search for "Web server," or you can go to ServerWatch (`serverwatch.internet.com`), a Web site devoted to keeping tabs on the latest developments in Web server software.

Keep in mind, however, that IIS and Apache are overwhelmingly the most popular Web servers available. As a result, you'll find plenty of books and Web sites devoted to them. If you choose a lesser-known Web server, you may have trouble finding the help you need to set it up and keep it running.

Registering Your Own Domain Name

An important part of setting up a Web site is obtaining your own domain name. You can choose any name your want for your domain name, provided that the name satisfies the basic rules for Internet domain names and no one else has already claimed the name. (For more information about domain names, refer to Chapter 17.)

Fortunately, getting your own domain name is easy and not very expensive. You can register a domain name for $35 per year. For a small additional charge, most domain name registration companies will also provide you with a one-page Web site you can use until you get your Web server up and running and may also throw in an e-mail account or two.

For a list of companies that can register a domain name for you, search for "Domain Registration" on an Internet search service such as Yahoo! or `msn.com`. One of the most popular domain registration companies is Network Solutions (`www.networksolutions.com`). With your credit card handy, you can easily register a domain name from the Network Solutions home page.

The bad news is that with so many companies and individuals already on the Web, odds are that the domain name you want has already been taken. Domain registration companies such as Network Solutions offer free search services that will tell you if the name you want is available. You may have to try several searches before you find a domain name that is available.

Understanding the Web Alphabet Soup

In addition to the Web server software such as IIS or Apache, there are many other Web services and features you need to contend with when you set up a Web server. Most of these features are three- or four-letter acronyms (TLAs and ETLAs). Occasionally you'll run into a five letter acronym (known as an AETLA, which stands for Augmented Extended Three Letter Acronym). The following sections highlight the more important TLAs, ETLAs, and AETLAs.

HTML

HTML, which stands for *HyperText Markup Language,* is what launched the Web. Although many people are mystified by HTML, HTML is actually a very simple. It's a way of adding special markup codes to a text file so that a Web browser knows how to display the text between the codes. For example, here's a small snippet of HTML:

```
This text is <b>bold</b>.
```

In this example, <b> and </b> are HTML markup codes that tells the Web browser that the text between the codes should be displayed in boldface.

HTML is used to display *static pages* — pages that don't change or interact with users. Most new Web pages use a more advanced dialect of HTML known as *DHTML,* which stands for *Dynamic HyperText Markup Language.* Pages created with DHTML often include fancy user-interface elements such as text that changes color or size when you roll the mouse over it.

HTTP

HTTP stands for *HyperText Transfer Protocol.* HTTP is the basic protocol that enables Web browsers to communicate with Web servers. When you type a Web address into the address bar of your Web browser and press the Enter key, the Web browser sends an HTTP message to the Web server at the address to request the HTML file that corresponds to the Web address you entered. The Web server retrieves the HTML file from its disk and sends an HTTP message that contains the page back to your browser. Your browser then displays the page.

FTP

FTP *(File Transfer Protocol)* is a method of exchanging files between a client and a server. FTP is often used to upload HTML files to a Web server. To use FTP, the server computer must have its FTP server software enabled, the client computer must have an FTP client program (Windows includes both a command-line FTP program and built-in FTP support in Internet Explorer), and the user must have an FTP account.

CGI

The earliest forms of HTML allowed only static information to appear on Web pages. Users could request the display of certain pages, but information flowed only in one direction: from the server to the client.

Then along came an HTML feature called *forms,* which enables Web developers to put simple data entry fields on their Web pages. Form fields were limited to simple text boxes, radio buttons, check boxes, and just two types of command buttons: one to send data to the server, the other to clear data entered on the form. This limited repertoire of controls allowed only simple interactions, but forms took off. The best Web sites used forms to create simple interactive applications.

Probably the best-known examples of Web sites that use forms are the search sites like Yahoo! and AltaVista. In a search site, you type a keyword into a text box and then click a command button. The search site then displays a list of Web sites that are related to the keyword you entered.

To use HTML forms, you have to contend with a feature called *CGI,* which stands for *Common Gateway Interface.* Here's how a form-based interaction using CGI works:

1. The client (that is, the Web browser) requests a page that contains a form. The server sends the requested page to the Web browser, which displays the page along with its form fields.

2. The user types information into the form fields and then clicks the Submit button. The Web browser gathers the information entered by the user and sends it back to the server.

3. The server receives the information sent from the Web browser, realizes that the information is data from a form, and runs a program that's specially designed to handle the form's data.

   This program is called a *CGI program.* You have to create the CGI program yourself, which means you have to understand the CGI scripting language if you want to use forms in your Web site.

4. The CGI program examines the data and does something worthwhile with it.

   In most cases, the CGI program retrieves information from a database.

5. The CGI program generates an HTML document that contains the results of the processing done in Step 4.

   For example, if the CGI program performed a database query, the HTML document contains the results of the query.

6. The server sends the HTML document generated by the CGI program to the Web browser.

7. The client displays the HTML document.

The key thing to note about CGI is that the CGI program itself always runs on the server. So, although CGI enables you to create interactive applications on the Web, it isn't very flexible or efficient.

Keep in mind that using CGI on your Web server opens up a can of security worms that you must deal with. For example, you must make sure that users cannot modify your CGI scripts or create their own CGI scripts to run on your server.

Java

For some reason, the movers and shakers of the Web world think that naming new Internet products after various types of coffee is cool. The whole thing started when Sun Microsystems released a revolutionary programming language for Web pages called *Java*. Everyone soon jumped on the bandwagon. Now you have JavaScript, Visual Café, Latte, Mocha, Hot Java (as if you want your Java cold), Star Buck, and JavaBeans. It all sounds like a scene from *L.A. Story*. ("I'll have a double decaf JavaBean Latte with a twist.")

So what exactly is Java? Java is a programming language that's used to create programs that run on an Internet user's computer rather than on the server computer. Java Web programs are called *applets* because they're not stand-alone programs. An applet must run within a Java-enabled Web browser, such as Navigator or Internet Explorer. (Java can also be used to create programs that run on the Web server rather than on the Internet user's computer.)

Java solves many of the problems inherent in the form-based CGI approach to building interactive Web applications. For starters, form-based applications can use only a limited range of controls: text boxes, radio buttons, check boxes, and Submit and Reset buttons. In contrast, you can build a Java applet to display any type of custom control that you want on a Web page. With Java, you can build interactive Web applications that sport fancy slider boxes, spin buttons, draggable objects, and any other type of control that you can imagine.

Scripts

Java is good, but its main drawback is that it's a complicated programming language that requires special tools to use. Enter scripts, which are simple programs that you can place directly into HTML documents without the need for any special type of programming tool. Scripts run much slower than Java applets but are much easier to create and use.

You have two competing scripting languages to choose from:

> ✔ **JavaScript:** This language was developed by Netscape and is the main scripting language for Navigator. Don't be fooled by the clever name: JavaScript bears little resemblance to Java. In fact, when Netscape first started developing JavaScript, it was called LiveScript. Netscape

changed the name to JavaScript in an attempt to capitalize on Java's popularity, even though JavaScript is not related in any way to Java.

✔ **VBScript:** This is Microsoft's scripting language for Internet Explorer. VBScript is based on Microsoft's popular Visual Basic programming language and is a tad bit easier to learn than JavaScript.

Note that Microsoft also ships Internet Explorer with its own version of JavaScript, called JScript. So with Internet Explorer, you have two scripting languages to choose from: JScript and VBScript. With Navigator, JavaScript is the only choice.

Web applications

Beyond just equipping HTML files with fancy JavaScript or VBScript scripts or using crude CGI for forms processing, modern Web servers let you create sophisticated *Web applications* in which programs run on the Web server to handle requests submitted by users.

To create a Web application, you have to go to Computer Geek school and learn how to write your own computer programs. Then, you can use one of these popular Web application environments to create your applications:

✔ **ASP**, which stands for *Active Server Pages.* ASP, which is from Microsoft, lets you create Web applications using a scripting language such as VBScript or JScript. ASP is included free with IIS.

✔ **ASP.NET**, the newest version of ASP. With ASP.NET, you can use more powerful programming languages such as Visual Basic .NET, C#, or Java. ASP.NET is also free.

✔ **JSP**, a Java-based system for developing Web application.

✔ **PHP**, a free Web application development environment that works with Apache. PHP is free and can be downloaded from www.php.net.

✔ **ColdFusion**, an application development system from Macromedia. You can find out more about ColdFusion at www.macromedia.com/software/coldfusion.

Chapter 19

Creating Your Own Web Pages

. . . .

. . . .

After you get your Web server set up, it's time to get to work putting pages on it so the world can visit your Web site. This chapter gets you pointed in the right direction so you can get started. You won't learn all the details of how to create Web pages, but you gain some insight into what kind of information to put on your Web site, what tools to use to create your pages, and some basics about working with HTML.

Planning Your Web Site

Before you dive in and start whipping out pages, you should spend some time designing the overall layout of your site. Think about what features you want to include in the site, what pages you'll have to create to implement those features, and how the pages will fit together.

For example, suppose the famous Cleaver family from *Leave It To Beaver* decides to put up a Web site. The site might include a mixture of personal and business features, such as:

✔ A catalog of Beaver's baseball card collection, with an online purchasing system for the cards the Beave is willing to part with.

✔ A recipe exchange section where June can post her favorite recipes — such as her famous meatloaf, pot roast, and peanut butter and jelly sandwiches — and visitors to the Web site can post their own recipes.

✔ Ward's latest golf scores and handicap information, and an online weekend golf scheduler that enables Ward's friends to schedule golf outings.

✔ An online newspaper subscription payment section, where Wally's newspaper customers can pay their monthly bill so that Wally doesn't have to go door-to-door collecting for the newspaper.

One good way to plan a Web site is to sketch a simple diagram (sometimes called a *storyboard*) on paper showing the various pages you want to create, with arrows showing the links between the pages. Or, you can create an outline that represents your entire site. You can be as detailed or as vague as you want. And you can be as sloppy or as neat as you want. Figure 19-1 shows a simple diagram of the Cleaver family Web site.

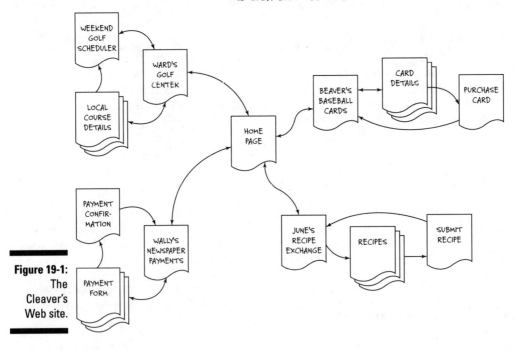

Figure 19-1:
The Cleaver's
Web site.

How to Organize Your Web Site

As you plan the content and appearance of your Web site, you'll need to come up with a scheme for organizing the site's pages. The following sections describe four common types of organizations for Web sites.

Sequential organization

If you want to guide your users through your Web site one page at a time, you can organize your pages sequentially like the pages in a book, as shown in Figure 19-2. Each page should include a link to the next page in sequence. In addition, you may want to include a link to the previous page to make it easy for the user to backtrack and a link to the first page so the user can start over.

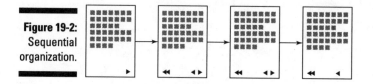

Figure 19-2:
Sequential
organization.

Hierarchical organization

In a hierarchical Web site, pages are arranged by categories and organized into a hierarchy, as shown in Figure 19-3. The topmost page services as a menu that enables users to access other pages directly. That way, users can go directly to the pages that interest them.

If necessary, your site can use several layers of menu pages. However, don't overdo the menus. Web sites that have numerous menus, each with only two or three links, are annoying. When a menu has more than a dozen or so choices, however, consider breaking the menu into two or more separate menus.

Web organization

Some Web sites lend themselves to pages that are linked to other related pages, without regard to a sequential or hierarchical organization. In extreme cases, every page has links to every other pages, creating a structure that resembles a spider web, as shown in Figure 19-4.

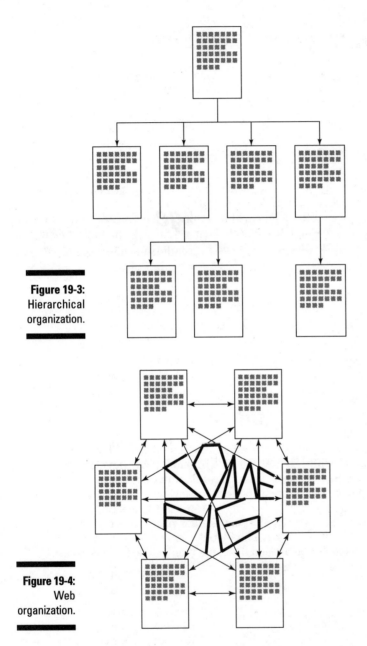

Figure 19-3:
Hierarchical
organization.

Figure 19-4:
Web
organization.

This is a good style of organization if the total number of pages in the site is limited and you can't predict the sequence in which users will want to view your pages.

Mixed organization

Most Web sites do not use a strictly sequential, hierarchical, or web organization, but rather a combination of the three. For example, the home page may serve as a menu to different sections of the site. Each section then uses whatever form of organization works best for its content. If one section is a tutorial on model airplane building, that section may be organized sequentially. If another section is a catalog of model kits, that section may be organized hierarchically by type of model (aircraft, cars, naval ships, and so on).

What to Include on Every Page

Although every Web page should contain unique and useful information, all Web pages should contain the following three elements:

- ✔ **Title:** Place a title at the top of every page. The title should identify not just the specific contents of the page but also the Web site itself. A specific title on each page is important because some users may not enter your site through your home page. Instead, they may go directly to one of the content pages in your site.

  Although the title can be simple text, most Web sites use an attractive graphic banner to display the title. That way, the banner creates a distinctive look for your pages.

  (Web pages also include a title that appears in the title bar of the browser window. This is separate from the title that appears at the top of the page.)

- ✔ **Navigation links:** All the pages of your Web site should have a consistent set of navigation links. At the minimum, provide a link to your home page on every page in your site. You may also want to include links to the major sections of your site on every page. And you may want to include links to the next and previous pages if your pages have a sequential organization.

  Place the navigation links in a consistent location on each page in your site. The two most popular locations for displaying navigation links are beneath the title or banner and in the left margin of the page.

- ✔ **Author and copyright information:** Every page should also include author credits and a copyright notice. Because users can enter your site by going directly to any page, placing the authorship and copyright notices on only the home page is not sufficient. This information is usually placed at the bottom of the page.

  It's also common to include an e-mail link on each page. That way, users can e-mail you to tell you how wonderful your site is or (more likely) to let you know about problems with your site.

What Kind of Pages to Include In Your Site

Although every Web site is different, you can find certain common elements on most Web sites. The following sections describe the items you should consider including on your Web site.

Home page

Every Web site should include a home page that serves as an entry point into the site. The home page is the first page that most users see when they visit your site (unless you include a cover page, as described in the next section). As a result, devote considerable time and energy to making sure your home page makes a good first impression.

Place an attractive title element at the top of the page. Remember that most users have to scroll down to see all of your home page. They see just the top of the page first, so you want to make sure that the title is immediately visible.

After the title, include a site menu that enables users to access the content available on your Web site. Here are a few other goodies you may want to include on your home page.

- **An indication of new content that is available on your Web site.** Users who return to your site often want to know right away when new information is available.

- **The date your site was last updated.**

- **A copyright notice.** You can include a link to a separate copyright page where you spell out whether others can copy the information you have placed on your site.

- **A reminder to bookmark the page so users can get back to the page easily.**

- **A hit counter.** If users see that 4 million people have visited your site since last Tuesday, they automatically assume that yours must be a hot site. On the other hand, if they see that only three people have visited since Truman was president, they'll yawn and leave quickly. If your site isn't very popular, you may want to skip the hit counter.

Avoid placing a huge amount of graphics on your home page. Your home page is the first page on your Web site most users see. If it takes more than 15 seconds for your page to load, users may lose patience and skip your page altogether. As a simple test, try holding your breath while your home page downloads. If you turn blue before the page finishes downloading, the page is too big.

Cover page

A cover page is displayed temporarily before your home page is displayed. Cover pages usually feature a flashy graphic logo or an animation. In most cover pages, the user must click the logo or some other element on the page to enter the site's home page. Or the page can be programmed so that it automatically jumps to the home page after a certain amount of time — say 10 or 15 seconds — has elapsed.

Many users are annoyed by cover pages, especially those that take more than a few seconds to download and display. Think carefully about whether the splashy cover page actually enhances your site or is more of an annoyance. If the cover page features a lengthy animation, include a link that allows impatient users to bypass the cover page and go directly into your site.

Site map

If your site has a lot of pages, you may want to include a site map. A site map is a detailed menu that provides links to every page on the site. By using the site map, a user can bypass intermediate menus and go directly to the pages that interest him or her.

Contact information

Be sure your site includes information about how to contact you or your company. You can easily include your e-mail address as a link right on the home page. When the user clicks this link, most Web browsers fire up the user's e-mail program, ready to compose a message with your e-mail address already filled in.

If you want to include complete contact information, such as your address and phone number, or if you want to list contact information for several individuals, you may want to place the contact information on a separate page that can be accessed from the home page.

Help page

If your Web site contains more than just a few pages, consider providing a help page that provides information about how to use the site. The help page can include information about how to navigate the site, as well as information such as how you obtained the information for the site, how often the site is updated, how someone would go about contributing to the site, and so on.

FAQ

Frequently Asked Questions (FAQ) pages are among the most popular sources of information on the Internet. You can organize your own FAQ page on any topic you want. Just come up with a list of questions and provide the answers. Or solicit answers from readers of your page.

Related links

At some sites, the most popular page is the links page, which provides a list of links to related sites. As the compiler of your own links page, you can do something that search engines such as Yahoo! cannot: You can pick and choose the links you want to include, and you can provide your own commentary about the information contained on each site.

Check your links to make sure they still work regularly. Web sites come and go, and little exacerbates a user more than clicking on a link and finding that it is broken.

Discussion group

A discussion group adds interactivity to your Web site by allowing visitors to post articles that can be read and responded to by other people who visit your site.

Choosing Tools to Create Your Web Pages

When you are ready to start creating Web pages for your site, you'll need to decide which Web page editor to use. There are many different alternatives to choose from. Some of the most popular are described in the following sections.

Notepad

Notepad is the free text editor that comes with all versions of Windows. Because HTML pages are nothing more than text files that contain special HTML codes intermingled with text, it is possible to build even complicated Web sites using nothing more than Notepad.

Notepad is the tool of choice for many die-hard HTML developers, but you should use Notepad only if the thought of learning HTML inside and out doesn't give you the hives. With Notepad, you have to type every jot and tiddle of HTML manually. You won't find out if you've made a mistake until you display your page in a Web browser.

FrontPage

FrontPage is a popular Web page editor that is a part of Microsoft Office, although it ships only with certain editions of Office. FrontPage is like a word processor for creating Web sites. It includes a WYSIWYG (What You See Is What You Get) Web page editor that lets you type information the way you want it to appear without worrying about the HTML.

If you have absolutely no experience with creating Web pages, FrontPage is a good place to start. However, the more you learn about Web development and HTML, the more FrontPage may end up frustrating you because of its limitations. When that happens, you'll want to move on to a more advanced Web development tool such as Dreamweaver.

Dreamweaver

Dreamweaver, from Macromedia (www.macromedia.com), is considered by many developers to be the best integrated tool for developing Web pages. It includes a sophisticated WYSIWYG editor, but also lets you work directly with the HTML. And it includes many powerful features for creating advanced Web sites.

Dreamweaver is not a simple program to learn, and it is not inexpensive. But if you're going to invest a lot of time developing a Web site, investing in Dreamweaver is worthwhile.

HTML text editors

Many Web developers shun WYSIWYG editors for powerful HTML-based editors that are designed to let you work directly with the HTML. These editors provide handy features such as built-in HTML help, integrated preview windows, and automatic completion of HTML elements as you type them. They offer the best of both worlds by letting you see how your pages will appear when viewed with a Web browser, but letting you work hands-on with the HTML codes.

One of the best known HTML editors is TextPad. You can download a free evaluation version at www.textpad.com. If you decide to buy it, the cost is only about $30.

Other tools you'll need

Besides an HTML editor, you'll need an arsenal of other software tools to develop a Web site. The following paragraphs describe some of the tools you may need:

- A graphics program such as Adobe Photoshop (www.adobe.com), CorelDraw (www.corel.com), or JASC Software's Paintshop Pro (www.jasc.com). You'll need a graphics program to create the graphics that appear on your Web site.

- One of each version of Web browser that users will view your site with. At the minimum, you'll need the most recent versions of Internet Explorer and Netscape Navigator.

- If you want to create downloadable documents in the popular PDF format, you'll need Adobe Acrobat (www.adobe.com) or some other program that can convert files to PDF format.

Tips for Creating a Successful Web Site

How will you measure the success of your Web site? By the number of people who visit it? By the number of customers you create through it? By comments you receive from people who say they like your site? By awards it wins?

There are a number of ways to measure the success of a Web site. But however you choose to evaluate your site's success, the following pointers give you some ideas on how to make your site appealing.

- **Check the competition.** Find out what other Web sites similar to yours have to offer. Don't create a "me too" Web site that offers nothing but information that is already available elsewhere. Instead, strive for unique information that can be found only on your Web site.

✔ **Offer something useful on every page.** Too many Web sites are filled with fluff — pages that don't have any useful content. Avoid creating pages that are just steps along the way to truly useful information. Instead, strive to include something useful on every page of your Web site.

✔ **Make it look good.** No matter how good the information at your Web site is, people will stay away if your site looks as if you spent no more than five minutes on design and layout. Yes, substance is more important than style. But an ugly Web site turns people away, whereas an attractive Web site draws people in. One of the keys to making a Web site look good is creating a consistent design that you follow throughout the site.

✔ **Proof it carefully.** If every third word in your Web site is misspelled, people will assume that the information on your Web site is as unreliable as your spelling. If your HTML editor has a spell-check feature, use it. Otherwise, proof your work carefully before you post it to the Web. Or better yet, have someone else proof it for you.

✔ **Keep it current.** Internet users will not frequent your site if it contains old, out-of-date information. Make sure that you frequently update your Web pages with current information. Obviously, some Web pages need to be changed more than others. For example, if you maintain a Web page that lists the team standings for a soccer league, you have to update the page after every game. On the other hand, a page that features medieval verse romances doesn't need to be updated very often, unless someone discovers a previously unpublished Chaucer text hidden in a trunk.

✔ **Don't tie it to a certain browser.** Exploiting the cool new features of the latest and greatest Web browser, whether it's Microsoft Internet Explorer or Netscape Navigator, is a good idea. But don't do so at the expense of users who may be using the *other* browser, or at the expense of users who are still working with an earlier version. Some people are still using browsers that don't even support frames. Make sure that any pages in which you incorporate advanced features of the newer browsers work well with older browsers as well.

✔ **Don't make hardware assumptions.** Remember that not everyone has a 21-inch monitor and a high-speed cable-modem connection to the Internet. Design your Web site so that it can be used by the poor sap who is stuck with a 14-inch monitor and — gasp — a dial-up modem connection to the Internet.

✔ **Publicize it.** Few people will stumble across your Web site by accident. If you want people to visit your Web site, you have to publicize it. Make sure that your site is listed in the major search engines, such as Google and Yahoo!. Also, you can promote your site by putting its address on all your advertisements, correspondences, business cards, e-mails, and so on.

Part V
More Ways to Network

The 5th Wave   By Rich Tennant

Despite its inclusion on the Hardware Compatability List, Martin shuddered at the thought of having to install Windows NT on the workstation from the early 1950s.

In this part . . .

After you've got the basics down, this part helps you do some of the more advanced stuff, which includes setting up a wireless network, creating a dial-up connection so that you can access your network while you're at home or on the road, using the network features of Microsoft Office, building a network that includes older MS-DOS and Windows computers as well as Macintosh computers, and setting up a server that runs the Linux operating system.

Chapter 20

Wireless Networking

· ·

· ·

Since the beginning of Ethernet networking, cable has been getting smaller and easier to work with. The original Ethernet cable was about as thick as your thumb, weighed a ton, and was difficult to bend around tight corners. Then came coax cable, which was lighter and easier to work with. Coax was supplanted by Unshielded Twisted Pair (UTP) cable, which is the cable used for most networks today. But coax and UTP cable is still cable, which means that you have to drill holes and pull cable through walls and ceilings to wire your entire home or office.

That's why wireless networking has become so popular. With wireless networking, you don't need cables to connect your computers. Instead, wireless networks use radio waves to send and receive network signals. As a result, a computer can connect to a wireless network at any location in your home or office.

Wireless networks are especially useful for notebook computers. After all, the main benefit of a notebook computer is that you can carry it around with you wherever you go. At work, you can use your notebook computer at your desk, in the conference room, in the break room, or even out in the parking lot. At home, you can use it in the bedroom, kitchen, den, gameroom, or out by the pool. With wireless networking, your notebook computer can be connected to the network no matter where you take it.

This chapter introduces you to the ins and outs of setting up a wireless network. I tell you what you need to know to use wireless network components instead of standard Ethernet components, how to create a network that mixes both wireless and cabled components, and what you need to know about the special security risks that going wireless entails.

Understanding Wireless Networking

A wireless network is a network that uses radio signals to exchange information rather than direct cable connections. A computer with a wireless network connection is like a cell phone. Just as you don't have to be connected to a phone line to use a cell phone, you don't have to be connected to a network cable to use a wireless networked computer.

The following paragraphs summarize some of the key concepts and terms you need to understand to set up and use a basic wireless network:

✔ A wireless network is often referred to as a *WLAN,* for *Wireless Local Area Network.* Some people prefer to switch the acronym around to *Local Area Wireless Network,* or *LAWN.* The term *Wi-Fi* is often used to describe wireless networks, although it technically refers to just one form of wireless network: the 802.11b standard. (See the sidebar, "802 Dot Eleventy Something.")

✔ A wireless network has a name, known as a *SSID.* SSID stands for *Service Set Identifier* — wouldn't that make a great *Jeopardy* question? (I'll take obscure four-letter acronyms for $400, please!) Each of the computers that belongs to a single wireless network must have the same SSID.

✔ Wireless networks can transmit over any of several channels. For computers to talk to one another, they must be configured to transmit on the same channel.

✔ The simplest type of wireless network consists of two or more computers with wireless network adapters. This type of network is called an *ad-hoc mode network.*

✔ A more complex type of network is an *infrastructure mode network.* All this really means is that a group of wireless computers can be connected not only to each other, but also to an existing cabled network via a device called a *Wireless Access Point,* or WAP. (I tell you more about ad-hoc and infrastructure networks later in this chapter.)

802 Dot Eleventy-Something

Although there are several different forms of wireless networking available, the most popular is wireless Ethernet, which is based on a standard known as 802.11. Actually, there are two versions of the 802.11 standard that are in widespread use: 802.11a and 802.11b. 802.11a is the more expensive of the two, so small office and home wireless networks tend to use 802.11b components.

You can't mix and match 802.11a and 802.11b in the same network, so be sure all of the components you buy are one or the other. 802.11a is faster and more reliable than 802.11b, so get 802.11a components if you can afford the extra cost. (You may be able to find wireless access points that support bot 802.11a and 802.11b.)

Warning: 802.11b networks operate on the same radio frequency as many cordless phones: 2.4GMHz. If you set up an 802.11b network in your home and you also have a 2.4GHz cordless phone, you may find that the network and phone occasionally interfere with one another. The only way to completely avoid the interference is to switch to a 900MHz phone or use more expensive 802.11a network components, which transmit at 5GHz rather than 2.4GHz.

Home on the Range

The maximum range of an 802.11b wireless device indoors is about 300 feet. This can have an interesting effect when you get a bunch of wireless computers together such that some of them are in range of each other, but others are not. For example, suppose Wally, Ward, and the Beaver all have wireless notebooks. Wally's computer is 200 feet away from Ward's computer, and Ward's computer is 200 feet away from Beaver's in the opposite direction (see Figure 20-1). In this case, Ward is able to access both Wally's and Beaver's computer, but Wally can access only Ward's computer, and Beaver can access only Ward's computer. In other words, Wally and Beaver won't be able to access each other's computers, because they're outside of the 300 feet range limit. (This is starting to sound suspiciously like an algebra problem. Now suppose Wally starts walking towards Ward at 2 miles per hour, and Beaver starts running towards Ward at 4 miles per hour . . . .)

Although the normal range for 802.11b is 300 feet, in actual practice the range may be less. Obstacles such as solid walls, bad weather, cordless phones, microwave ovens, backyard nuclear reactors, and so on can all conspire together to reduce the effective range of a wireless adapter. If you're having trouble connecting to the network, sometimes just adjusting the antenna helps.

Figure 20-1:
Ward,
Wally, and
the Beaver
playing with
their
wireless
network.

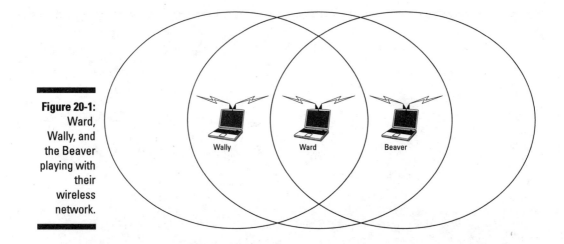

Also, wireless networks tend to slow down when the distance increases.
802.11b network devices claim to operate at 11Mbps, but they usually achieve
that speed only at ranges of 100 feet or less. At 300 feet, they often slow down
to 1Mbps. You should also realize that when you're at the edge of the wireless
device's range, you're more likely to suddenly lose your connection due to
bad weather.

Wireless Network Adapters

Each computer that will connect to your wireless network needs a *wireless
network adapter*. The wireless network adapter is similar to the Network
Interface Card (NIC) that is used for a standard Ethernet connection.
However, instead of having a cable connector on the back, a wireless network
adapter has an antenna.

There are several basic types of wireless network adapters you can get,
depending on your needs and the type of computer you will use it with:

- A wireless PCI card is a wireless network adapter that you install into an
  available slot inside a desktop computer. In order to install this type of
  card, you need to take your computer apart. So use this type of card
  only if you have the expertise and the nerves to dig into your computer's guts.

- A wireless USB adapter is a separate box that plugs into a USB port on
  your computer. Because the USB adapter is a separate device, it takes up
  extra desk space. However, you can install it without taking your computer apart.

✔ A wireless PC card is designed to slide into the PC card slot found in most notebook computers. This is the type of card to get if you want to network your notebook.

You can purchase an 802.11b wireless adapter for about $100. 802.11a adapters cost about $150 each.

At first, you may think that wireless network adapters are prohibitively expensive. After all, you can buy a regular Ethernet adapter for as little as $20. But when you consider that you don't have to purchase and install cable to use a wireless adapter, the price of wireless networking becomes more palatable.

Wireless Access Points

Unlike cabled networks, wireless networks do not need a hub or switch. If all you want to do is network a group of wireless computers, you just purchase a wireless adapter for each computer, put them all within 300 feet of each other, and *voila!* — instant network.

But what if you already have an existing cabled network? For example, suppose you work at an office with 15 computers all cabled up nicely, and you just want to add a couple of wireless notebook computers to the network. That's where a Wireless Access Point, also known as a WAP, comes in. A WAP connects your wireless computers to your existing cabled network so that all of your computers get along like one big happy family. Figure 20-2 shows how this works.

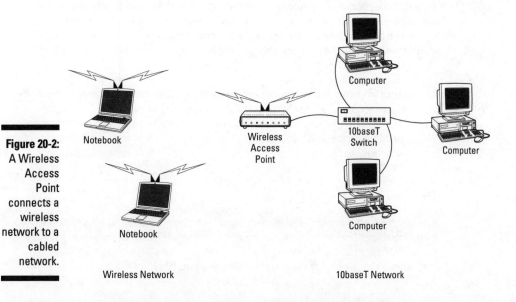

Figure 20-2:
A Wireless Access Point connects a wireless network to a cabled network.

A Wireless Access Point is a box that has an antenna (or often a pair of antennae) and an RJ-45 Ethernet port. You just plug the WAP into a network cable, plug the other end of the cable into a hub or switch, and your wireless network should be able to connect to your cabled network.

Multifunction WAPs

Wireless Access Points often include other built-in features. For example, some WAPs double as Ethernet hubs or switches. In that case, the WAP will have more than one RJ-45 ports. In addition, some WAPs include broadband cable or DSL firewall routers that enable you to connect to the Internet. For my network at home, I use a Linksys Wireless Access Point Router that includes the following features:

- ✔ An 802.11b Wireless Access Point that lets me connect a notebook computer and a computer located on the other side of the house because I didn't want to run cable through the attic.

- ✔ A four-port 10/100MHz switch that I can connect up to four computers to via twisted-pair cable.

- ✔ A DSL/Cable router that I connect to my cable modem. This enables all the computers on the network (cabled and wireless) to access the Internet.

Roaming

Two or more Wireless Access Points can be used to create a large wireless network in which computer users can roam from area to area and still be connected to the wireless network. As the user moves out of the range of one WAP, another WAP automatically picks the user up and takes over without interrupting the user's network service.

To set up two or more WAPs for roaming, you must carefully place the WAPs so that all areas of the office or building being networked are in range of at least one of the WAPs. Then, just make sure that all of the computers and WAPs use the same SSID and channel.

Wireless bridging

Suppose you have two separate computer networks in nearby sections of a building, but no easy way to run cable between them. In that case, you could use a pair of wireless access points to create a *wireless bridge* between the two networks. Connect one of the WAPs to the first network and the other

WAP to the second network. Then, configure both WAPs to use the same SSID and channel. (As an alternative, you can use a single WAP with a more powerful antenna to extend the range.)

Dealing with Security Issues

Before you dive headfirst into the deep end of the wireless networking pool, you should first consider the security risks that are inherent in setting up a wireless network. With a cabled network, the best security tool you have is the lock on the front door of your office. Unless someone can physically get to one of the computers on your network, he or she can't get into your network. (Well, we're sort of ignoring your wide-open broadband Internet connection for the sake of argument.)

If you go wireless, an intruder doesn't have to get into your office to hack into your network. He or she can do it from the office next door. Or the lobby. Or the parking garage beneath your office. Or the sidewalk outside.

In fact, the recent explosion of wireless networking has led to a whole new world of wireless network hackers. Some even practice the art of *wardriving*, which means they drive around town with notebook computers just looking for open access to wireless networks. Some of them even make maps and put them on the Internet.

The term *wardriving* has nothing to do with combat. It derives from the popular hacker word *warez* (pronounced *wayrz*), which refers to pirated software. Thus, wardriving refers to looking for pirated wireless network access. Another related term, *warchalking*, refers to marking the location of open access points with special chalk symbols.

How can you protect your network from such access? The following guidelines get you started in the right direction:

✔ Enable the WEP security feature of all your wireless devices. WEP stands for *Wired Equivalent Privacy* and is designed to make wireless transmission as secure as transmission over a network cable. It turns out that WEP is not completely bulletproof, but it does help keep out casual hackers.

✔ Impose sensible file sharing and user-access security by choosing good passwords, sharing only specific folders rather than entire drives, and so on.

✔ Change the default passwords for everything, especially the WAP and the administrator accounts for your servers. Security experts estimate that as many as 75 percent of all computer security failures are due to weak passwords.

✔ If your WAP supports it, use the MAC-address based access feature. This lets you limit access to only specific computers based on their MAC addresses.

✔ Change the SSID of your network from the default values.

✔ Be careful of rogue Wireless Access Points. Because WAPs are so inexpensive and easy to hook up, it's not uncommon for a savvy network user to install one on his or her own, without permission or help from the network administrator. Such rogue WAPs often expose the entire network to outsiders.

✔ Back up!

Chapter 21

Dialing In to Your Network

· ·

In This Chapter

▶ Using Dial-Up Networking to dial in to your network

▶ Setting up callback on a Windows 2000 Pro dial-up server

▶ Finding out about Remote Access Service on a Windows NT or 2000 Server

· ·

*W*ith portable computers and home computers becoming more and more popular, many computer users take work home with them to work on in the evening or over the weekend and bring back to the office the following weekday. This arrangement works reasonably well, except that exchanging information between a portable or home computer and your office computer is far from easy.

One way to exchange files is to copy them from one computer to a diskette and then copy the files from the diskette to the other computer. However, this approach has its drawbacks. What if the files you want to exchange won't fit on a single floppy disk? And what if, in the rush to get out of the house the following morning, you forget to put the disk in your pocket or bag? (You can get around the size limitation of floppy disks by using removable ZIP disks with capacities up to 250MB or tiny USB removable storage devices that are the size of a keychain and can hold up to 1GB. But you still have the problem of forgetting the disks or losing them in the subway on the way to work.)

If you use a laptop computer, you can add a network interface card to the laptop computer and then connect the laptop computer to your office network and exchange files with your office computer. But Ethernet cards for laptop computers are not cheap, and you have to enable file sharing on the laptop computer, your office computer, or both.

Alternatively, you can use a program, such as LapLink, which allows you to connect your portable computer to your office computer using a cable connected to both computers' serial, parallel, or USB ports. After you connect the computers, you can then transfer files over the cable. This process is much more efficient than copying the files using diskettes but still has drawbacks. What if you get home and discover that you forgot to copy one important file?

If you must work from home, the best way to access your work at the office is to create a dial-up connection that uses modems to connect your home computer directly to your office network. Using this setup, you can access from your home computer any shared disk drives available on the office network, just as if your home computer were a part of the office network.

This chapter shows you how to create a remote connection using a feature of Windows called Dial-Up Networking. This feature provides a simple but limited modem link between a remote computer and a networked computer. I also point out some advantages of using a more sophisticated approach to remote access, such as Windows NT/2000 Remote Access Service or NetWare Connect.

Security is a major concern whenever you enable dial-up networking. If you can dial in to your office computer and access your files, so can anybody else. Passwords offer some measure of protection, but serious computer hackers can get past simple password protection as easy as experienced car thieves can hotwire a car. For that reason, I suggest you do not use Windows 98 or Millennium Edition as a dial-up server if security is a concern.

Throughout this chapter, I assume that you're using remote access to call in to your work computer from a home computer. Of course, this isn't the only way to use dial-up connections. You can do it the other way around, call up your home computer from the office. Or you can call your office or home computer from a hotel room using a laptop computer. The point is that I refer to the computer that you use to call in to another computer as the *home computer,* and I refer to the other computer — the one that you're calling in to — as the *office computer.*

Understanding Dial-Up Networking

All versions of Windows since Windows 95 include a feature called *Dial-Up Networking,* which enables you to connect to a network using modems and a phone line. With Dial-Up Networking, you can easily set up a dial-up connection between your home computer and your office computer so you can access your office computer's disk drives and printers while you're at home. In addition, any network resources that are available to your office computer will also become available to your home computer.

Because computer geeks love confusing us with three-letter acronyms, they have designated *DUN* as the official three letter acronym for Dial-Up Networking. I promise not to use the term *DUN* again in this chapter.

To use DUN — oops, I mean Dial-Up Networking — to connect from home to office, both your home and office computers must have a modem, and they must both be connected to a phone line.

In Dial-Up Networking terminology, the computer that you dial in to — that is, your office computer — is referred to as a *dial-up server*. Likewise, the computer you dial in from — your home computer — is called a *dial-up client*. Note that the dial-up server computer doesn't have to be a dedicated server computer. The computer in your office can function as a dial-up server, provided that it has a modem connected to a phone line.

Because Dial-Up Networking uses modems and phone lines rather than Ethernet cards to connect your home computer to your office computer, the connection will be slow. The slow speed of the Dial-Up Networking connection won't bother you too much if you just want to access a couple of small Excel files or send a short document to your printer, but if you try to copy a 20MB file over a dial-up, you'll have enough time to watch a couple of Kevin Costner movies while you're waiting.

The ability to create a dial-up server is built in to Windows 2000 Professional and Windows XP, so you don't have to install it separately. But if you're using an older version of Windows, you have to install the dial-up server software from the Windows CD before you can set up dial-up networking. You can install the necessary software from the Windows Setup tab of the Add/Remove Programs dialog box, which you can access from the Control Panel.

Before you can use a dial-up connection, you must configure both your home and office computers for Dial-Up Networking. First, you must configure your office computer to work as a dial-up server. Then you must configure your home computer to function as a dial-up client. After you configure both computers, you can use the dial-up client computer at home to call in to the dial-up server computer at work. I describe how to configure the dial-up server and client in the following sections.

Configuring a Dial-Up Server

To set up a dial-up server in Windows XP, click the Start button and choose All Programs➪Accessories➪Communications➪Network Connections. Then, click Create a New Connection to start the New Connection Wizard. When the Welcome screen appears, click Next. The Wizard asks what type of network connection you want to create; choose Set Up an Advanced Connection, then click Next. The New Connection Wizard then asks what type of advanced connection you want to create, as shown in Figure 21-1. Choose Accept Incoming Connections, then click Next.

For Windows 2000, open My Computer, then open the Network and Dial-Up Connections folder and double-click the Make a New Connection icon to start the Network Connection Wizard. After the welcome screen, the wizard asks what type of connection you want to create. Choose Accept Incoming Connections, then click Next.

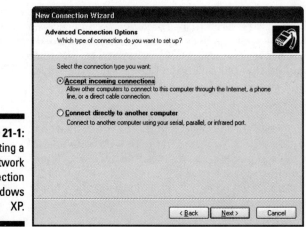

Figure 21-1:
Creating a
network
connection
in Windows
XP.

In both Windows XP and 2000, the wizard next displays a series of dialog
boxes asking for the following information:

- ✔ **The device you want to allow incoming connections on.** In most cases,
  a modem and a LAN connection will be listed. Choose the modem to
  allow dial-up connections.

- ✔ **Whether to allow Virtual Private Networking.** For a simple dial-up
  connection, choose No.

- ✔ **Which users to allow access.** All of the user accounts authorized to use
  your computer will be listed. Choose the user account you want to use
  for the dial-up connection.

  Creating a separate user account that you can use for dial-up access is a
  good idea. Then, you can give this account access just to the folders and
  printers you need to access from home.

- ✔ **The network protocols you want to use for the dial-up connection.** The
  default is to use TCP/IP, Microsoft File and Printer Sharing, and Client for
  Microsoft Networks. Change these settings only if you have a reason and
  you know what you're doing.

- ✔ **A name for your connection.**

Here are a few additional points to ponder when you use a dial-up server:

- ✔ Don't, under any circumstances, set up a Dial-Up Server without a
  password! Yes, I know I already warned you about this, but it's worth a
  second warning.

- ✔ If you shut down your computer while it's in Dial-Up Server mode, the
  Dial-Up Server is automatically restarted when you restart your computer.

✔ If you're using Windows 98 or Millennium Edition, the procedure for configuring the dial-up networking connection is slightly different. Open the My Computer icon, then double-click the Network Connections icon. You can then configure a dial-up network connection by choosing the Connections⇨Dial-Up Server command.

✔ If you're a network administrator, the thought of users creating Dial-Up Servers to gain remote access to your network may give you the willies. If so, you can ban the Dial-Up Server function by using a Windows program called the System Policy Editor.

Configuring Your Home Computer for Dial-Up Networking

To configure your home computer to act as a dial-up client, you must create a new dial-up connection that is set up to dial in to you office computer. You can follow these steps for Windows XP:

1. **Click the Start button, then choose All Programs⇨Accessories⇨ Communications⇨Network Connections.**

   The Network Connections folder appears.

2. **Click Create a New Connection.**

   The New Connection Wizard comes to life.

3. **Click Next to dismiss the Welcome screen, then choose Connect to the Network at my Workplace and click Next.**

   The Wizard asks whether you want to connect with a dial-up connection or with a Virtual Private Network connection that works over the Internet.

4. **Choose Dial-Up Connection, then click Next.**

   The Wizard asks for a name for your connection.

5. **Type a name for the connection to your office computer, then click Next.**

   Use a simple name, such as *Office.* Next, the wizard asks for your office computer's phone number.

6. **Type the phone number for the phone line that's connected to your office computer's modem and then click Next.**

   The wizard displays a confirmation dialog box saying that it's ready to create the connection, as shown in Figure 21-2.

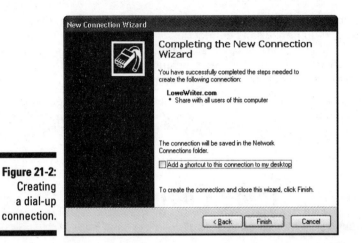

Figure 21-2:
Creating
a dial-up
connection.

7. **Click Finish.**

The wizard creates the new connection.

The procedure for Windows 98 or Me is almost the same. Start by choosing Start➪Programs➪Accessories➪Communications➪Dial-Up Networking. When the Dial-Up Networking folder appears, double-click the Make New Connection icon. Then pick up the procedure beginning at Step 5.

Here are a few tidbits to consider when setting up your home computer for Dial-Up Networking:

✔ The New Connection Wizard may ask for additional information if it discovers that you have not yet configured your modem for Windows. If this happens, just follow the bouncing ball and answer whatever questions it asks as best you can. If you become confused, just act like you know what you're doing, and the wizard won't notice. In almost all cases, the wizard can automatically detect and configure your modem properly, so all you have to do is sit and watch.

✔ If you can't find Dial-Up Networking anywhere on your computer, you may not have installed it. Find your Windows CD and then double-click the Add/Remove Programs icon in the Control Panel. Click the Windows Setup tab in the Add/Remove Programs dialog box and then double-click the Communications icon and make sure that Dial-Up Networking is selected. Click OK and then insert your Windows CD in your CD-ROM drive to install Dial-Up Networking.

✔ If you plan on calling your office computer often, drag the office computer connection icon from the Dial-Up Networking window onto your desktop. Then you won't have to wade through My Computer every time you want to connect.

Making the Connection

After you configure your office and home computers for Dial-Up Networking, you undoubtedly want to call your office computer and put Dial-Up Networking to work. Here's how:

1. **When you leave work to go home, make sure you leave the dial-up server computer turned on.**

   You can't dial in to the dial-up server from home if you turn the dial-up server computer off.

2. **On your home computer, choose the Start⇨All Programs⇨ Accessories⇨Communications⇨Network Connections, and then double-click the icon for the office computer's connection.**

   Or if you dragged a copy of the icon to your desktop, just double-click the icon on your desktop. Either way, the Connect Office dialog box appears, as shown in Figure 21-3.

Figure 21-3: The Connect Office dialog box.

3. **Make sure that the phone number, user name, and password are correct. Then click Connect.**

   Windows calls in to your office computer and establishes a connection. This process may take a minute or so, so be patient. You see various messages on the screen while the connection is being made, such as

Dialing, Verifying User Name and Password, Waiting for Godot, Twiddling Thumbs, **and so on. Eventually, the message says** Connected, at which point you're officially connected to your office computer.

Using Network Resources with a Dial-Up Connection

After you're connected to the dial-up server, you can access the dial-up server's disk drives and printers as if they were on a local network. However, because file transfers over a modem are slow, your computer may slow down dramatically for certain operations. For example, opening even a small Word document might take 10 or 15 seconds.

Because dial-up connections are slower than local network connections, you should avoid browsing the network using My Network Places (or Network Neighborhood in Windows 98 or Me). Instead, follow these steps to access your office computer's resources when connected over the phone:

1. **Choose the Start⇨Run command.**

2. **Type two backward slashes followed by the name of your office computer.**

   For example, type **Office**.

3. **Click OK.**

   Your home computer takes a while to access your office computer over the phone. Eventually, though, a window, such as the one shown in Figure 21-4, appears. You can access your office computer's shared disk drives and printers from this window.

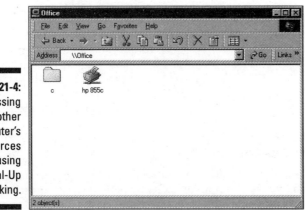

Figure 21-4:
Accessing
another
computer's
resources
using
Dial-Up
Networking.

To disconnect from the office computer, double-click the modem icon that appears in the taskbar and then click Disconnect. Or if you prefer, right-click the modem icon and choose Disconnect from the pop-up menu that appears.

You can also access files on your dial-up server's disk drive by using the standard Open and Save As dialog boxes. To see how, refer to the section about accessing network files in Chapter 23.

Don't Call Us — We'll Call You

One of the advantages of using Windows 2000 or XP for your dial-up server is that you can use the callback feature. Callback is both a security feature and a cost-cutting feature. It works like this:

1. From your remote computer, you dial in to the dial-up server computer.

2. The dial-up server verifies your user name and password.

3. The dial-up server hangs up on you.

4. The dial-up server then calls you back.

5. Your computer answers the phone and verifies the connection.

6. You can then use the network.

When used as a security feature, the dial-up server calls you back using a pre-arranged number. That way, you can only dial in to the network from a fixed location, such as your home. For a hacker to break in to your network using a callback connection, he or she would have to break into your home and call in using your phone line.

The callback feature can also be used as a simple cost-cutting measure for users who need to connect to the office computer while they are on the road. For example, suppose you are in your hotel room in St. Louis and you need to connect to your office computer in Detroit. With a callback connection, you can place a short long distance call from the hotel room to the dial-up server computer in the Detroit office. Before it hangs up on you, the dial-up server asks you what number to call you back at. Then, the dial-up server hangs up and calls you right back, your computer answers and reconnects, and you can use the network while the call is billed to the dial-up servers' phone rather than to your hotel room's phone.

Callback for a Windows 2000 dial-up server is set on a user-by-user basis, because each user can have a different phone number to call back. To configure callback, follow these steps:

1. **Double-click My Computer; then click the Network and Dial-up Connections link.**

   The Network and Dial-up Connections folder appears.

2. **Right-click the Incoming Connections icon; then choose Properties from the pop-up menu that appears.**

   This brings up the Incoming Connections Properties dialog box.

3. **Click the Users tab.**

   A list of user accounts appears in the dialog box, as shown in Figure 21-5.

4. **Click the user account you will use to call in to the dial-up server and then click Properties.**

   The User Properties dialog box appears. This dialog box has two tabs: General and Callback. The General tab is shown first.

5. **Click the Callback tab.**

   The callback options appear, as shown in Figure 21-6.

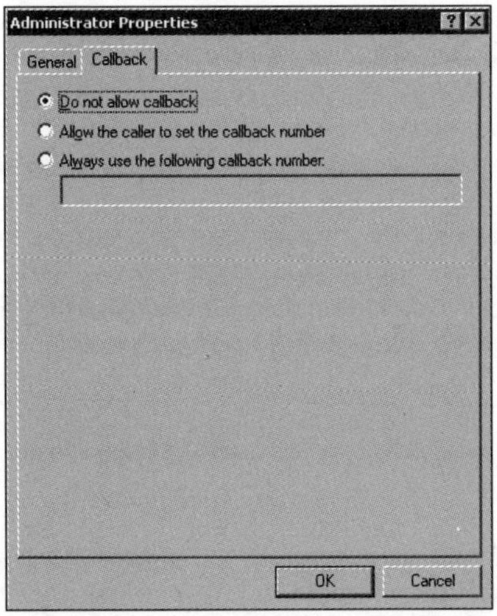

Figure 21-6:
Setting the
callback
options for a
dial-up user.

6. **Set the callback option you want to use.**

   The choices are

   - **Do Not Allow Callback**, which disables the callback feature for this user. (This is the default setting.)

   - **Allow the Caller to Set the Callback Number**, which means that the dial-up server will ask you to enter a number before hanging up, then call you back at the number you provide.

   - **Always Use the Following Callback Number**, which means that the dial-up server will call you back at a fixed number.

7. **If you choose Always Use the Following Callback Number, type the number you want the server to call back in the text box.**

   For example, if you will be dialing in to the dial-up server from your home, type the number your home computer's modem is connected to.

8. **Click OK.**

   You are returned to the Incoming Connections Properties dialog box.

9. **Repeat Steps 4 through 8 for any other users you want to configure callback options for.**

   In most cases, you'll configure just one user for the dial-up server. However, if you are setting up the dial-up server so that several users can access it, repeat Steps 4 through 8 for each user.

10. **Click OK to dismiss the Incoming Connections Properties dialog box.**

You're done! Now, when you call in to the dial-up server, the server will hang up on you and call you back.

Using Remote Access Service

Both Windows NT 4 and 2000 Server include built-in support for remote access, with a feature called *Remote Access Service,* also known as *RAS.* With RAS, you equip a server computer with one or more modems (standard modems or ISDN modems) and dedicate it as a remote access server. Remote users can then dial in to the network and, once connected, use the network as if they were connected with an Ethernet cable. Of course, the connection is much slower because it operates over phone lines rather than real Ethernet cable.

Remote Access Service has several advantages over a simple Windows dial-up server:

- RAS can work with more than one modem to allow more than one user to connect simultaneously. With special modem pooling equipment, RAS can service hundreds of dial-up users.

- RAS has better security features than a simple Windows dial-up server. With RAS, you can encrypt data that is transmitted over the phone line, and you can use more reliable authentication methods to verify that dial-up users arc really who they say they are.

- RAS can use Caller ID to verify that a user is calling from a predetermined number. This provides the same protection as callback to a fixed number but is more convenient.

- RAS can limit dial-in access to specified times and days.

- RAS also supports Virtual Private Network (VPN) connections, which enable a user to connect to your network via the Internet rather than by dialing directly into your network.

Novell offers a similar remote access program called NetWare Connect.

Hardware-Based Remote Access

An alternative to devoting a server computer for remote access is to use specialized remote access hardware, which connects directly to your network and allows users to dial in. That way, you don't have to contend with setting up and maintaining a Windows NT, 2000, or NetWare server, and you don't have to dedicate an entire PC to the task of sharing modems for remote access.

One of the most popular remote access servers is LanRover, made by Shiva (which is owned by Intel). LanRover is a self-contained remote access server that includes an Ethernet port so that you can connect LanRover to your network and eight serial ports for plug-in modems. Or you can get LanRover Plus, which includes built-in modems. LanRover can use normal modem connections or high-speed ISDN connections for faster connections.

For more information about LanRover, check out Shiva's home page on the Internet at `www.shiva.com`.

Virtual Private Networking

An alternative to using a dial-up connection to access your office network from home is to use a technique called *Virtual Private Networking,* or *VPN.* VPN lets you create the equivalent of a private connection between two computers or networks using the Internet instead of a separate dial-up connection. For example, suppose you already have an Internet connection at home, either via a dial-up line or with a fast cable or DSL connection, and the network at your office also has an Internet connection. Rather than use dial-up networking to access the office network from home, you could use the Internet to create a VPN connection between your home computer and your office network.

To use VPN, you must first set up a VPN connection on a Windows NT or 2000 Server computer running RAS or a NetWare server with NetWare Connect. (For more information, see the section "Using Remote Access Service" earlier in this chapter.) Then, you can configure a VPN connection on your home computer.

 VPN uses a special protocol known as *PPTP,* which stands for *Point-to-Point Tunneling Protocol.* The process of creating a private connection between two computers over an intermediate network such as the Internet is often called tunneling because the connection is similar to a tunnel through the Internet that connects the two computers directly.

Chapter 22

Using Microsoft Office
on a Network

*M*icrosoft Office is far and away the most popular suite of application programs used on personal computers, and it includes the most common types of application programs used in an office: a word processing program (Word), a spreadsheet program (Excel), a presentation program (PowerPoint), and an excellent e-mail program (Outlook). Depending on the version of Office you purchase, you may also get a database program (Access), Web site development program (FrontPage), a desktop publishing program (Publisher), a set of Ginsu knives (KnifePoint), and a slicer and dicer (ActiveSalsa).

This chapter describes the networking features of Microsoft OfficeXP, the latest and greatest version of Office. Most of these features also work with previous versions of Office as well.

To get the most from using Office on a network, you should purchase the Microsoft Office Resource Kit. The Office Resource Kit, also known as *ORK,* contains information about installing and using Office on a network and comes with a CD that has valuable tools. If you don't want to purchase the ORK, you can view it online and download the ORK tools from Microsoft's TechNet Web site (`technet.microsoft.com`). Nanu-nanu.

Installing Office on a Network — Some Options

You need to make two basic decisions when you prepare to install Microsoft Office on a network. The first is whether you want to copy the Office program files onto each computer's local hard disk or place some or all of the Office program files on a shared server disk. Here are the pros and cons of each option:

✔ Installing the Office program files onto each computer's hard disk is usually the best choice. However, this option requires that each computer have enough free disk space to hold the Office program files. Office XP can require more than 500MB of disk space if you install all of its components.

✔ Placing Office program files on the server frees up disk space on the client computers' hard drives. However, network users will notice that Office runs slower because network files are slower to access than local files. To alleviate this, you can install the most frequently needed Office program files on each computer's local disk and the less frequently used files on the network server.

The second choice to make when installing Office on a network is which of several alternative installation methods to use. Here are the options:

✔ Ignore the fact that you have a network, purchase a separate copy of Office for each user on the network, and install Office from the CD on each computer. This option works well if your network is small, if each computer has ample disk space to hold the necessary Office files, and if each computer has its own CD-ROM drive.

✔ Buy a separate copy of Office for each computer but install Office onto each computer from a shared CD-ROM drive located on a server computer. This option works well when you have network client computers that do not have their own CD-ROM drives.

✔ Copy the entire Office CD into a shared folder on a network server. Then from each network computer, connect to the shared folder and run the Office Setup program to install Office onto each computer on the network.

✔ Use the Office Setup program in Administrative Setup mode. This option lets you create a special type of setup on a network server disk, from which you can install Office onto network computers. Administrative Setup enables you to control the custom features selected for each network computer and reduce the amount of user interaction required to install Office onto each computer.

If you choose to use Administrative Setup, you can use the Network Installation Wizard that comes with the Office Resource Kit. The Network Installation Wizard lets you customize settings for installing Office onto client computers. For example, you can choose which Office components to install, provide default answers to yes/no questions that Setup asks the user while installing Office, and select the amount of interaction you want the Setup program to have with the user while installing Office.

No matter which option you choose for installing Office on your network, you must purchase either a copy of Office or a license to install Office for every computer that uses Office. Purchasing a single copy of Office and installing it on more than one computer is illegal.

Accessing Network Files

Opening a file that resides on a network drive is almost as easy as opening a file on a local drive. All Office programs use the File⇨Open command to summon the Open dialog box, as shown in its Excel incarnation in Figure 22-1. (The Open dialog box is nearly identical in other Office programs.)

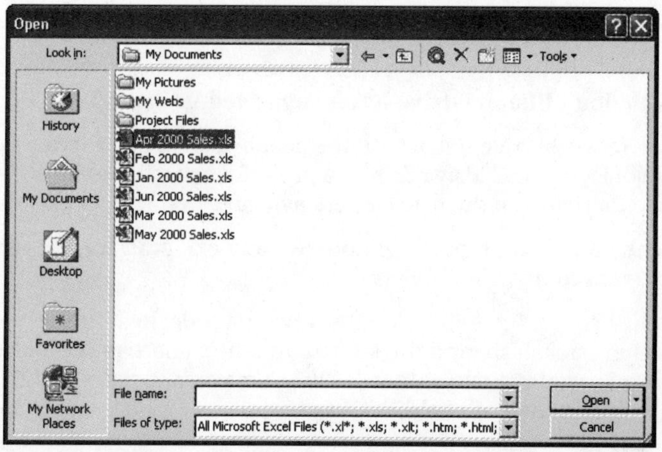

Figure 22-1:
The Open dialog box in Excel 2002.

To access a file that resides on a network volume that has been mapped to a drive letter, all you have to do is use the Look In drop-down list to select the network drive. If the network volume has not been mapped to a drive, click My Network Places near the bottom left corner of the Open dialog box.

You can map a network drive directly from the Open dialog box by following these steps:

1. **Choose the File⇨Open command.**

   This summons the Open dialog box.

2. **Click Tools in the Open dialog box and then choose Map Network Drive.**

   The Map Network Drive dialog box appears, as shown in Figure 22-2.

Figure 22-2:
Mapping a network drive.

Map Network Drive

Windows can help you connect to a shared network folder and assign a drive letter to the connection so that you can access the folder using My Computer.

Specify the drive letter for the connection and the folder that you want to connect to:

Drive: Z:

Folder: | Browse...

Example: \\server\share

☑ Reconnect at logon

Connect using a different user name.

Sign up for online storage or connect to a network server.

< Back   Finish   Cancel

3. **If you don't like the drive letter suggested in the Drive field, change it.**

   Map Network Drive defaults to the next available drive letter — in the case of Figure 22-2, drive Z:. If you prefer to use a different drive letter, you can choose any of the drive letters available in the Drive drop-down list.

4. **In the Path field, type the complete network path for the shared drive you want to map.**

   In most cases, the network path is two backslashes, the server name, another backslash, and the shared volume's share name. For example, to map a shared volume named MYDOCS on a server named WALLY, type the following in the Path field:

   ```
   \\WALLY\MYDOCS
   ```

   This type of filename, with the double backslashes, the server name, and the share name, is known as a *UNC name*. (*UNC* stands for *Universal Naming Convention*.)

5. **If you want this drive to be mapped automatically each time you log on to the network, check the Reconnect at Logon option.**

   If you leave this option unchecked, the drive mapping vanishes when you log off the network.

6. Click OK.

You return to the Open dialog box. The Look In field automatically shows the newly mapped network drive, so the Open dialog box lists the files and folders in the network drive.

If you try to open a file that another network user already has opened, Office tells you that the file is already in use and offers to let you open a read-only version of the file. You can read and edit the read-only version, but Office won't let you overwrite the existing version of the file. You'll have to use the Save As command instead to save your changes to a new file.

Using Workgroup Templates

A *template* is not a place of worship, though an occasional sacrifice to the Office gods may make your computing life a bit easier. Rather, a template is a special type of document file that holds formatting information, boilerplate text, and other customized settings that you can use as the basis for new documents.

Three Office programs — Word, Excel, and PowerPoint — enable you to specify a template whenever you create a new document. When you create a new document in Word, Excel, or PowerPoint by choosing the File➪New command, you see a dialog box that lets you choose a template for the new document. For example, Figure 22-3 shows the dialog box that appears when you create a new document from a template in Word 2002.

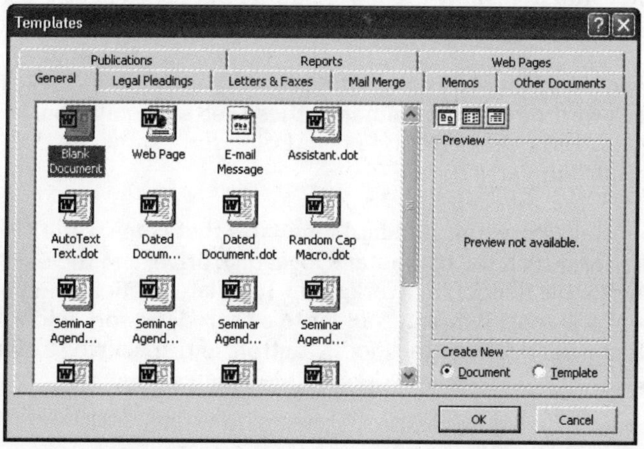

Figure 22-3:
The
Templates
dialog box in
Word 2002.

Templates				? X
Publications		Reports		Web Pages
General	Legal Pleadings	Letters & Faxes	Mail Merge	Memos	Other Documents

Blank Document   Web Page   E-mail Message   Assistant.dot

AutoText Text.dot   Dated Docum...   Dated Document.dot   Random Cap Macro.dot

Seminar Agend...   Seminar Agend...   Seminar Agend...   Seminar Agend...

Preview

Preview not available.

Create New
○ Document   ○ Template

OK   Cancel

Office comes with a set of templates for the most common types of documents. These templates are grouped under the various tabs that appear across the top of the New dialog box.

In addition to the templates that come with Office, you can create your own templates in Word, Excel, and PowerPoint. Creating your own templates is especially useful if you want to establish a consistent look for documents prepared by your network users. For example, you can create a Letter template that includes your company's letterhead or a Proposal template that includes a company logo.

Office enables you to store templates in two locations. The first location, referred to as the User Templates folder, usually resides on the user's local disk drive. The second location, called the Workgroup Templates folder, is usually a folder on a shared network drive. This arrangement lets you store templates that you want to make available to all network users on a network server, but still allows each user to create his or her own templates that are not available to other network users.

When you use both a User Templates folder and a Workgroup Templates folder, Office combines the templates from both folders and lists them in alphabetical order in the New dialog box. For example, suppose that the User Templates folder contains templates called Blank Document and Web Page, and the Workgroup Templates folder contains a template called Company Letterhead. In this case, three templates appear in the New dialog box, in this order: Blank Document, Company Letterhead, and Web Page.

To set the User Templates and Workgroup Templates folders, choose Tools⇨Options in Word to summon the Options dialog box. Then click the File Locations tab to display the file location options, such as those shown in Figure 22-4.

Although the User Templates and Workgroup Templates settings affect Word, Excel, and PowerPoint, you can change these settings only from Word. The Options dialog boxes in Excel and PowerPoint don't show the User Templates or Workgroup Templates options.

When you install Office, the standard templates that come with Office are copied into a folder on the computer's local disk drive, and the User Templates option is set to this folder. The Workgroup Templates option is left blank. You can set the Workgroup Templates folder to a shared network folder by clicking Network Templates, clicking the Modify button, and specifying a shared network folder that contains your workgroup templates.

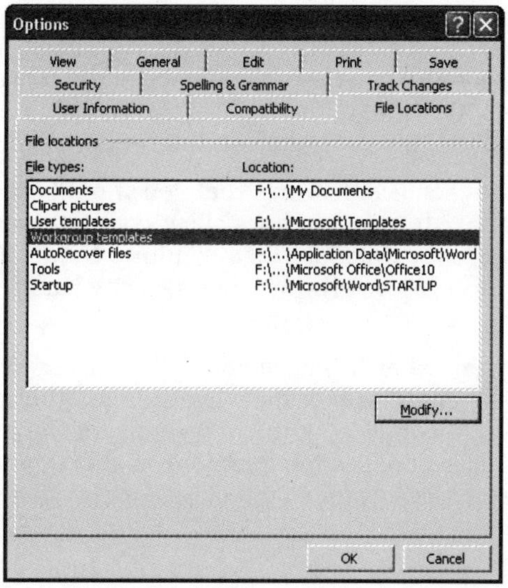

Figure 22-4:
The Options
dialog box.

Networking an Access Database

If you want to share a Microsoft Access database among several network users, you should be aware of a few special considerations. Here are the more important ones:

✔ When you share a database, more than one user may try to access the same record at the same time. This situation can lead to problems if two or more users try to update the record. To handle this, Access locks the record so that only one user at a time can update it. Access uses one of three methods to lock records:

- **Edited Record:** Locks a record whenever a user begins to edit a record. For example, if a user retrieves a record in a form that allows the record to be updated, Access locks the record while the user edits it so that other users can't edit the record until the first record is finished.

- **No Locks:** This doesn't really mean that the record isn't locked. Instead, No Locks means that the record is not locked until a user actually writes a change to the database. This method can be confusing to users because it enables one user to overwrite changes made by another user.

- **All Records:** Locks an entire table whenever a user edits any record in the table.

✔ Access lets you split a database so that the forms, queries, and reports are stored on each user's local disk drive, but the data itself is stored on a network drive. This feature can make the database run more efficiently on a network but is a little more difficult to set up. To split a database, use the Tools⇨Database Utilities⇨Database Splitter command.

✔ Access includes built-in security features that you should use if you share an Access database from a Windows client computer such as Windows XP. If you store the database on a Windows NT/2000 server or on a NetWare server, you can use the server's security features to protect the database.

✔ Access automatically refreshes forms and datasheets every 60 seconds. That way, if one user opens a form or datasheet and another user changes the data a few seconds later, the first user sees the changes within one minute. If 60 seconds is too long (or too short), you can change the refresh from the Advanced tab of the Options dialog box.

Chapter 23

Networking Older Computers

. . . .

. . . .

*W*ouldn't it be great if every computer on your network had a shiny new Pentium 4 processor, 512MB of RAM, and a 40GB disk drive? Managing a network like this would be a breeze. Everyone could take advantage of the latest networking features of Windows XP, you wouldn't have to worry about incompatible network cards or software conflicts, and the users would never complain about lousy performance.

Unfortunately, few networks in the real world have the luxury of working with only the most current computers. Most networks consist of a hodgepodge of computers, ranging from brand-new Pentium 4 computers with plenty of RAM and disk space, to older Pentium III computers with adequate RAM and disk space, to ancient Pentium computers with barely enough RAM and disk space. Some even have prehistoric 486 computers with RAM numbered in the single digits. Getting all these computers to work on your network is the topic of this chapter.

Networking Older Computers Presents Challenges

Accommodating older computers on your network presents you with a plethora of challenges to overcome. The following list highlights the major areas of difficulty you face when networking computers that are less than state-of-the-art:

✔ Your client computers may run several different versions of Windows. You may find computers with Windows XP, Millennium Edition (Windows Me), Windows 98 (first and second edition), Windows 95, Windows 3.1, and Windows for Workgroup computers in your network. You may also find Windows NT 4 Workstation and Windows 2000 Professional. Windows 95, 98, and Me as well as Windows NT 4 and Windows 2000 have built-in networking support, but configuring older versions of Windows for networking can be a challenge.

✔ Some of the client computers may not even run Windows. You may have to figure out how to incorporate computers running DOS without Windows into your network.

✔ Older computers are probably very tight on disk space. Not long ago, 650MB of disk space seemed like a lot. Now it's barely enough to hold Windows, let alone any application programs or data files. Users of these computers will crave disk space on your network servers.

✔ Older computers have hardware limitations that make installing and configuring network cards difficult. (For more info, see the section "Configuring a Network Card in an Older Computer," later in this chapter.)

✔ When you mix old computers with new computers on the network, software incompatibilities are bound to arise. For example, some users may use Microsoft Office 2000, while others use older version of Office. Some may even still use DOS versions of WordPerfect and Lotus 1-2-3.

Dealing with Older Computers in Two Ways

The following sections summarize two basic approaches to handling the challenges of networking older computers.

Option 1: Don't include older computers in the network

One option is to simply state a minimum configuration that you will support on your network and refuse even to attempt to network any computer that doesn't meet that minimum. For example, you may say that you won't network any computer that doesn't already run at least Windows 95. Anyone who is still using Windows 3.1 or plain old DOS is out of luck.

Of course, this approach can make a lot of people mad — especially the ones with the older computers. To make these people happy, you have two options: upgrade their old computers so that they can run Windows XP, or throw the old computers away and replace them with new computers.

If the computer isn't too old, you may be able to upgrade it to Windows XP without much trouble. According to Microsoft, the minimum system requirements for Windows XP are as follows:

- A Pentium or better processor running at 233 MHz or faster
- 128MB of RAM
- 1.5G MB of available disk space

If you have a computer that doesn't meet these requirements, you might be able to purchase an older version of Windows, such as Windows 98 or even Windows 95. The computer will be slow, but at least you'll be able to network it.

The biggest trick is installing and configuring a network card to work in a 486-based computer. For tips on how to do this, see the section "Configuring a Network Card in an Older Computer," later in this chapter.

A computer with a 486 (or older) requires a more substantial overhaul to bring it up to Windows XP standards. In fact, to upgrade a 486 computer to run Windows , you probably need to replace almost every major component of the computer: the motherboard, power supply and case, disk drive, video card, and maybe even the monitor. By the time you finish, you have spent as much or actually more than a new computer costs. Better to just discard these computers and replace them with new ones.

Although it is possible to run Windows 98 on a 486 computer, I wouldn't try it. By the time you invest the hours it will take to install any needed upgrades, manually configure the network card, install Windows 98 (which will take a long time because of the slow speed of the computer), you'll realize that in the long run, replacing the 486 computer with a new computer would be less expensive.

Option 2: Use your network's DOS support

If you have computers that run MS-DOS, with or without old-fashioned Windows 3.1, you can include them in your network by using your network operating system's built-in support for MS-DOS client computers. Both Windows NT/2000 Server and NetWare support MS-DOS client computers. An MS-DOS client computer can access shared network disk drives and printers, but cannot share its own drives or printers with other network users.

For more information about using a DOS computer on a network, see the section "Using a DOS Client Computer," later in this chapter.

Using a DOS Client Computer

Both Windows NT/2000 Server and NetWare enable you to use DOS computers as clients on the network. A DOS client computer cannot share its own disk drives or printers with other network users, but it can access network drives and printers. The following sections describe the basics of using a DOS computer on a network.

Logging on to the network

To use network resources, a DOS client computer must first log on to the network. Usually, the logon process is started automatically by the computer's AUTOEXEC.BAT file when you start up your computer. You see a prompt similar to the following:

```
Enter your login name:
```

Type your user ID and press Enter. Then a prompt similar to this one appears:

```
Enter your password:
```

When you type your password, the password doesn't appear on the screen, which prevents someone looking over your shoulder from learning your password, unless of course they watch your fingers while you type.

After the network verifies your user ID and password, a special *login script* runs. The login script sets up your computer so that you can use network drives and printers.

Using a network drive

After you log on to the network, you have access to one or more network drives. Just like local drives, network drives are accessed using drive letters that are assigned to the network drives by the login script.

Every network is set up differently, so I can't tell you what your network drive letters are or what restrictions are in place for accessing your network drives. But you can find out easily enough. If you work on a Windows Server network, just type the following command at an MS-DOS prompt:

```
NET USE
```

This command displays a list of the network drives that are available to you. To see a similar list for a NetWare network, use this command:

```
MAP
```

This displays a list of all mapped network drives.

Network printing with NetWare

If your network is Novell NetWare and you're using NetWare's DOS client software, you set up redirection for a network printer by using the CAPTURE command. This command tells the NetWare software to capture everything sent to a particular printer port and redirect it to a network print queue. You'll probably want to put the CAPTURE command in the computer's AUTOEXEC.BAT file or a login script.

Here's a typical CAPTURE command:

```
CAPTURE Q=LJET TI=10
```

This command redirects any printer output you send to LPT1 to a print queue named LJET. TI=10 sets the time-out value to ten seconds. If your program stops sending output to the printer for ten seconds, NetWare assumes the print job is finished.

Network printing with Windows NT/2000 Server

If your network is Windows NT or 2000 Server and you use Microsoft MS-DOS client software, you set up printer redirection by using the NET USE command. This command tells the MS-DOS client software to use a particular network printer whenever you send output to a printer.

Here's a typical NET USE command to set up a network printer:

```
NET USE LPT1: \\WARD\LASER
```

This command redirects any printer output that you send to LPT1 to a printer named LASER on the server named WARD.

Logging off the network

When you have finished using the network, you should log off. Logging off the network makes the network drives and printers unavailable, so strangers can't walk up to your computer and access the network.

If you just turn off your computer, you are automatically logged off the network. If you want to log off the network but keep your computer on so that you can continue using it, type the command **LOGOUT** if you use a NetWare network or **NET LOGOFF** if your network uses Windows NT/2000 Server.

Configuring a Network Card in an Older Computer

One of the best features about modern versions of Windows is *Plug and Play,* which makes installing new devices, such as a network interface card, a snap. Plug and Play automatically recognizes your network card, configures it, and installs any special device drivers that the card needs to operate.

To install a network card in a computer that runs Windows 3.1 or plain DOS, you have to configure the card manually. You may have to fiddle with confusing software configuration settings, or, worse yet, you may actually have to make changes on the card itself before you install it into your computer. If that's the case, the following tips should prove helpful:

✔ If possible, use good name-brand network cards (such as Intel or 3Com) for older computers. Name-brand cards may cost more, but they are usually easier to configure, which can be a major plus for older computers.

✔ On some cards, configuration settings are made by changing special switches called *DIP switches* or moving a *jumper block.* Figure 23-1 shows what a DIP switch and jumper block look like. The switch or block must be set *before* you install the card into your computer.

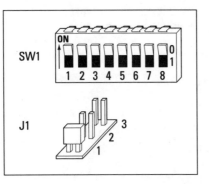

Figure 23-1:
A DIP switch and a jumper block.

✔ A straightened-out paper clip is the ideal tool for setting DIP switches.

✔ To change a jumper block, you move the *plug* from one set of pins to another. You need fingernails to do it properly. Or a good set of tweezers.

✔ If you're lucky, your network cards have been preconfigured for you with the most likely settings. You need to double-check, though, because *(1)* the factory settings are not always appropriate, and *(2)* sometimes they make mistakes at the factory and configure the cards incorrectly.

✔ If you're even luckier, your cards don't use DIP switches or jumper blocks at all. These cards still have to be configured, but the configuration is done with software rather than with a paper clip or your fingernails.

✔ Most network cards have two configuration settings: IRQ number and I/O port address. Some cards also enable you to configure a DMA channel. The trick in configuring these settings is to make sure the card doesn't conflict with settings used by another card already installed in the computer. You can find out what settings are already in use by running the MSD program from a DOS command prompt.

✔ Network cards that support more than one type of cable connector also have to be configured for the proper cable type. For example, if your card supports both 10baseT and coax connectors, you have to configure the card depending on the type of cable you use.

✔ When you configure a network card, write down the settings you select. You need these settings later when you install the client software. Store your list of network card settings in your network binder.

✔ Adding a joke about DIP switches here would be too easy. Insert your own joke if you're so inclined.

Chapter 24

Welcoming Macintosh Computers to Your Network

. . . .

In This Chapter

▶ Hooking up a Macintosh network

▶ Using a Macintosh network

▶ Mixing Macs and PCs

. . . .

*T*his book dwells on networking PCs as if IBM were the only game in town. To be politically correct, I should at least acknowledge the existence of an altogether different breed of computer: the Apple Macintosh.

Apple prides itself on its ability to include stuff in its Macintosh computers that Windows users have to purchase separately. Network support is an example. Every Macintosh comes with a built-in Ethernet port that's already configured to access the network. All you have to do to network your Macintosh is plug in a network cable.

Well, you actually discover that networking your Macintosh involves a lot more than that. This chapter presents what you need to know to hook up a Macintosh network, use a Macintosh network, and mix Macintoshes and PCs on the same network. This chapter is not a comprehensive tome on networking Macintoshes, but it should be enough to get you started.

What You Need to Know to Hook Up a Macintosh Network

The following sections present some key things you should know about networking Macintosh computers before you start plugging in cables.

AppleTalk and Open Transport

Every Macintosh ever built, even an original 1984 model, includes networking support. Of course, newer Macintosh computers have better built-in networking features than older Macintosh computers. The newest Macs include built-in 10/100Mbps Ethernet adapters and sophisticated networking support built in to the operating system, similar to the networking features that come with Windows XP. The beauty of Macintosh networking is that the network card is built in, so you don't have to worry about installing and configuring the network.

Macintosh computers use a set of networking protocols collectively known as *AppleTalk*. Because AppleTalk is built in to every Mac, it has become an inarguable networking standard among Macintosh users. You don't have to worry about the differences between different network operating systems, because all Macintosh networking is based on AppleTalk.

AppleTalk has gone through several major revisions since it was first introduced back in 1984. Originally, AppleTalk supported only small networks that operated only over low-speed connections. In 1989, Apple enhanced AppleTalk to support larger networks and faster connections.

In 1996, with the release of MacOS System 7.5.3, Apple folded AppleTalk into a grander networking scheme known as Open Transport. The idea behind Open Transport is to bring all the different types of communications software used on Macintoshes under a common umbrella and make them easy to configure and use. Currently, two types of networking are handled by Open Transport:

- ✔ **Open Transport/AppleTalk:** Handles local area networks (LANs) based on the AppleTalk protocols. Open Transport/AppleTalk is a beefed-up version of AppleTalk that's more efficient and flexible.

- ✔ **OpenTransport/TCP:** Handles TCP/IP communications, such as Internet connections.

Open Transport is standard fare on all new Macintosh computers, and old Macintosh computers can be upgraded to Open Transport, provided that they're powerful enough. (The minimum system requirements for Open Transport are a 68030 processor, 5MB RAM, and MacOS System 7.5.3.)

AppleTalk enables you to subdivide a network into *zones,* which are similar to workgroups in Windows for Workgroups. Each zone consists of the network users who regularly share information.

Although basic support for networking is built in to every Macintosh, you still have to purchase cables to connect the computers to one another. You have several types of cables to choose from. You can use AppleTalk with two different cabling schemes that connect to the Macintosh printer port, or you can use AppleTalk with faster Ethernet interface cards.

Who's winning in the AFP West?

AFP is not a division of the NFL, but an abbreviation for AppleTalk Filing Protocol. It's the part of AppleTalk that governs how files are stored and accessed on the network. AFP allows files to be shared with non-Macintosh computers. You can integrate Macintoshes into any network operating system that recognizes AFP.

NetWare and all versions of Windows since Windows 95 use AFP to support Macintoshes in their networks.

In case you're interested (and you shouldn't be), AFP is a presentation-layer protocol. See Chapter 30 if you don't have a clue what I'm talking about.

LocalTalk: The cheap way to network

LocalTalk is an older method of connecting Macintosh computers that don't have built-in network adapters. LocalTalk connects Macintosh computers using special cables that attach to each computer's printer port.

Here are the details:

- LocalTalk connectors are self-terminating, which means that separate terminators are not required on both ends of the cable segment.

- Each LocalTalk connector comes with a 2-meter-long LocalTalk cable (that's about 6 ½ feet). You can also purchase 10-meter cables if your computers aren't that close together.

- LocalTalk uses shielded twisted-pair cable. The shielding protects the cable from electrical interference but limits the total length of a cable that is used in a network segment to 300 feet.

- No more than 32 computers and printers can be connected to a single segment.

- A popular alternative to LocalTalk is PhoneNET, made by Farallon Computing. PhoneNET uses inexpensive telephone cable rather than the shielded twisted-pair cable used by LocalTalk.

Ethernet with Macintosh computers

LocalTalk is popular because it's cheap. But LocalTalk has one major problem: It's unbearably slow. LocalTalk uses the Macintosh serial printer ports and therefore transmits data over the network at a paltry 230,400 bits per second (bps). This transmission rate is acceptable for casual use of a network printer and for occasionally copying a small file to or from another computer but not for serious networking.

Fortunately, AppleTalk also supports Ethernet network adapters and cables. With Ethernet, data travels at 10 or 100 megabits per second (Mbps) — much more suitable for real-life networking.

When you use Ethernet, you have access to all the cabling options described in Chapter 10: 10base5 (yellow cable), 10base2 (thinnet), and 10baseT (twisted pair). Fast (100Mbps) Ethernet works as well.

Here are some additional points to ponder when you use Ethernet to network your Macintosh computers:

- ✔ AppleTalk running on an Ethernet network is sometimes referred to as *EtherTalk*.

- ✔ Ethernet interface cards for Macintoshes are a bit more expensive than their PC counterparts, mostly because they aren't as widely used. However, most Macs built within the last few years have Ethernet built in, so if your Macs are new, you probably don't need cards. All the current Apple Macintosh computers come with built-in 10/100MHz Ethernet adapters.

- ✔ Some Macintosh computers that do not have built-in Ethernet adapters have standard PCI expansion slots — the same expansion slots that modern PCs have. That means you can use any PCI Ethernet card in a PCI-equipped Macintosh. (Well, almost any. The manufacturer of the card must supply a Macintosh driver for the card, and some manufacturers don't.)

- ✔ Some older Macintosh computers used a special interface for Ethernet cards called the *Ethernet cabling system*. When the Ethernet cabling system is used, the network cards themselves don't have coax or 10baseT connectors. Instead, they have a special type of connector called an *Apple Attachment Unit Interface* (AAUI). You must plug a device called a transceiver into the AAUI connector so that you can attach the computer to a coax or twisted-pair cable. Newer Macintosh computers with built-in Ethernet adapters use standard RJ-45 connectors.

- ✔ You can use a router to connect a LocalTalk network to an Ethernet network. This arrangement often connects a small group of Macintosh users to a larger network or connects an existing LocalTalk network to an Ethernet network.

AppleShare

AppleShare turns any Macintosh computer that runs the Mac OS 9 operating system into a dedicated file server. AppleShare can support up to 250 users connected to the server simultaneously using AppleTalk or 500 users with TCP/IP.

The current version of AppleShare, called AppleShare IP 6.3, offers the following features:

- ✔ File server using AppleTalk's standard file protocol, AFP
- ✔ Print server
- ✔ Mail server
- ✔ Web server
- ✔ FTP server
- ✔ Support for both AppleTalk and TCP/IP protocols

You need to purchase AppleShare only if you want to set up a Macintosh computer to act as a dedicated file server. All Macintosh computers come with the ability to connect to a network, access network printers and drives, and share their own printers and disk drives with other network users.

Mac OS X Server

Apple also offers a dedicated network operating system known as Mac OS X Server (the *X* is pronounced "Ten," not "Ex"), which is designed for PowerMac G3 or later computers. Mac OS X Server is based on a UNIX operating system kernel known as Mach. As a result, Mac OS X Server can handle many network server tasks as efficiently as any other network operating system, including Windows 2000, NetWare, and UNIX.

(Mac OS X Server is the server version of the Mac OS X operating system, which is the current operating system version for client Macintosh computers.)

The Mac OS X Server includes the following features:

- ✔ Apache Web server
- ✔ NetBoot, a feature that simplifies the task of managing network client computers
- ✔ File services using AFP
- ✔ WebObjects, a high-end tool for creating Web sites
- ✔ QuickTime Streaming Server, which lets the server broadcast multimedia programs over the network

What You Need to Know to Use a Macintosh Network

Here are some of the most common questions that come up after you install the network cable. Note that the following sections assume that you're working with AppleTalk networking using Mac OS X. The procedures may vary somewhat if you're using Open Transport networking or an earlier version of the Macintosh Operating System.

Configuring a Mac for networking

Before you can access the network from your Mac, you must configure your Mac for networking by activating AppleTalk and assigning your network name and password.

Activating AppleTalk

After all the cables are in place, you have to activate AppleTalk. Here's how:

1. **Choose the Chooser desk accessory from the Apple menu.**

2. **Click the Active button.**

3. **Close the Chooser.**

That's all there is to it.

Assigning your name and password

Next, assign an owner name, a password, and a name for your computer. This process allows other network users to access your Mac. Here's how:

1. **Choose the File Sharing control panel from the Apple menu (Apple⇨Control Panels⇨File Sharing).**

2. **Type your name in the Owner Name field.**

3. **Type a password in the Owner Password field.**

   Don't forget what the password is.

4. **Type a descriptive name for your computer in the Computer Name field.**

   Other network users will know your computer by this name.

5. **Click the Close button.**

Piece of cake, eh?

Accessing a network printer

Accessing a network printer with AppleTalk is no different than accessing a printer when you don't have a network. If more than one printer is available on the network, you use the Chooser to select the printer you want to use. Chooser displays all the available network printers — just pick the one you want to use. And keep the following points in mind:

✔ **Be sure to enable Background Printing for the network printer.** If you don't, your Mac is tied up until the printer finishes your job — that can be a long time if someone else sent a 500-page report to the printer just before you. When you enable Background Printing, your printer output is captured to a disk file and then sent to the printer later while you continue with other work.

To enable Background Printing:

1. **Choose Apple⇨Chooser desk accessory.**

2. **Select the printer you want to use from the Chooser.**

3. **Click the Background Printing On button.**

✔ **Do not enable Background Printing if a dedicated print server has been set up.** In that case, print data is automatically spooled to the print server's disk so that your Mac doesn't have to wait for the printer to become available.

Sharing files with other users

To share files on your Mac with other network users, you must set up a shared resource. You can share an entire disk or just individual folders and restrict access to certain users, if you want.

Before you can share files with other users, you must activate the AppleTalk file-sharing feature. Here's how:

1. **Choose the File Sharing control panel from the Apple Menu.**

2. **Click the Start button in the File Sharing section of the control panel.**

3. **Click the Close button.**

To share a file or folder, click the file or folder once. Then open the File menu, choose Get Info, and then choose Sharing from the submenu that appears. You can also use the Sharing section of the Info window to set access privileges to restrict access to the file or folder.

Accessing shared files

To access files on another Macintosh, follow this procedure:

1. **Choose the Chooser from the Apple menu.**

2. **Click the AppleShare icon from the Chooser window.**

3. **Click the name of the computer you want to access. (If your network has zones, you must first click the zone you want to access.)**

4. **Click OK.**

   A login screen appears.

5. **If you have a user account on the computer, click the Registered User button and enter your user name and password. Otherwise, click the Guest button and then click OK.**

   A list of shared folders and disks appears.

6. **Click the folders and disks you want to access.**

   A check box appears next to each item on the list. If you check this box, you connect to the folder or disk automatically each time you start your computer.

7. **Click OK.**

 With Mac OS 8.5 and later, you can also use the Network Browser, found in the Apple menu, to access network drives or folders. Just open the Network Browser from the Apple menu, double-click the server that contains the shared disk or folder, and then double-click the drive or folder you want to use.

What You Need to Know to Network Macintoshes with PCs

Life would be too boring if Macs lived on one side of the tracks and PCs lived on the other. If your organization has a mix of both Macs and PCs, odds are you eventually want to network them together. Fortunately, you have several ways to do so:

✔ If your network has an AppleShare server, you can use the Windows client software that comes with AppleShare to connect any version of Windows to the AppleShare server. Doing so enables Windows users to access the files and printers on the AppleShare server.

✔ If you have Windows NT/2000 Server, you can use a feature called Services for Macintosh to allow Macintosh computers to access files and printers managed by the Windows NT/2000 Server without having to install special client software on the Macintosh computers.

✔ If you use NetWare, you must purchase separate NetWare client software for your Macintosh computers. After you install this client software, the Macs can access files and printers managed by your NetWare servers.

The biggest complication that occurs when you mix Macintosh and Windows computers on the same network is that the Mac OS and Windows have slightly different rules for naming files. For example, Macintosh filenames are limited to 31 characters, but Windows filenames can be up to 255 characters. And although a Macintosh filename can include any characters other than a colon, Windows filenames can't include backslashes, greater than or less than signs, and a few other oddball characters.

The best way to avoid filename problems is to stick with short names (under 31 characters) and limit your filenames to letters, numbers, and common symbols such as the hyphen or pound sign. Although you can translate any filenames that violate the rules of the system being used into a form that is acceptable to both Windows and the Macintosh, doing so sometimes leads to cryptic or ambiguous filenames.

Chapter 25

Using a Linux Server

*L*inux, the free operating system based on UNIX, is becoming more and more popular as an alternative to expensive server operating systems such as Windows 2000 Server and NetWare. In fact, by some estimates, there are more computers now running the Linux operating system than there are running the Macintosh operating system. You can use Linux as a Web server for the Internet or for an intranet, and you can use it as a firewall or a file and print server on your local area network.

Linux was started in 1991 by a Linus Torvalds, who was at the time an under-graduate student at the University of Helsinki in Finland. Linus thought it would be fun to create his own operating system for his brand-new PC, based on UNIX. In the nearly ten years since Linux was first conceived, Linux has become a full-featured operating system that is fast and reliable.

In this chapter, you find out the basics of setting up a Linux server on your network and using it as a file server, as a Web server for the Internet or an intranet, as an e-mail server, and as a router and firewall to help connect your network to the Internet.

Linux is a complicated operating system. Learning how to use it can be a daunting task, especially if your only prior computer experience is with Windows. Fortunately, Wiley Publishing, Inc. has a plethora of *For Dummies* books that make learning Linux less painful. Check out *Linux For Dummies,* 2nd Edition by Jon "maddog" Hall, *Linux For Dummies Quick Reference,* 2nd Edition by Phil Hughes, and *Linux Administration For Dummies* by Michael Bellomo.

Comparing Linux with Windows

If your only computer experience is with Windows, you are in for a steep learning curve when you first start working with Linux. There are many fundamental differences between the Linux operating system and Windows. Here are some of the more important differences:

- ✔ **Linux is a multiuser operating system.** That means that more than one user can log on and use a Linux computer at the same time. Two or more users can log on to a Linux computer from the same keyboard and monitor by using virtual consoles, which let you switch from one user session to another with a special key combination. Or, users can log on to the Linux computer from a terminal window running on another computer on the network.

  In contrast, most versions of Windows are single-user systems. Only one user at a time can log on to a Windows computer and run commands. (Windows 2000 can be configured as a multiuser system with terminal services.)

- ✔ **Linux does not have a built-in graphical user interface (GUI) as Windows does.** Instead, the GUI in Linux is provided by an optional component called *X Window System*. You can run Linux without X Window, in which case you interact with Linux by typing commands. If you prefer to use a GUI, you must install and run X Window.

  X Window is split into two parts: a server component, called an *X server,* which handles the basic chores of managing multiple windows and providing graphics services for application programs, and a user interface component, called a *window manager,* which provides user interface features such as menus, buttons, toolbars, a taskbar, and so on. Several different window managers are available, each with a different look and feel. With Windows, you are stuck with the user interface that Microsoft designed. With Linux, you can use the user interface of your choosing.

- ✔ **Linux cannot run Windows programs.** That means you cannot run Microsoft Office on a Linux system; instead, you must find a similar program that is written specifically for Linux. Many Linux distributions come with an office suite called StarOffice, which provides word processing, spreadsheet, presentation, graphics, database, e-mail, calendar, and scheduling software. Thousands of other programs are available for Linux. (There are Windows emulator programs — the best known is Wine — that can run some Windows programs on Linux. But the emulators can run only some Windows programs, and it runs them slower than they would run on a Windows system.)

- ✔ **Linux doesn't do Plug and Play like Windows does.** Although the major Linux distributions come with configuration programs that can automatically detect and configure the most common hardware components,

Linux does not have built-in support for Plug-and-Play hardware devices. As a result, you're more likely to run into a hardware configuration problem with Linux than with Windows.

✔ **Linux uses a different system for accessing disk drives and files than Windows does.** For an explanation of how the Linux file system works, see the sidebar "I can't see my C drive!" below.

✔ **Linux runs better on older hardware than the current incarnations of Windows do.** Linux is an ideal operating system for an older Pentium computer with at least 32MB of RAM and 2GB of hard disk. However, with a bit of juggling, you can get Linux to run well even on a 486 computer with as little as 4MB of RAM and a few hundred MB of disk space.

I can't see my C drive!

Linux and Windows have a completely different method of referring to your computer's disk drives and partitions. The differences can take some getting used to for experienced Windows users.

Windows uses a separate letter for each drive and partition on you system. For example, if you have a single drive formatted into three partitions, Windows identifies the partitions as drives C, D, and E. Each of these drives has its own root directory, which can in turn contain additional directories used to organize your files. As far as Windows is concerned, drives C, D, and E are completely separate drives, even though the drives are actually just partitions on a single drive.

Linux does not use drive letters. Instead, Linux combines all the drives and partitions into a single directory hierarchy. In Linux, one of the partitions is designated as the *root* partition. The root is roughly analogous to the C drive on a Windows system. Then, the other partitions can be *mounted* on the root partition and treated as if they were directories on the root partition. For example, you might designate the first partition as the root partition and then mount the second partition as /user and the third partition as

/var. Then, any files stored in the /user directory would actually be stored in the second partition, and files stored in the /var directory would be stored on the third partition.

The directory which a drive mounts to is called the drive's *mount point.*

Notice that Linux uses regular forward slash characters (/) to separate directory names rather than the backward slash characters (\) used by Windows. Typing backslashes instead of regular slashes is one of the most common mistakes made by new Linux users.

While we're on the subject, Linux uses a different convention for naming files, too. In Windows, file names end in a three-letter extension that is separated from the rest of the file name by a period. The extension is used to indicate the file type. For example, files that end in .exe are program files, but files that end in .doc are word processing documents.

Linux doesn't use file extensions, but periods are often used in Linux file names to separate different parts of the name and the last part often indicates the file type. For example, ldap.conf, and pine.conf are both configuration files.

Choosing a Linux Distribution

Because the kernel (that is, the core operating functions) of the Linux operating system is free, several companies have created their own *distributions* of Linux, which include the Linux operating system along with a bundle of packages to go along with it, such as administration tools, Web servers, and other useful utilities, as well as printed documentation. These distributions are inexpensive — ranging from $25 to $100 — and are well worth the small cost.

The following are some of the more popular Linux distributions:

- **Red Hat** is by most counts the most popular Linux distribution. Red Hat comes in three versions: Red Hat Standard Edition ($29.95), which includes the basic Linux operating system and tools; Deluxe Edition ($79.95), which adds a collection of workstation tools and additional printed documentation; and Professional Edition ($179.95), which adds advanced server and e-commerce tools. If you prefer, you can also download Red Hat Linux free from the Red Hat Web site. For more information, see www.redhat.com.

  All of the examples in this chapter are based on Red Hat Linux.

- **Linux-Mandrake** is another popular Linux distribution, one that is often recommended as the easiest for first-time Linux users to install.

- **SuSE** (pronounced "Soo-zuh," like the famous composer of marches) is a popular Linux distribution that comes on six CD-ROM disks and includes more than 1,500 Linux application programs and utilities, including everything you need to set up a network, Web, e-mail, or electronic commerce server. You can find more information at www.suse.com.

- **Caldera OpenLinux** emphasizes Linux's role as an electronic commerce server for the Internet with its OpenLinux distributions. With Caldera, you get just about everything you need to set up an online Web store. Check out www.caldera.com for more information.

- **Slackware**, one of the oldest Linux distributions, is still popular especially among Linux old-timers. A full installation of Slackware gives you all the tools you need to set up a network or Internet server. See www.slackware.com for more information.

- **Corel** offers not only the Corel Linux distribution but also a Linux version of its office suite, WordPerfect Office 2000. Although Corel Linux was designed with desktop users in mind, it comes with Web, mail, and news servers so you can use it as an Internet or intranet server. You can find more information about Corel Linux at linux.corel.com.

All distributions of Linux include the same core components — the Linux kernel, an X Server, popular windows managers such as GNOME and KDE, compilers, Internet programs such as Apache, Sendmail, and so on. However, not all Linux distributions are created equal. In particular, the manufacturer of each distribution creates it own installation and configuration programs to install and configure Linux.

The installation program is what makes or breaks a Linux distribution. All the distributions I list in this section have easy-to-use installation programs that automatically detect the hardware that is present on your computer and configure Linux to work with that hardware, eliminating most if not all manual configuration chores. The installation programs also let you select the Linux packages you want to install and let you set up one or more user accounts besides the root account.

The most enjoyable installation program overall comes with the Caldera distribution: It lets you play PacMan while it copies files from the CD-ROM disk to your hard disk!

Installing Linux

All the Linux distributions described in the section "Choosing a Linux Distribution" include an installation program that simplifies the task of installing Linux on your computer. The installation program asks you a series of questions about your hardware, what components of Linux you want to install, and how you want to configure certain features. Then it copies the appropriate files to your hard disk and configures your Linux system.

If the thought of installing Linux gives you hives, you can buy computers with Linux preinstalled, just as you can buy computers with Windows already installed.

Before you begin to install Linux, you should make a list of all the hardware components on your computer and how they are configured. Be as specific as you can: Write down each component's manufacturer and model number as well as configuration information such as the component's IRQ and I/O address, if appropriate.

Next, decide how you want to partition your hard disk for Linux. Although Windows is usually installed into a single disk partition, Linux installations typically require three or more hard disk partitions:

- **A boot partition:** This should be small — 16MB is recommended. The boot partition contains the operating system kernel and is required to start Linux properly on some computers.

- **A swap partition:** This should be about twice the size of your computer's RAM. For example, if the computer has 64MB of RAM, allocate a 128MB swap partition. Linux uses this partition as an extension of your computer's RAM.

✔ **A root partition:** This, in most cases, uses up the remaining free space on the disk. The root partition contains all the files and data used by your Linux system.

You can also create additional partitions if you wish. The installation program includes a disk-partitioning feature that lets you set up your disk partitions and indicate the mount point for each partition. (For more information about disk partitions, see the sidebar "I can't see my C drive!" earlier in this chapter.)

Linux is happy to share your hard disk with another operating system, such as Windows. However, you may have to repartition your disk to install Linux without erasing your existing operating system. If you need to repartition your hard drive, I recommend you pick up a copy of PowerQuest's PartitionMagic (www.powerquest.com) or a similar partitioning program, which will allow you to juggle your partitions without losing your existing operating system.

You'll also need to decide which optional Linux packages to install along with the Linux kernel. If you have enough drive space, I recommend you install all the packages that come with your distribution. That way, if you decide you need to use a package, you won't have to figure out how to install the package outside of the installation program. If you're tight on space, make sure that you at least install the basic network and Internet server packages, including Apache, Sendmail, FTP, and Samba.

Finally, you'll need to set the password for the root account and, in most distributions, choose whether or not to create one or more user accounts. I suggest you create at least one user account during installation, so you can log on to Linux as a user rather with the root account. That way, you can experiment with Linux commands without accidentally deleting or corrupting an important system file

Managing User Accounts

After you get your Linux server up and running, it will probably chug along for days, weeks, or even months at a time without any attention from you. However, on occasion you will have to put on your Network Administrator cap and perform some basic Linux system management chores. One of the most common network administration tasks is adding a user account.

Each Linux user account has the following information associated with it:

✔ **User name:** The name the user types to log on to the Linux system.

✔ **Full name:** The user's full name.

✔ **Home directory:** The directory which the user will be placed in when he or she logs in. In Red Hat Linux, the default home directory is /home/ username. For example, if the user name is blowe, the home directory will be /home/blowe.

✔ **Shell:** The program used to process Linux commands. Several shell programs are available. In most distributions, the default shell is /bin/bash.

✔ **Group:** You can create group accounts, which make it easy to apply identical access rights to groups of users.

✔ **User ID:** The internal identifier for the user.

You can add a new user by using the useradd command. For example, to create a user account named slowe and using default values for the other account information, type this command:

```
# useradd slowe
```

The useradd command has many optional parameters you can use to set account information such as the user's home directory and shell.

Fortunately, most Linux distributions come with special programs that simplify routine system management tasks. For example, Figure 25-1 shows the linuxconf program, which comes with the Red Hat Linux distribution. From this one program, you can manage network settings, user accounts, file system rights, and other system configuration options. Other Linux distributions include similar programs.

Figure 25-1:
Using linuxconf to manage a Red Hat Linux server.

In Linux, the user ID for the system administrator account is called `root`. You set the password for the root account when you install Linux. The root account is a very powerful account, as it has unrestricted access to all the files, directories, and programs on your Linux system. When you are logged on with the root account, be careful that you don't accidentally delete or modify any important system files.

Do not get into the habit of logging on to your Linux system using the root account! Instead, log on with your normal user account. Then, when you need to perform some type of system administration, use the `su` command (with no arguments) to switch to the root user. (`su` stands for Switch User.) The `su` command asks you to enter the root user password and then temporarily switches you to the root user account. When you are finished performing your administrator duties, type **exit** to return to your regular user account.

Configuring Linux Network Settings

In most cases, the installation program for your Linux distribution will automatically detect your network interface card and install the necessary drivers for the card. Linux refers to your Ethernet card as device `eth0`. (If you have more than one Ethernet card, the second card is `eth1`, the third card is `eth2`, and so on.)

You can check to see if your Ethernet card is working properly by using the `ifconfig` command. If your Ethernet card is working, `ifconfig` will display something similar to the following:

```
eth0      Link encap:Ethernet  Hwaddr 00:20:78:16:7C:16
          inet addr:192.168.1.103  Bcast:192.168.1.255
                    Mask:255.255.255.0
          UP BROADCAST RUNNING MULTICAST  MTU:1500  Metric:1
          RX packets:3441 errors:0 dropped:0 overruns:0
             frame:0
          TX packets:2622 errors:0 dropped:0 overruns:0
             carrier:0
          collisions:0 txqueuelen:100
          Interrupt:9 Base addr:0x600

lo        Link encap:Local Loopback
          inet addr:127.0.0.1  Mask:255.0.0.0
          UP LOOPBACK RUNNING  MTU:3924  Metric:1
          RX packets:44 errors:0 dropped:0 overruns:0 frame:0
          TX packets:44 errors:0 dropped:0 overruns:0
             carrier:0
          collisions:0 txqueuelen:100
```

The first section shows information for your Ethernet card (device `eth0`), such as the card's IP address (192.168.1.103) and the number of packets it has received (3,441). The second section shows information for an internal loopback device, which is used for testing and diagnostic purposes.

If `ifconfig` does not show an IP address for your card and you want to manually configure an address, you can do so by using an `ifconfig` command similar to this one:

```
ifconfig eth0 192.168.1.103
```

The `ifconfig` command has numerous arguments that let you set other network options besides the IP address. Fortunately, the system configuration program included with most Linux distributions provides an easier way to configure network settings. For example, Figure 25-2 shows one of several network configuration screens displayed by the `linuxconf` program that comes with Red Hat Linux.

Figure 25-2:
Configuring
network
settings
using the
Red Hat
`linuxconf`
program.

A basic test to see if your network is up and running is to use the `ping` command to see if your Linux computer can contact other computers on the network, and vice-versa. All you need to know is the IP address of the computer you want to contact. Here is an example of a `ping` session attempting to contact a computer whose IP address is 192.168.1.1:

```
# ping 192.168.1.1 -c 5
PING 192.168.1.1 (192.168.1.1) from 192.168.1.103 : 56(84)
          bytes of data.
64 bytes from 192.168.1.1: icmp_seq=0 ttl=64 time=1.2 ms
64 bytes from 192.168.1.1: icmp_seq=1 ttl=64 time=1.0 ms
64 bytes from 192.168.1.1: icmp_seq=2 ttl=64 time=1.0 ms
64 bytes from 192.168.1.1: icmp_seq=3 ttl=64 time=1.0 ms
64 bytes from 192.168.1.1: icmp_seq=4 ttl=64 time=1.0 ms
--- 192.168.1.1 ping statistics ---
5 packets transmitted, 5 packets received, 0% packet loss
round-trip min/avg/max = 0.9/1.0/1.2 ms
```

In this example, I used a `ping` command to ping the computer at 192.168.1.1 five times. The output from the `ping` command shows that each of the five attempts to contact 192.168.1.1 were successful. If any of the `ping` attempts failed, an error message would be displayed.

Running the Apache Web Server

All the popular Linux distributions come with Apache, the most popular Web server on the Internet today. In most cases, Apache is installed and configured automatically when you install Linux. Then, setting up a Web server for the Internet or an intranet is simply a matter of tweaking a few Apache configuration settings and copying your HTML document files to Apache's home directory.

An easy way to find out if Apache is up and running is to try to display the default home page shipped with Apache from another computer on your network. You can do that by firing up a Web browser such as Internet Explorer and typing the IP address of your Linux server in the Address bar. If Apache is running on the server, a page such as the one shown in Figure 25-3 will be displayed.

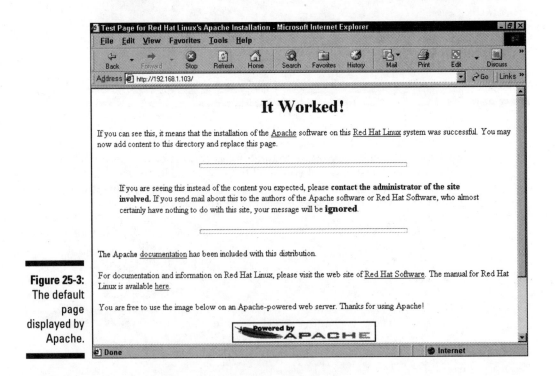

Figure 25-3:
The default page displayed by Apache.

Apache should run fine using the default configuration settings made when you install it. However, you can change various configuration settings either by editing the Apache configuration files or by using your distribution's configuration program. For example, Figure 25-4 shows some of the Apache configuration settings available from Red Hat's linuxconf program.

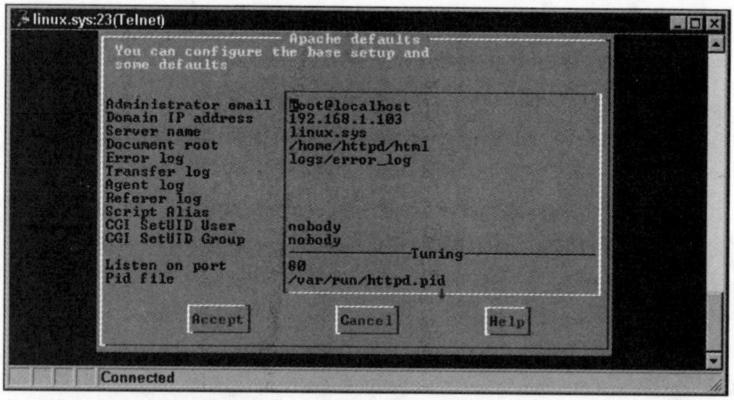

Figure 25-4: Apache configuration options.

From this screen, you can change the following Apache settings:

✔ The e-mail address of the server administrator

✔ The IP address of the server

✔ The server's name

✔ The location of the server's HTML documents

✔ The location of the server's log files

✔ CGI settings

✔ The TCP/IP port number

If you prefer, you can configure your Apache server by directly editing the configuration files. Apache's configuration settings are found in three separate configuration files, named httpd.conf, srm.conf, and access.conf. These files are located in /etc/httpd/conf in Red Hat Linux, but might be in a different location in other Linux distributions. Be sure to study the Apache documentation before you start messing with these files!

For more information about running Apache, see *Apache Server For Dummies* by Ken A.L. Coar, published, of course, by Wiley Publishing, Inc.

Running the Sendmail Mail Server

Sendmail, which comes with all of the Linux distributions mentioned in this chapter, is one of the most popular mail server programs on the Internet. You can also use Sendmail as an alternative to expensive mail server programs such as Microsoft Exchange Server to provide email services for your LAN.

Red Hat's `linuxconf` program has several screens that let you configure Sendmail settings. Figure 25-5 shows the basic Sendmail configuration screen, where you can set such options as the name of the mail server, the name of a mail gateway to forward outgoing mail to, and other basic options. Other distributions include similar configuration programs.

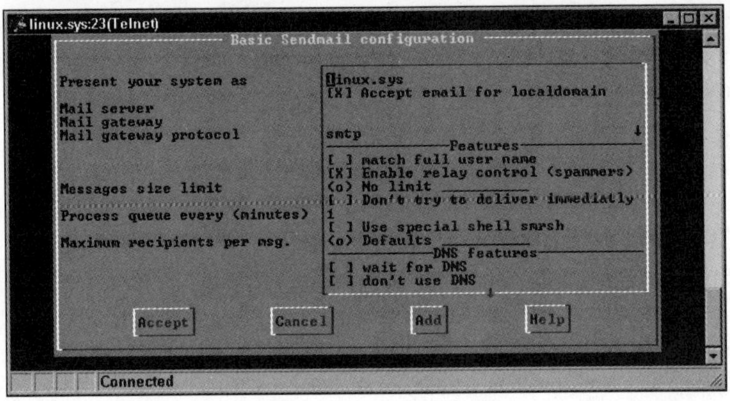

Figure 25-5:
Configuring
Sendmail in
Red Hat
Linux.

For more control over Sendmail configuration, you can edit special configuration macro files that contain detailed configuration settings. You must first run the configuration macro files through a program called m4 before Sendmail can use them.

Spam artists — unscrupulous marketers who clutter the Internet with tens of thousands of unsolicited e-mails — are constantly on the prowl for unprotected Sendmail servers, which they can use to launch their spam campaigns. If you don't protect your server, sooner or later a spammer will coax your computer into spending almost all its time sending out the spammer's e-mail. To protect your server from becoming an indentured spam servant, you can configure it to refuse any mail that merely wants to use your computer to relay messages to other computers.

Doing the Samba Dance

Until now, you probably thought of Samba as a Brazilian dance with intricate steps and fun rhythms. But in the Linux world, Samba refers to a file and printer sharing program that allows Linux to mimic a Windows file and print server so that Windows computers can use shared Linux directories and printers. If you want to use Linux as a file or print server in a Windows network, you'll have to learn how to dance the Samba.

Why did Samba's developers choose to call their program *Samba?* Simply because the protocol that Windows file and print servers use to communicate with one another is called *SMB,* which stands for *Server Message Block.* Add a couple of vowels to *SMB* and you get *Samba.* One way to describe Samba is to say that Samba is a Linux implementation of SMB.

You can configure Samba by editing the smb.conf file located in /etc in Red Hat installations. (Different distributions may place this file elsewhere.) Or, you can use a configuration program such as Red Hat's linuxconf to configure Samba settings. Figure 25-6 shows the linuxconf screen used to configure basic Samba settings. You can use this screen to set basic options such as the server name, the workgroup name, and a brief description of the server.

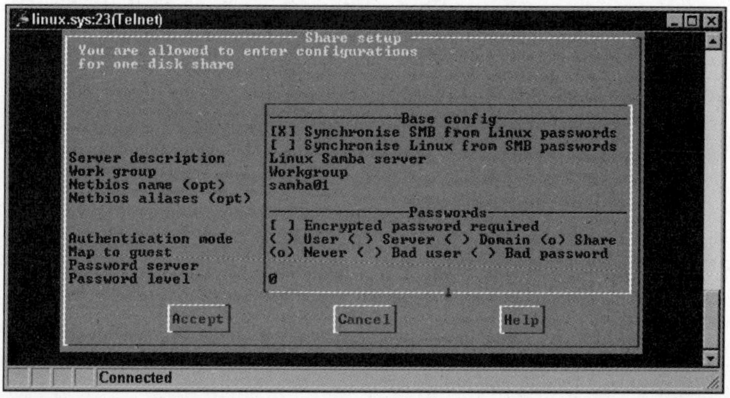

Figure 25-6: Configuring Samba with Red Hat's linuxconf program.

Red Hat's linuxconf program also makes it easy to share directories on your Samba server. Figure 25-7 shows the screen you use to share a directory.

Figure 25-7:
Sharing a
Linux
directory
using
linuxconf.

On this screen, you supply the following information:

✔ The share name, which other users will use to access the directory.

✔ Whether or not to enable the share. If you leave this option unchecked, the shared directory will not be accessible by network users.

✔ Whether or not the share should be browsable. If the share is browsable, users can access it via Network Neighborhood or My Network Places. If not, users must know the share name to access the directory.

✔ The directory to be shared.

✔ Access controls, which enable you to restrict access to certain users, make the share read-only, prevent certain users from accessing the share, and so on.

Using Linux as a Firewall

If your network is connected to the Internet, you should use some type of firewall to protect your LAN from unauthorized access from unfriendly Internet users. You can purchase special firewall devices for this purpose, or you can create your own inexpensive firewall using Linux.

A Linux firewall is a type of router that performs two functions:

✔ The firewall selectively allows certain TCP/IP packets to pass from the Internet to your LAN and prevents other packets from passing through. This is known as *packet filtering.*

✔ The firewall hides all knowledge of the individual computers that are on your network by representing all your computers to the Internet using a single IP address. This is known as *IP masquerading.*

Fortunately, packet filtering and IP masquerading are standard features of Linux.

To create a Linux firewall, the Linux computer must have two network interfaces: an Ethernet card to connect to your LAN and a modem or other type of high-speed connection (such as cable or DSL) to connect to the Internet. The firewall computer must have two IP addresses: one for its connection to the Internet and the other for its connection to your LAN.

The first step in setting up a Linux firewall is to install Linux on the firewall computer and get both the network interfaces up and running. Then, setting up the firewall is a matter of telling Linux what types of TCP/IP packets to block and which types to let through and instructing Linux how to handle IP masquerading. Both tasks are performed using the ipchains command.

Unfortunately, the details of using ipchains to set up a Linux firewall are complicated enough to make most normal people either scream or cry. To do it properly, you must create a script containing perhaps dozens of ipchains commands, each one setting up a rule that blocks or allows a particular type of TCP/IP packet.

If you are a TCP/IP expert, you can probably set up the necessary ipchains commands yourself. Fortunately, the good folks at Red Hat have created a script that you can download and customize to create a basic firewall. You can find the firewall script at the following Web page:

```
www.redhat.com/support/docs/tips/firewall/firewallservice.html
```

Read the script over carefully (it has lots of comments) and then modify it carefully to suit your firewall needs.

Part VI
The Part of Tens

The 5th Wave — By Rich Tennant

"Sure, at first it sounded great — an intuitive network adapter that helps people write memos by finishing their thoughts for them."

In this part . . .

1f you keep this book in the bathroom, the chapters in this section are the ones that you'll read most. Each chapter consists of ten (more or less) things that are worth knowing about various aspects of networking. Without further ado, here they are, direct from the home office in sunny Fresno, California.

Chapter 26

Ten Big Network Mistakes

*J*ust about the time you figure out how to avoid the most embarrassing computer mistakes, such as using your CD drive's tray as a cupholder, the network lands on your computer. Now you have a whole new list of dumb things you can do, mistakes that can give your average computer geek a belly laugh because they seem so basic to him. Well, that's because he's a computer geek. Nobody had to tell him not to fold the disk — he was born with an extra gene that gave him an instinctive knowledge of such things.

Here's a list of some of the most common mistakes made by network novices. Avoid these mistakes and you deprive your local computer geek of the pleasure of a good laugh at your expense.

Skimping on Cable

If your network consists of more than a few computers or has computers located in different rooms, you should invest in a professional-quality cable installation, complete with wall-mounted jacks, patch panels, and high-quality hubs. It is tempting to cut costs by using the cheapest hubs and by stringing inexpensive cable directly from the hubs to each computer on the network. But in the long run, that approach will actually prove to be more expensive than investing in a good cable installation in the first place.

Here are just a few of the reasons it pays to do the cabling right in the first place:

- A good cable installation will last much longer than the computers it services. A good cable installation can last 10 or 15 years, long after the computers on your network have been placed on display in a computer history museum.

- Installing cable is hard work. No one enjoys going up in the attic, poking his or her head up through ceiling panels and wiping fiberglass insulation out of his or her hair, or fishing cables through walls. If you're going to do it, do it right so that you don't have to do it again in just a few years. Build your cable installation so that it lasts.

- Your network users may be satisfied with 10BaseT networking now, but it won't be long before they demand 100BaseT. And a few years after that, they'll want Gigahertz speed. If you cut costs by using Category 3 instead of Category 5 cable or by installing less than Cat 5 patch panels or modular jacks, you'll have to replace them later.

- You might be tempted to skip the modular wall jacks and patch cables and instead just run the cable down the wall, out through a hole, and then directly to the computer or hub. That's a bad idea because the wires inside the network cable are solid wire, which is designed to last for a long time, provided it doesn't get handled much. If you run solid-wire cable directly to a computer, the wire will be stressed each time someone unplugs the cable. Even just dusting behind the computer (which some people actually do) can jostle the cable. Sooner or later, one of the wires inside the cable will break. Patch cables are made with stranded rather than solid wire, so they can tolerate a lot of handling without breaking. And if a patch cable does fail, you can replace it yourself for just a few dollars.

For more information about professional touches for installing cable, see Chapter 10.

Turning Off or Restarting a Server Computer While Users Are Logged On

The fastest way to blow your network users to kingdom come is to turn off a server computer while users are logged on. Restarting it by pressing its reset button can have the same disastrous effect.

If your network is set up with a dedicated file server, you probably won't be tempted to turn it off or restart it. But if your network is set up as a true peer-to-peer network, where each of the workstation computers — including your own — also doubles as a server computer, be careful about the impulsive urge to turn your computer off or restart it. Someone may be accessing a file or printer on your computer at that very moment.

Before turning off or restarting a server computer, find out whether anyone is logged on. If so, politely ask him or her to log off.

Deleting Important Files on the Server

Without a network, you can do anything you want to your computer, and the only person you can hurt is yourself. Kind of like the old "victimless crime" debate. Put your computer on a network, though, and you take on a certain amount of responsibility. You must find out how to live like a responsible member of the network society.

That means you can't capriciously delete files from a network server just because you don't need them. They may not be yours. You wouldn't want someone deleting your files, would you?

Be especially careful about files that are required to keep the network running. For example, some versions of Windows use a folder named wgpo0000 to hold e-mail. Delete this folder and your e-mail is history.

Copying a File from the Server, Changing It, and Then Copying It Back

Sometimes working on a network file is easier if you first copy the file to your local hard drive. Then you can access it from your application program more efficiently because you don't have to use the network. This is especially true for large database files that have to be sorted to print reports.

You're asking for trouble, though, if you copy the file to your PC's local hard drive, make changes to the file, and then copy the updated version of the file back to the server. Why? Because somebody else may be trying the same thing at the same time. If that happens, the updates made by one of you — the one who copies the file back to the server first — are lost.

Copying a file to a local drive is an okay thing to do, but not if you plan on updating the file and copying it back.

Sending Something to the Printer Again Just Because It Didn't Print the First Time

What do you do if you send something to the printer and nothing happens? *Right answer:* Find out why nothing happened and fix it. *Wrong answer:* Send it again and see whether it works this time. Some users keep sending it over and over again, hoping that one of these days, it'll take. The result is rather embarrassing when someone finally clears the paper jam and then watches 30 copies of the same letter print.

Unplugging a Cable While the Computer Is On

Bad idea! If for any reason you need to unplug a cable from behind your computer, turn your computer off first. You don't want to fry any of the delicate electronic parts inside your computer, do you?

If you need to unplug the network cable, you should wait until all the computers on the network are off. This is especially true if your network is wired with thinnet coax cable; it's not such a big deal with twisted-pair cable.

Note: With thinnet cable, you can disconnect the T connector from your computer as long as you don't disconnect the cable itself from the T connector.

Assuming That the Server Is Safely Backed Up

Some users make the unfortunate assumption that the network somehow represents an efficient and organized bureaucracy worthy of their trust. Far from the truth. Never assume that the network jocks are doing their jobs backing up the network data every day. Check up on them. Conduct a surprise inspection one day: Burst into the computer room wearing white gloves and demand to see the backup tapes. Check the tape rotation to make sure that more than one day's worth of backups are available.

If you're not impressed with your network's backup procedures, take it upon yourself to make sure that you never lose any of your data. Back up your most valued files to floppy disks frequently or, better yet, a CD-R disc.

Connecting to the Internet without Considering Security Issues

If you connect a non-networked computer to the Internet and then pick up a virus or get yourself hacked into, only that one computer is affected. But if you connect a networked computer to the Internet, the entire network becomes vulnerable. As a result, never connect a networked computer to the Internet without first considering the security issues. How will you protect yourself and the network from viruses? How will you ensure that the files located on your file server do not suddenly become accessible to the entire world? How can you prevent evil hackers from sneaking into your network, stealing your customer file, and selling your customer's credit card data on the black market?

For answers to these and other Internet security questions, see Chapter 17.

Plugging in a Wireless Access Point without Asking

For that matter, plugging any device into your network without first getting permission from the network administrator is a big no-no. But Wireless Access Points (WAPs) are particularly insidious. Many users fall for the marketing line that wireless networking is as easy as plugging one of these devices into the network. Then, your wireless notebook PC or hand-held device can instantly join the network.

The trouble is, so can anyone else within about ¼ mile of the wireless access point. That means that extra security measures must be employed to make sure that hackers can't get into your network by using a wireless computer located in the parking lot or across the street.

If you think that's unlikely, think again. There are several underground Web sites on the Internet that actually display maps of unsecured wireless networks in major cities. For more information about securing a wireless network, see Chapter 20.

Thinking You Can't Work Just Because the Network Is Down

A few years back, I realized that I can't do my job without electricity. Should power failure occur and I find myself without electricity, I can't even light a candle and work with pencil and paper because the only pencil sharpener I have is electric.

Some people have the same attitude about the network: They figure that if the network goes down, they may as well go home. That's not always the case. Just because your computer is attached to a network doesn't mean that it won't work when the network is down. True — if the wind flies out of the network sails, you can't access any network devices. You can't get files from network drives, and you can't print on network printers. But you can still use your computer for local work: accessing files and programs on your local hard drive and printing on your local printer (if you're lucky enough to have one).

Always Blaming the Network

Some people treat the network kind of like the village idiot who can be blamed whenever anything goes wrong. Networks do cause problems of their own, but they aren't the root of all evil.

If your monitor displays only capital letters, it's probably because you pressed the Caps Lock key. Don't blame the network.

If you spill coffee on the keyboard, well, that's your fault. Don't blame the network.

If your toddler sticks Play-Doh in the floppy drive, kids will be kids. Don't blame the network.

Get the point?

Chapter 27

Ten Networking Commandments

"Blessed is the network manager who walks not in the council of the ignorant, nor stands in the way of the oblivious, nor sits in the seat of the greenhorn, but delights in the Law of the Network and meditates on this Law day and night."

—*Networks 1:1*

And so it came to pass that these Ten Networking Commandments were passed down from generation to generation, to be worn as frontlets between the computer geeks' eyes (taped on the bridge of their broken glasses) and written upon their doorposts. Obey these commandments and it shall go well with you, with your children, and with your children's children.

I. Thou Shalt Back Up Thy Hard Drive Religiously

Prayer is a wonderful thing, but when it comes to protecting the data on your network, nothing beats a well-thought-out schedule of backups followed religiously. If this were an actual network Bible, a footnote here would refer you back to related verses in Chapter 15.

II. Thou Shalt Protect Thy Network from Infidels

Remember Colonel Flagg from *M*A*S*H,* who hid in trashcans looking for Commies? You don't exactly want to become him, but on the other hand, you don't want to ignore the possibility of getting zapped by a virus or your network being invaded by hackers. Make sure that your Internet connection is properly secured, and do not allow the use of modems to access the Internet unless you have provided adequate security.

As for virus threats, start by making sure that every user realizes that any floppy disk from the outside can be infected, and after one computer on the network is infected, the entire network is in trouble. Then show the users how easily they can scan suspicious disks before using them.

If possible, install an antivirus program on every computer on the network and show your users how to use it.

Also, make sure your users are aware of the danger posed by viruses that can infiltrate your network via e-mail attachments.

III. Thou Shalt Keepeth Thy Network Drive Pure and Cleanse It of Old Files

Don't wait until your 40GB network drive is down to just one cluster of free space before thinking about cleaning it up. Set up a routine schedule for disk housekeeping, where you wade through the files and directories on the network disk to remove old junk.

IV. Thou Shalt Not Tinker with Thine Network Configuration Files Unless Thou Knowest What Thou Art Doing

Networks are finicky things. After yours is up and running, don't mess around with it unless you know what you're doing. And be especially careful if you think you know what you're doing. It's people who think they know what they're doing who get themselves into trouble!

V. Thou Shalt Not Covet Thy Neighbor's Network

Network envy is a common malady among network managers. If your network uses plain old Windows 98 and it works, nothing can be gained by coveting someone else's network. If you run NetWare 4.2, resist the urge to upgrade to 5 unless you have a really good reason. And if you run Windows NT Server, fantasizing about Windows 2000 Enterprise Server is a venial sin.

You're especially susceptible to network envy if you're a gadget freak. There's always a better hub to be had or some fancy network protocol gizmo to lust after. Don't give in to these base urges! Resist the devil, and he will flee!

VI. Thou Shalt Schedule Downtime before Working upon Thy Network

As a courtesy, try to give your users plenty of advance notice before you take down the network to work on it. Obviously, you can't predict when random problems strike. But if you know you're going to add a new computer to the network on Thursday morning, you earn points if you tell everyone about the inconvenience two days before rather than two minutes before.

VII. Thou Shalt Keep an Adequate Supply of Spare Parts

There's no reason that your network should be down for two days just because a cable breaks. Always make sure that you have at least a minimal supply of network spare parts on hand. As luck would have it, Chapter 28 suggests ten things you should keep in your closet.

VIII. Thou Shalt Not Steal Thy Neighbor's Program without a License

How would you like it if Inspector Clouseau barged into your office, looked over your shoulder as you ran Lotus 1-2-3 from a network server, and asked, "Do you have a liesaunce?"

"A liesaunce?" you reply, puzzled.

"Yes of course, a liesaunce, that is what I said. The law specifically prohibits the playing of a computer program on a network without a proper liesaunce."

You don't want to go against the law, do you?

IX. Thou Shalt Train Thy Users in the Ways of the Network

Don't blame the users if they don't know how to use the network. It's not their fault. If you're the network administrator, your job is to provide training so that the network users know how to use the network.

X. Thou Shalt Write Down Thy Network Configuration upon Tablets of Stone

If you cross the river Jordan, who else will know diddly-squat about the network if you don't write it down somewhere? The back of a napkin won't cut it. Write down everything and put it in an official binder labeled *Network Bible* and protect the binder as if it were sacred.

Your hope should be that 2,000 years from now, when archaeologists are exploring caves in your area, they find your network documentation hidden in a jar and marvel at how meticulously the people of our time recorded their network configurations.

They'll probably draw ridiculous conclusions such as we offered sacrifices of burnt data packets to a deity named TCP/IP, but that makes it all the more fun.

Chapter 28

Ten Things You Should Keep in Your Closet

. . . .

In This Chapter

▶ Tools

▶ Extra cable

▶ Duct tape

▶ Extra connectors

▶ Patch cables

▶ Twinkies

▶ An extra network card

▶ Complete documentation of the network on tablets of stone

▶ The network manuals and disks

▶ Ten copies of this book

. . . .

*W*hen you first network your office computers, you need to find a closet where you can stash some network goodies. If you can't find a whole closet, shoot for a shelf, a drawer, or at least a sturdy cardboard box.

Here's a list of what stuff to keep on hand.

Tools

Make sure that you have at least a basic computer toolkit, the kind you can pick up for $15 from just about any office supply store. You also should have wire cutters, wire strippers, and cable crimpers that work for your network cable type.

Extra Cable

When you buy network cable, never buy exactly the amount you need. In fact, buying at least twice as much cable as you need isn't a bad idea, because half the cable is left over in case you need it later. You will. Something will go wrong, and you'll suspect a cable problem, so you'll need extra cable to replace the bad cable. Or you may add a computer or two to the network and need extra cable.

If your network is glued together with preassembled 25-foot lengths of thin-net coax cable, having at least one 25-foot segment lying around in the closet is a good idea.

Duct Tape

It helped get the crew of Apollo 13 back from their near-disastrous moon voyage. You won't actually use it much to maintain your network, but it serves the symbolic purpose of demonstrating that you realize things sometimes go wrong and you are willing to improvise to get your network up and running.

If you don't like duct tape, a little baling wire and chewing gum will serve the same purpose.

Extra Connectors

Don't run out of connectors, either. If you use twisted-pair cabling, you'll find that connectors go bad more often than you'd like. Buy the connectors 25, 50, or 100 at a time so that you have plenty of spares lying around.

If you use thinnet cable, keep a few spare BNC connectors handy, plus a few T connectors and a few terminators. Terminators have been known to mysteriously disappear. Rumor has it that they are sucked through some kind of time vortex into the distant future, where they're refabricated and returned to our time in the form of Arnold Schwarzenegger.

Patch Cables

If you wired your network the professional way, with wall jacks in each office, keep a few patch cables of various lengths in the closet. That way, you won't have to run to the store every time you need to change a patch cable. And trust me, you will need to replace patch cables from time to time.

Twinkies

If left sealed in their little individually wrapped packages, Twinkies keep for years. In fact, they'll probably outlast the network itself. You can give 'em to future network geeks, ensuring continued network support for generations to come.

Extra Network Cards

Ideally, you want to use identical network cards in all your computers. But if the boss's computer is down, you'd probably settle for whatever network card the corner network street vendor is selling today. That's why you should always keep at least one spare network card in the closet. You can rest easy knowing that if a network card fails, you have an identical replacement card sitting on the shelf, just waiting to be installed — and you won't have to buy one from someone who also sells imitation Persian rugs.

Obviously, if you have only two computers on your network, justifying spending the money for a spare network adapter card is hard. With larger networks, it's easier to justify.

The Complete Documentation of the Network on Tablets of Stone

I've mentioned several times in this book the importance of documenting your network. Don't spend hours documenting your network and then hide the documentation under a pile of old magazines behind your desk. Put the binder in the closet with the other network supplies so that you and everyone else always know where to find it. And keep backup copies of the Word, Excel, or other documents that make up the network binder in a fireproof safe or at another site.

Don't you dare chisel passwords into the network documentation, though. Shame on you for even thinking about it!

If you do decide to chisel the network documentation in stone tablets, consider using sandstone. It's attractive, inexpensive, and easy to update (just rub out the old info and chisel in the new). Keep in mind, however, that sandstone is subject to erosion from spilled Diet Coke. Oh, and make sure that you store it on a reinforced shelf.

The Network Manuals and Disks

In the land of Oz, a common lament of the Network Scarecrow is "If I only had the manual." True, the manual probably isn't a Pulitzer-prize candidate, but that doesn't mean you should toss it in a landfill, either. Put the manual where it belongs: in the closet with all the other network tools and artifacts.

Likewise, the disks. You may need them someday, so keep them with the other network stuff.

Ten Copies of This Book

Obviously, you want to keep an adequate supply of this book on hand to distribute to all your network users. The more they know, the more they stay off your back. Sheesh, 10 copies may not be enough — 20 may be closer to what you need.

Chapter 29

Ten Network Gizmos
Only Big Networks Need

. . . .

In This Chapter

▶ Repeaters

▶ Managed hubs

▶ Switches

▶ Bridges

▶ Gateways

▶ RAIDs

▶ Server farms

▶ Gigabit Ethernet

▶ Protocol analyzers

. . . .

*P*eople who compile statistics on things, such as the ratio of chickens to humans in Arkansas and the likelihood of the Mets losing when the other team shows up, report that more than 40 percent of all networks have fewer than ten computers and that this percentage is expected to increase in coming years. A Ross Perot-style pie chart would be good here, but my editor tells me I'm running long, so I have to pass on that.

The point is that if you're one of the lucky 40 percent with fewer than ten computers on your network, you can skip this chapter altogether. Here, I briefly describe various network gizmos that you may need if your network is really big. How big is big? There's no hard-and-fast rule, but the soft-and-slow rule is that you should look into this stuff when your network grows to about 25 computers.

The exceptions to the soft-and-slow rule are as follows: (1) Your company has two or more networks that you want to hook together, and these networks were designed by different people who refused to talk to each other until it was too late; (2) your network needs to connect computers that are more than a few hundred yards apart, perhaps in different buildings or via the Internet.

Repeaters

A *repeater* is a gizmo that gives your network signals a boost so that the signals can travel farther. It's kind of like the Gatorade stations in a marathon. As the signals travel past the repeater, they pick up a cup of Gatorade, take a sip, splash the rest of it on their heads, toss the cup, and hop in a cab when they're sure that no one is looking.

You need a repeater when the total length of a single span of network cable is larger than the maximum allowed for your cable type:

Cable	Maximum Length
10Base2 (Coax)	185 meters or 606 feet
10/100baseT (Twisted Pair)	100 meters or 328 feet

For coax cable, the preceding cable lengths apply to cable segments, not individual lengths of cable. A segment is the entire run of cable from one terminator to another and may include more than one computer. In other words, if you have ten computers and you connect them all with 25-foot lengths of thin coax cable, the total length of the segment is 225 feet. (Made you look! Only nine cables are required to connect ten computers — that's why it's not 250 feet.)

For 10baseT or 100baseT cable, the 100-meter length limit applies to the cable that connects a computer to the hub or the cable that connects hubs to each other when hubs are daisy-chained with twisted-pair cable. In other words, you can connect each computer to the hub with no more than 100 meters of cable, and you can connect hubs to each other with no more than 100 meters of cable.

Figure 29-1 shows how you can use a repeater to connect two groups of computers that are too far apart to be strung on a single segment. When you use a repeater like this, the repeater divides the cable into two segments. The cable length limit still applies to the cable on each side of the repeater.

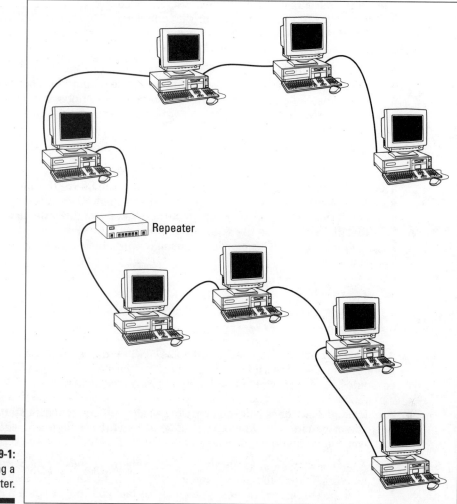

Figure 29-1:
Using a
repeater.

Here are some points to ponder when you lie awake tonight wondering about repeaters:

✔ Repeaters are used only with Ethernet networks wired with coax cable. 10/100baseT networks don't use repeaters.

Actually, that's not quite true: 10/100baseT does use repeaters. It's just that the repeater isn't a separate device. In a 10/100baseT network, the hub is actually a multiport repeater. That's why the cable used to attach each computer to the hub is considered a separate segment.

- ✔ Some 10/100baseT hubs have a BNC connector on the back. This BNC connector is a thinnet repeater that enables you to attach a full 185-meter thinnet segment. The segment can attach other computers, 10baseT hubs, or a combination of both.

- ✔ A basic rule of Ethernet life is that a signal cannot pass through more than three repeaters on its way from one node to another. That doesn't mean you can't have more than three repeaters or hubs, but if you do, you have to carefully plan the network cabling so that the three-repeater rule isn't violated.

- ✔ A two-port 10Base2 repeater costs about $200. Sheesh! I guess that's one of the reasons few people use coax cable anymore.

- ✔ Repeaters are legitimate components of a by-the-book Ethernet network. They don't extend the maximum length of a single segment; they just enable you to tie two segments together. Beware of the little black boxes that claim to extend the segment limit beyond the standard 185-meter limit for thinnet. These products usually work, but playing by the rules is better.

Managed Switches

A *managed switch* is a 10baseT or 100baseT switch that allows you to monitor and control various aspects of the switch's operation from a remote computer. Here are some of the benefits of managed switches:

- ✔ Managed switches can keep network usage and performance statistics, so you can find out which parts of your network are heavily used and which are not.

- ✔ A managed switch can alert you when something goes wrong with your network. In fact, the management software that controls the switch can even be configured to send you e-mail or dial your pager when a network error occurs.

- ✔ You can reconfigure a managed switch from any computer on the network, without having to actually go to the switch.

Inexpensive switches do not include management features. An unmanaged switch is fine for a small network, but for larger networks, you should invest in managed switches. A typical managed switch can cost two or three times as much as an equivalent unmanaged switch, but for larger networks, the benefits of switch management are well worth the additional cost. However, if your network has only one or two switches, you probably don't need management.

Bridges

A bridge is a device that connects two networks so that they act as if they are one network. Bridges are used to partition one large network into two smaller networks for performance reasons. You can think of a bridge as a kind of smart repeater. Repeaters listen to signals coming down one network cable, amplify them, and send them down the other cable. They do this blindly, paying no attention to the content of the messages they repeat.

In contrast, a bridge is a little smarter about the messages that come down the pike. For starters, most bridges have the capability to listen to the network and automatically figure out the address of each computer on both sides of the bridge. Then the bridge can inspect each message that comes from one side of the bridge and broadcast it on the other side of the bridge only if the message is intended for a computer that's on the other side.

This key feature enables bridges to partition a large network into two smaller, more efficient networks. Bridges work best in networks that are highly segregated. For example (humor me here — I'm a Dr. Seuss fan), suppose that the Sneetches networked all their computers and discovered that, although the Star-Bellied Sneetches' computers talked to each other frequently and the Plain-Bellied Sneetches' computers also talked to each other frequently, rarely did a Star-Bellied Sneetch computer talk to a Plain-Bellied Sneetch computer.

A bridge can partition the Sneetchnet into two networks: the Star-Bellied network and the Plain-Bellied network. The bridge automatically learns which computers are on the Star-Bellied network and which are on the Plain-Bellied network. The bridge forwards messages from the Star-Bellied side to the Plain-Bellied side (and vice versa) only when necessary. The overall performance of both networks improves, although the performance of any network operation that has to travel over the bridge slows down a bit.

Here are a few additional things to consider about bridges:

✔ As I mentioned, some bridges also have the capability to translate the messages from one format to another. For example, if the Star-Bellied Sneetches build their network with Ethernet and the Plain-Bellied Sneetches use Token Ring, a bridge can tie the two together.

✔ You can get a basic bridge to partition two Ethernet networks for about $500 from mail-order suppliers. More sophisticated bridges can cost as much as $5,000 or more.

✔ If you've never read Dr. Seuss's classic story of the Sneetches, you should.

✔ If you're not confused yet, don't worry. Read on.

Gateways

No, not the Bill Gates way. This kind of gateway is a super-intelligent router, which is a super-intelligent bridge, which is a super-intelligent repeater. Notice a pattern here?

Gateways are designed to connect radically different types of networks together. They do this by translating messages from one network's format to another's format, much like the Universal Translator that got Kirk and Spock out of so many jams. (Ever notice how all those planets with gorgeous females never seemed to have a word for *kiss,* so Kirk had to demonstrate?)

Gateways usually connect a network to a mainframe or minicomputer. If you don't have a mainframe or minicomputer, you probably don't need a gateway.

Keep the following points in mind:

- Gateways are necessary only because of the mess that computer manufacturers got us into by insisting on using their own proprietary designs for networks. If computer manufacturers had talked to each other 20 years ago, we wouldn't have to use gateways to make their networks talk to each other today.
- Gateways come in several varieties. My favorite is ornamental wrought iron.

It's a RAID!

In most small networks, it's a hassle if a disk drive goes south and has to be sent to the shop for repairs. In some large networks, a failed disk drive is more than a hassle: It's an outright disaster. Big companies don't know how to do anything when the computer goes down. Everyone just sits around, looking at the floor, silently keeping vigil 'til the computers come back up.

A *RAID system* is a fancy type of disk storage that hardly ever fails. It works by lumping several disk drives together and treating them as if they were one humongous drive. RAID uses some fancy techniques devised by computer nerds at Berkeley. These computer nerds guarantee that if one of the disk drives in the RAID system fails, no data is lost. The disk drive that failed can be removed and repaired, and the data that was on it can be reconstructed from the other drives.

Here are a few additional thoughts on RAID:

- ✔ RAID stands for Redundant Array of Inexpensive Disks, but that doesn't matter. You don't have to remember that for the test.

- ✔ A RAID system is usually housed in a separate cabinet that includes its own RAID disk controller. It's sometimes called a disk subsystem.

- ✔ In the coolest RAID systems, the disk drives themselves are *hot swappable*. That means that you can shut down and remove one of the disk drives while the RAID system continues to operate. Network users won't even know that one of the disks has been removed because the RAID system reconstructs the data that was on the removed disk using data from the other disks. After the failed disk has been replaced, the new disk is brought online without a hitch.

Server Farms

Large networks with multiple servers often have their servers bunched together in one room, known as a *server farm*. If you have more than two or three servers, you might want to consider some or all of the following methods of dealing with them:

- ✔ You can use inexpensive wire shelving to hold your servers. You can get special wire shelves designed to hold keyboards, monitors, and processors, providing easy access to cabling. For a more professional look, you can get customized LAN management furniture that is designed to hold multiple server computers in just about any configuration you need.

- ✔ If you have limited space, you can use a device known as a *KVM Switch* to connect several server computers to a single keyboard, monitor, and mouse. (*KVM* stands for Keyboard, Video, and Mouse.) That way, you can control any of the servers from the same keyboard, monitor, and mouse by turning a dial or pressing a button on the KVM switch.

- ✔ To save even more space, you can get rack-mounted servers instead of servers built in standard computer cases. Rack-mounted servers can be attached to the same standard 19-inch racks that rack-mounted hubs and patch panels mount to.

- ✔ The latest trend in server farms is the use of *blade servers*. These are complete servers that fit on a single card, which can be mounted vertically in a special rack-mounted case that is designed to hold several servers. For example, Hewlett Packard makes a blade chassis that can hold up to 16 blade servers in a single cabinet.

Gigabit Ethernet

Most small networks operate just fine with standard 10baseT or 100baseT Ethernet connections. However, if your network is large enough to merit a high-speed backbone connection, you may want to look into Gigabit Ethernet. Gigabit Ethernet is a relatively new version of Ethernet, which runs at 1000Mbps instead of 10 or 100Mbps.

Gigabit Ethernet, also known as 1000baseX, was initially designed to operate over fiber-optic cables but will eventually be able to work over Category 5 UTP cable as well. That's one of the reasons you should take care to install only top-quality Category 5 cable and keep the cable lengths under 100 meters.

Of course, Gigabit Ethernet is more expensive than 10baseT or 100baseT. A Gigabit Ethernet switch can cost several thousand dollars, and you need one at each end of the backbone.

Protocol Analyzer

A *protocol analyzer* is a device that attaches to your network and examines all of the packets that are zipping along inside the cables. In the hands of a seasoned pro, a protocol analyzer can help diagnose all kinds of networking problems: performance problems, security breaches, broken connections, and so on.

But to use a protocol analyzer, you need a low-level understanding of how networking works. You need to understand about protocols, the differences between the data-link and MAC layers, and the details that lurk inside the packets that make up your network traffic.

So although a protocol analyzer can be a nifty tool, it's usually found only in the hands of network technicians who work with large networks.

Gadgets that used to be in this chapter

Over the years, as I've revised this book to keep up with current technology, I've had the privilege of dropping items from this chapter. I've dropped some items because they aren't even used in large networks anymore. Others I've dropped because their cost has come down so dramatically that they are now used in even the smallest networks.

Here are a few of the goodies that I've retired from this chapter:

✔ **Fast Ethernet.** When 100Mbps Ethernet was new, it was expensive enough that only large organizations could justify it. Now it's dirt cheap. Even the least expensive network cards and components support 100BaseT. So I've retired Fast Ethernet from this chapter. (Gigabit Ethernet is another story. Most networks are fine with 100Mbps. Only really large networks need 1,000 times that much speed.)

✔ **Switches.** In the old days, inexpensive 10BaseT networks used cheap hubs, and switches were used only for large networks where network performance was a driving factor. However, the price of switches has come down so much lately that I now recommend you build all 10BaseT networks using switches rather than hubs.

✔ **Routers.** Routers were once required only for large networks. However, now that broadband Internet access is the norm, many small networks — even networks with just two or three computers — use inexpensive routers to connect to the Internet.

✔ **Firewalls.** Again, because of the proliferation of cheap and fast Internet access, I can no longer say that only large networks need firewalls. Nowadays, *any* network that has a broadband Internet connection needs a firewall.

✔ **Superservers.** This is one of my favorite archaic buzzwords. Once upon a time, computer makers coined this phrase to refer to big servers with multiple processors that could handle work that used to require several servers. The idea was that network servers would become more like the mainframe computers of old, where a single computer handled the workload for an entire organization. Fortunately, this idea didn't catch on.

Chapter 30

Ten Hot Network Buzzwords Guaranteed to Enliven a Cocktail Party

. . . .

. . . .

*T*ired of boring cocktail parties where everyone talks about the latest prime time game show or who's going to play Anakin Skywalker in the next *Star Wars* movie? Here are some conversation topics guaranteed to liven things up a bit or get you thrown out. Either way, they work. Try 'em.

Intranet

What it means: I've grown weary of the Internet, and now I want to create my own little private Internet on my LAN. An intranet uses the tools of the Internet: TCP/IP, HTTP, HTML, and Web-server software, but it isn't connected to the Internet. Intranets are used to create "internal" home pages that can be accessed from the company LAN but not from outside the company.

Used in a sentence: I won't be home for supper tonight, honey. I've got to finish uploading the third-quarter results to the company intranet!

Wi-Fi

What it means: A wireless network that uses the 802.11b wireless network standard.

Used in a sentence: Now that we've got our wi-fi network running, our parking lot has been overrun by kids toting notebook computers who are free-loading off our Internet connection!

Client/Server

What it means: A computer system in which part of the work happens on a client computer, and part of it happens on a server computer. To be a true client/server application, real work must be done on the server. Any server-based network can be loosely called client/server, but in a true client/server system, at least part of the real work — not just file access — is done on the server. For example, in a true client/server database, a database query is processed on the server computer, and just the results of the query are sent back to the client computer. If you want to know more, get a copy of my very own book, *Client/Server Computing For Dummies,* 3rd Edition (Wiley Publishing, Inc.).

Used in a sentence: I heard that it took your company five years to replace your old mainframe invoicing system to client/server! You should have gotten a copy of *Client/Server Computing For Dummies,* 3rd Edition, by that fabulous author Doug Lowe.

Enterprise Computing

What it means: The complete computing needs of a business enterprise. In the past, computing was too often focused on the individual needs of small departments or workgroups. The result was a hodgepodge of incompatible systems: Marketing had a minicomputer, sales had a NetWare network, and accounting had an abacus. Enterprise computing views the computing needs of the organization as a whole. Very smart.

Used in a sentence: Our Enterprise computing effort is sailing along at warp 9; I hear you guys are still stuck at one-quarter impulse. Fascinating.

Interoperability

What it means: Fitting round pegs into square holes. Literally, linking estranged networks together so that they work well together. This one is so hot that a whole trade show called Interop is devoted to making different networks work together.

Used in a sentence: We've finally solved our interoperability problems — we fired the guy who bought the stuff that wasn't interoperable.

Fiber

What it means: The fastest form of network cable, where signals are transmitted by light rather than by electricity. This type of cable used to be called Fiber-Optic, but now is just referred to as *fiber* as if it's something you should get more of in your diet. Fiber is typically used to form the backbone of large networks or to link networks in separate buildings, where the 500-meter limit of yellow cable just won't do. Fiber cables hum along at a cool 100 Mbps or 1,000 Mbps.

Used in a sentence: If your diet is low in fiber, you should try eating old network cables. Many parts are edible.

E-commerce

What it means: Conducting business over the Internet — that is, actually selling products or services, collecting the money via the Internet, and possibly even delivering the product via the Net.

Used in a sentence: Our profitability has shot up so much since we put in our e-commerce system that we've decided to retire and move to Vail.

Broadband

What it means: Broadband is a networking technology that allows more than one signal to travel over a cable at the same time. One use of broadband is on those new cable TV systems that can send more than just TV: They can also handle your phone lines and an Internet connection. Broadband cable is lightning fast. In fact, an Internet connection over broadband cable is just as fast as an Ethernet connection on a local area network.

Used in a sentence: No, uh, I don't have broadband yet. Boy, weird weather we've been having lately, don't you think?

Dot-Com

What it means: A dot-com is a business that doesn't actually have any products to sell and doesn't actually make any money, but somehow manages to attract investors. Unfortunately, someone recently pulled the covers off the whole dot-com craze and the whole thing sort of fell apart.

Used in a sentence: I invested way too much money in Dot-Coms last year. Now they're all Not-Coms.

.Net

What it means: It's pronounced "dot-Net" and it refers to the latest thing from Microsoft, which is supposed to completely revolutionize the way we use computers. Kind of like the previous latest thing did, and much like the next latest thing probably will.

Used in a sentence: Stop the presses! Microsoft just released another beta test of .NET server.

Glossary

10base2: The type of coax cable most often used for Ethernet networks. Also known as *thinnet* or *cheapernet*. The maximum length of a single segment is 185 meters (600 feet).

10base5: The original Ethernet coax cable, now used mostly as the backbone for larger networks. Also known as *yellow cable* or *thick cable*. The maximum length of a single segment is 500 meters (1,640 feet).

10baseT: Twisted-pair cable, commonly used for Ethernet networks. Also known as *UTP, twisted pair,* or *twisted sister* (just kidding!). The maximum length of a single segment is 100 meters (330 feet). Of the three Ethernet cable types, this one is the easiest to work with.

100baseFX: The Ethernet standard for high-speed fiber-optic connections.

100baseTX: The leading standard for 100Mbps Ethernet, which uses two-pair Category-5 twisted-pair cable.

100baseT4: An alternative standard for 100Mbps Ethernet using four-pair Category-3 cable.

100VG AnyLAN: A standard for 100Mbps Ethernet that isn't as popular as 100baseT. Like 100baseT, 100VG AnyLAN uses twisted-pair cable.

1000baseT: A new standard for 1,000Mbps Ethernet using four-pair Category-5 unshielded twisted pair cable. 1000baseT is also known as Gigabit Ethernet.

1000000000BaseT: Well, not really. But if current trends continue, we'll get there soon.

802.2: The forgotten IEEE standard. The more glamorous 802.3 standard relies upon 802.2 for moral support.

802.3: The IEEE standard known in the vernacular as *Ethernet*.

802.11: The IEEE standard for wireless networking. Two popular variants are 802.11a and 802.11b.

8088 processor: The microprocessor chip around which IBM designed its original PC, marking the transition from the Bronze Age to the Iron Age.

80286 processor: *Computo-habilis,* an ancient ancestor of today's modern computers.

80386 processor: The first 32-bit microprocessor chip used in personal computers, long since replaced by newer, better designs but still used by far too many people.

80486 processor: The last of Intel's CPU chips to have a number instead of a name. Replaced years ago by the Pentium processor.

AAUI: *Apple Attachment Unit Interface,* a type of connector used in some Apple Ethernet networks.

access rights: A list of rights that tell you what you can and can't do with network files or directories.

account: You can't get into the network without one of these. The network knows who you are and what rights you have on the network by virtue of your account.

acronym: An abbreviation made up of the first letters of a series of words.

Active Directory: The directory service in Windows 2000.

Active Server Pages: An Internet feature from Microsoft that enables you to create Web pages with scripts that run on the server rather than on the client. Also known as *ASP.* The newest version is called ASP.NET.

adapter card: An electronic card that you can plug into one of your computer's adapter slots to give it some new and fabulous capability, such as displaying 16 million colors, talking to other computers over the phone, or accessing a network.

address book: In an e-mail system, a list of users with whom you regularly correspond.

administrator: The big network cheese who is responsible for setting things up and keeping them running. Pray that it's not you. Also known as the *network manager.*

AFP: *Apple Filing Protocol,* a protocol for filing used by Apple. (That helps a lot, doesn't it?)

AGP: *Advanced Graphics Port,* a high-speed graphics interface used on most new computer motherboards.

allocation unit: Windows allocates space to files one allocation unit at a time; the allocation unit is typically 2,048 or 4,096 bytes, depending on the size of the disk. Also known as *cluster.* NetWare and Windows NT/2000 can use allocation schemes that are more efficient than standard Windows.

antivirus program: A program that sniffs out viruses on your network and sends them into exile.

Apache: The most popular Web server on the Internet. It comes free with most versions of Linux.

AppleTalk: Apple's networking system for Macintoshes.

application layer: The highest layer of the OSI reference model, which governs how software communicates with the network.

archive bit: A flag that's kept for each file to indicate whether the file has been modified since it was last backed up.

ARCnet: A slow but steady network topology developed originally by Datapoint. ARCnet uses a token-passing scheme similar to Token Ring.

Athlon: A competitor to Intel's Pentium CPU chip manufactured by AMD.

attributes: Characteristics that are assigned to files. DOS alone provides four attributes: system, hidden, read-only, and archive. Network operating systems generally expand the list of file attributes.

AUI: *Attachment Unit Interface,* the big connector found on older network cards and hubs that's used to attach yellow cable via a transceiver.

AUTOEXEC.BAT: A batch file that DOS executes automatically every time you start your computer.

AUTOEXEC.NCF: A batch file that NetWare executes automatically every time you load the server software.

backbone: A trunk cable used to tie sections of a network together. The backbone is often 100Mbps Fast Ethernet.

BackOffice: A suite of Microsoft programs designed to run on server computers based on Windows NT/2000 Server.

backup: A copy of your important files made for safekeeping in case something happens to the original files; something you should make every day.

banner: A fancy page that's printed between each print job so that you can easily separate jobs from one another.

batch file: In DOS, a file that contains one or more commands that are executed together as a set. You create the batch file by using a text editor (like the DOS EDIT command) and run the file by typing its name at the command prompt.

benchmark: A repeatable test you use to judge the performance of your network. The best benchmarks are the ones that closely duplicate the type of work you routinely do on your network.

BNC connector: The connector that's used with 10base2 cable.

bottleneck: The slowest link in your network, which causes work to get jammed up. The first step in improving network performance is identifying the bottlenecks.

bridge: Not the popular card game, but a device that enables you to link two networks together. Bridges are smart enough to know which computers are on which side of the bridge, so they only allow those messages that need to get to the other side to cross the bridge. This device improves performance on both sides of the bridge.

buffer: An area of memory that holds data en route to somewhere else. For example, a disk buffer holds data as it travels between your computer and the disk drive.

bus: A type of network topology in which network nodes are strung out along a single run of cable called a *segment.* 10base2 and LocalTalk networks use a bus topology. *Bus* also refers to the row of expansion slots within your computer.

cache: A sophisticated form of buffering in which a large amount of memory is set aside to hold data so that it can be accessed quickly.

Category-3: An inexpensive form of unshielded twisted pair that is suitable only for 10Mbps networks (10baseT). Avoid using Category-3 cable for new networks.

Category-5: The higher grade of 10baseT cable that is suitable for 100Mbps networks (100baseTX) and gigabit Ethernet (1000baseT).

CD-R drive: A CD drive that can read and write CDs.

CD-ROM: A high-capacity disc that uses optical technology to store data in a form that can be read but not written over.

CD-RW drive: A CD drive that can read, write, and then rewrite CDs.

Certified NetWare Engineer: Someone who has studied hard and passed the official exam offered by Novell. Also known as *CNE.*

Certified Network Dummy: Someone who knows nothing about networks but nevertheless gets the honor of installing one. Also known as *CND.*

chat: What you do on the network when you talk *live* with another network user.

Chaucer: A dead English dude.

cheapernet: See *10base2.*

CHKDSK: A DOS command that checks the record-keeping structures of a DOS disk for errors.

click: What you do in Windows to get things done.

client: A computer that has access to the network but doesn't share any of its own resources with the network. See *server.*

client/server: A vague term meaning roughly that the work load is split between a client and server computer.

Clouseau: The most dangerous man in all of France. Some people say he only plays the fool.

cluster: See *allocation unit.*

coaxial cable: A type of cable that contains two conductors. The center conductor is surrounded by a layer of insulation, which is then wrapped by a braided-metal conductor and an outer layer of insulation.

COM1: The first serial port on a computer.

CompuServe: An online information network that you can access to talk with other users about issues such as NetWare, Windows NT/2000, politics, and the latest reality-based TV show.

computer name: A unique name assigned to each computer on a network.

CONFIG.SYS: A file on every DOS computer that contains configuration information. `CONFIG.SYS` is processed every time you start your computer.

console: In NetWare, the file server's keyboard and monitor. Console commands can be entered only at the server console.

console operator: In NetWare, a user working at the file server's console.

Control Panel: In Windows, an application that enables you to configure various aspects of the Windows operating system.

conventional memory: The first 640KB of memory on a DOS-based computer.

CPU: The *central processing unit,* or brains, of the computer.

crimp tool: A special tool used to attach connectors to cables. No network manager should be without one. Try not to get your fingers caught in it.

CSMA/CD: *Carrier Sense Multiple Access with Collision Detection,* the traffic management technique used by Ethernet.

daisy-chain: A way of connecting computer components in which the first component is connected to the second, which is connected to the third, and so on. In 10baseT and 100baseT Ethernet, you can daisy-chain hubs together.

DAT: *Digital audiotape,* a type of tape often used for network backup.

data-link layer: The second layer of the OSI model, responsible for transmitting bits of data over the network cable.

dedicated server: A computer used exclusively as a network server.

delayed write: A disk-caching technique in which data written to disk is placed in cache memory and actually written to disk later.

differential backup: A type of backup in which only the files that have changed since the last full backup are backed up.

DIP switch: A bank of switches used to configure an old-fashioned adapter card. Modern cards configure themselves automatically, so DIP switches aren't required. See *jumper block*.

directory hash: A popular breakfast food enjoyed by NetWare managers.

disk: A device that stores information magnetically on a disk. A hard disk is permanently sealed in an enclosure and has a capacity usually measured in thousands of megabytes. Also known as *gigabytes*. A *floppy disk* is removable and can have a capacity of 360KB, 720KB, 1.2MB, 1.44MB, or 2.88MB.

DMA channel: A direct pipeline for I/O that's faster than normal I/O. Network cards use DMA for fast network access.

DNS: See *Domain Name System*.

domain: (1) In a Windows NT/2000 network, one or more network servers that are managed by a single network directory. (2) In the Internet, a name assigned to a network.

Domain Name System (DNS): The naming system used on the Internet, in which a network is given a domain name and individual computers are given host names.

DOS: *Disk Operating System,* the original operating system for IBM and IBM-compatible computers. DOS isn't used as much now that Windows has taken over.

dot-matrix printer: A prehistoric type of printer that works by applying various-colored pigments to the walls of caves. Once the mainstay printer for PCs, dot-matrix printers have given way to laser printers and inkjet printers. High-speed matrix printers still have their place on the network, though, and matrix printers have the advantage of being able to print multipart forms.

DriveSpace: A disk compression feature of Windows 9*x*/Me (and MS-DOS 6.2). DriveSpace compresses file data so that files require less disk space. This compression increases the effective capacity of the disk, often by a factor of 2:1 or more.

dumb terminal: Back in the heyday of mainframe computers, a monitor and keyboard attached to the central mainframe. All the computing work occurred at the mainframe; the terminal only displayed the results and sent input typed at the keyboard back to the mainframe.

DVD drive: A new type of CD-ROM drive with much higher storage capacity than a standard CD-ROM drive — as much as 17GB on a single disk compared to the 600MB capacity of a standard CD.

Eddie Haskell: The kid who's always sneaking around, poking his nose into other people's business, and generally causing trouble. Every network has one.

editor: A program for creating and changing text files. DOS 5 and later versions come with a basic editor called EDIT. Other editors are available, but EDIT is good enough for most network needs.

EGA: The color monitor that was standard with IBM AT computers, based on 80286 processors. Now obsolete, but some are still in use.

EISA bus: *Extended Industry Standard Architecture,* an improved I/O bus that is compatible with the standard ISA bus but provides advanced features. Computers with an EISA bus were often used as file servers until the PCI bus became more popular. See *ISA bus* and *PCI.*

e-mail: Messages that are exchanged with other network users.

emoticon: A shorthand way of expressing emotions in e-mail and chats by combining symbols to create smiles, frowns, and so on.

Enterprise computing: A trendy term that refers to a view of an organization's complete computing needs, rather than just a single department's or group's needs.

Ethernet: The World's Most Popular Network Standard.

EtherTalk: What you call Ethernet when you use it on a Macintosh.

ETLA: _Extended Three-Letter Acronym,_ an acronym with four letters. See _TLA._

Exchange Server: The software that handles e-mail services on a Windows NT or 2000 server.

Fast Ethernet: 100Mbps Ethernet. Also known as 100baseT or 100baseTX.

FAT: _File allocation table,_ a record-keeping structure that DOS uses to keep track of the location of every file on a disk.

FAT32: An improved way of keeping track of disk files that can be used with Windows 98 and later.

FDDI: _Fiber Distributed Data Interface,_ a 100Mbps network standard used with fiber-optic backbone. When FDDI is used, FDDI FDDI/Ethernet bridges connect Ethernet segments to the backbone.

ferrule: The outer metal tube that you crimp on to attach a BNC connector to the cable.

fiber-optic cable: A blazingly fast network cable that transmits data using light rather than electricity. Fiber-optic cable is often used as the backbone in large networks, especially where great distances are involved.

file rights: The ability of a particular network user to access specific files on a network server.

file server: A network computer containing disk drives that are available to network users.

firewall: A special type of router that connects a LAN to the Internet while preventing unauthorized Internet users from accessing the LAN.

FTP: _File Transfer Protocol,_ a method for retrieving files from the Internet.

full backup: A backup of all the files on a disk, whether or not the files have been modified since the last backup. See *differential backup*.

gateway: A device that connects dissimilar networks. Gateways often connect Ethernet networks to mainframe computers or to the Internet.

GB: *Gigabyte,* roughly a billion bytes of disk storage (1,024MB to be precise). See *KB*, *MB*, and *TB*.

generation backup: A backup strategy in which several sets of backup disks or tapes are retained; sometimes called grandfather-father-son.

generation gap: What happens when you skip one of your backups.

glass house: The room where the mainframe computer is kept. Symbolic of the mainframe mentality, which stresses bureaucracy, inflexibility, and heavy iron.

group account: A grouping of user accounts that share common access rights.

groupware: A relatively new category of application programs that are designed with networks in mind to enable and even promote collaborative work.

guru: Anyone who knows more about computers than you do.

HTML: *HyperText Markup Language,* the language used to compose pages that can be displayed via the World Wide Web.

HTTP: *HyperText Transfer Protocol,* the protocol used by the World Wide Web for sending HTML pages from a server computer to a client computer.

HTTPS: A secure form of HTTP that is used to transmit sensitive data such as credit card numbers.

hub: In Ethernet, a device that is used with 10baseT and 100baseT cabling to connect computers to the network. Most hubs have from 5 to 24 ports. See also *switch*.

IACI: *International Association of the Computer Impaired.*

IDE: *Integrated Drive Electronics,* the most common type of disk interface in use today, popular because of its low cost and flexibility. For server computers, SCSI is the preferred drive interface. See *SCSI*.

IEEE: *Institute of Electrical and Electronic Engineers,* where they send computer geeks who've had a few too many parity errors.

incremental backup: A type of backup in which only the files that have changed since the last backup are backed up. Unlike a differential backup, an incremental backup resets each file's archive bit as it backs it up. See ***archive bit***, ***differential backup***, and ***full backup***.

inkjet printer: A type of printer that creates full-color pages by spraying tiny jets of ink onto paper.

Internet: A humongous network of networks that spans the globe and gives you access to just about anything you could ever hope for, provided that you can figure out how to work it.

Internet Explorer: Microsoft's popular Web browser.

interoperability: Providing a level playing field for incompatible networks to work together, kind of like NAFTA.

intranet: A network that resembles the Internet but is accessible only within a company or organization. Most intranets use the familiar World Wide Web interface to distribute information to company employees.

intranetWare: A funny name that Novell used for NetWare when the term *intranet* was the hottest buzzword.

I/O port address: Every I/O device in a computer — including network interface cards — must be assigned a unique address. In the old days, you had to configure the port address using DIP switches or jumpers. Newer network cards automatically configure their own port addresses so that you don't have to mess with switches or jumper blocks.

IP address: A string of numbers used to address computers on the Internet. If you enable TCP/IP on your network, you must provide an IP address for each computer on the network.

IPX: A transport protocol used by NetWare.

IPX.COM: The program file that implements IPX.

IRQ: *Interrupt ReQuest*, network interface cards must be configured for the proper IRQ in order to work. In olden times, you had to use DIP switches or jumper blocks to set the IRQ. Nowadays, network cards configure themselves.

ISA bus: *Industry Standard Architecture,* a once popular type of expansion bus for accommodating adapter cards. Now replaced by PCI.

ISDN: A digital telephone connection that lets you connect to the Internet at about twice the speed of a regular phone connection.

ISO: *International Standards Organization,* whom we can thank for OSI.

ISP: *Internet service provider,* a company that provides access to the Internet for a fee.

Java: A programming language popular on the Internet.

JavaScript: A popular scripting language that can be used on Web pages.

JetDirect: A device made by Hewlett-Packard that enables printers to connect directly to the network without the need for a separate print server computer.

jumper block: A device used to configure an old-fashioned adapter card. To change the setting of a jumper block, you remove the jumper from one set of pins and place it on another.

KB: *Kilobytes,* roughly one thousand bytes (1,024 to be precise). See *GB*, *MB*, and *TB*.

LAN: *Local area network,* what this book is all about.

LAN Manager: An obsolete network operating system that Microsoft used to sell. Microsoft long ago put all its networking eggs in the Windows NT/2000 basket, so LAN Manager exists only on isolated islands along with soldiers who are still fighting World War II.

LAN Server: IBM's version of LAN Manager.

LANcache: The disk caching program that comes with LANtastic.

LANtastic: A peer-to-peer network operating system that was once the most popular choice for small networks. When the good folks at Microsoft saw how popular LANtastic was, they decided to add free networking features to Windows. As a result, not too many people use LANtastic anymore.

laser printer: A high-quality printer that uses lasers and photon torpedoes to produce beautiful output.

lemon-pudding layer: A layer near the middle of the OSI reference model that provides flavor and moistness to an otherwise dry and tasteless fruitcake.

Linux: An almost-free version of the UNIX operating system that is becoming popular as a network server.

LLC sublayer: The *logical link sublayer* of layer 2 of the OSI model. The LLC is addressed by the IEEE 802.2 standard.

local area network: See *LAN*.

local bus: A fast expansion bus found on 486 and Pentium computers that operates at a higher speed than the old ISA bus and allows 32-bit data transfers. Two types are commonly found: VESA and PCI. Many 486 computers include several VESA local bus slots, but newer Pentium computers use PCI slots. For best network performance, all servers should have VESA or PCI disk I/O and network interface cards.

local resources: Disk drives, printers, and other devices that are attached directly to a workstation rather than accessed via the network.

LocalTalk: Apple's scheme for cabling Macintosh networks by using the Mac's printer ports. PhoneNET is a cabling scheme that's compatible with LocalTalk but less expensive.

log in: Same as *log on*.

log on: The process of identifying oneself to the network (or a specific network server) and gaining access to network resources.

log out: The process of leaving the network. When you log out, any network drives or printers you were connected to become unavailable to you.

LOGIN: The NetWare command used to log on to a NetWare network.

LOGIN directory: In NetWare, a network directory that's mapped to the workstation before the user has logged on. The `LOGIN` directory contains commands and programs that are accessible to every computer on the network, regardless of whether a user has logged on. Chief among these commands is the `LOGIN` command.

logon name: In a Windows network, the name that identifies a user uniquely to the network. Same as *user name* or *user ID*.

logon script: A file of NetWare commands that is executed when a user logs in.

LOGOUT: In NetWare, the command you use to log out.

LPT1: The first printer port on a PC. If a computer has a local printer, it more than likely is attached to this port. That's why you should set up printer redirections using LPT2 and LPT3.

Mac OS X: The latest and greatest operating system for Macintoshes.

Mac OS X Server: Apple's most powerful server operating system for Macintosh computers.

MAC sublayer: The *media access control* sublayer of layer 2 of the OSI model. The MAC is addressed by the IEEE 802.3 standard.

Macintosh: A cute little computer that draws great pictures and comes with built-in networking.

mail server: The server computer on which e-mail messages are stored. This same computer also may be used as a file and print server, or it may be dedicated as a mail server.

mainframe: A huge computer housed in a glass house on raised floors and cooled with liquid nitrogen. The cable that connects the disk drives to the CPU weighs more than most PCs.

mapping: Assigning unused drive letters to network drives or unused printer ports to network printers. See *redirection*.

MB: *Megabytes,* roughly one million bytes (1,024K to be precise). See *GB*, *KB*, and *TB*.

memory: The electronic storage where your computer stores data that's being manipulated and programs that are running. See *RAM*.

metaphor: A literary construction suitable for Shakespeare and Steinbeck but a bit overused by writers of computer books.

modem: A device that converts signals the computer understands into signals that can be accurately transmitted over the phone to another modem, which converts the signals back into their original form. Computers use modems to talk to each other. *Modem* is a combination of *modulator-demodulator.*

mouse: The obligatory way to use Windows. When you grab it and move it around, the cursor moves on the screen. After you get the hand-eye coordination down, using it is a snap. *Hint:* Don't pick it up and talk into it like Scotty did in *Star Trek IV.* Very embarrassing, especially if you've traveled millions of miles to get here.

Mr. McFeeley: The nerdy-looking mailman on *Mr. Rogers' Neighborhood.* He'd make a great computer geek. Speedy delivery!

MSD: *Microsoft Diagnostics,* a program that comes with DOS 6 and 6.2 and Windows 3.1. MSD gathers and displays useful information about your computer's configuration. In Windows 9*x*/Me, you can get similar information from a program called Microsoft System Information.

My Network Places: An icon on Windows XP, Windows 2000 and Window Millennium desktops that enables you to access network servers and resources. In Windows 95 and 98, this icon is known as *Network Neighborhood.*

NE2000: The standard by which network interface cards are judged. If your card is NE2000 compatible, you can use it with just about any network.

.NET: A new Windows application environment that promises to simplify the task of creating and using applications for Windows and for the Web.

NETBIOS: *Network basic input output system,* a high-level networking standard developed by IBM and used by most peer-to-peer networks. It can be used with NetWare as well.

Netscape: The company that makes Navigator, a popular program for browsing the World Wide Web.

NetWare: A popular network operating system, the proud child of Novell, Inc.

NetWare Directory Services: A feature of NetWare first introduced with Version 4, in which the resources of the servers are pooled together to form a single entity.

NetWare Loadable Module: A program that's loaded at the file server. Also known as *NLM.* NLMs extend the functionality of NetWare by providing additional services. Btrieve runs as an NLM, as do various backup, antivirus, and other utilities.

network: What this book is about. For more information, see Chapters 1 through 30.

network drive: A drive that resides somewhere out in the network rather than on your own computer.

network interface card: An adapter card that lets the computer attach to a network cable. Also known as *NIC.*

network layer: One of the layers somewhere near the middle of the OSI reference model. It addresses the interconnection of networks.

network manager: Hope that it's someone other than you.

Network Neighborhood: An icon on a Windows 95 or 98 desktop that enables you to access network servers and resources. In Windows 2000 and Windows Millennium, this icon is known as *My Network Places.*

network operating system: An operating system for networks, such as NetWare or Windows 2000 Server. Also known as *NOS.*

network resource: A disk drive, printer, or other device that's located in a server computer and shared with other users, in contrast with a *local resource,* which is located in a user's computer.

newsgroup: Internet discussion groups in which people leave messages which can be read and responded to by other Internet users.

NIC: See *network interface card*.

NLM: See *NetWare Loadable Module*.

node: A device on the network, typically a computer or printer. A router is also a node.

Norton Utilities: A big box chock-full of useful utilities, all for one affordable price. Get it.

NOS: See *network operating system*.

Novell: The folks you can thank or blame for NetWare, depending on your mood.

NTFS: A special type of disk format that you can use on Windows NT/2000 Server and Windows XP disk drives for improved performance and security.

offline: Not available on the network.

online: Available on the network.

operator: A user who has control over operational aspects of the network, but doesn't necessarily have the power to grant or revoke access rights, create user accounts, and so on.

OSI: The agency Lee Majors worked for in *The Six Million Dollar Man*. Also, the *Open System Interconnection* reference model, a seven-layer fruitcake framework upon which networking standards are hung.

packets: Data is sent over the network in manageable chunks called *packets*, or *frames*. The size and makeup of a packet is determined by the protocol being used.

parallel port: A port normally used to connect printers, sometimes called a *printer port*. Parallel ports send data over eight "parallel" wires, one byte at a time. See *serial port*.

partition: A division of a single disk drive into several smaller units that are treated by the operating system as if they were separate drives.

password: The only thing protecting your files from an impostor masquerading as you. Keep your password secret, and you'll have a long and happy life.

patch cable: A short cable used to connect a computer to a wall outlet, or one running from a patch panel to a hub.

PCI: *Peripheral Component Interconnect,* the high-speed bus design found in modern Pentium computers.

PCONSOLE: The NetWare command you use from a DOS command prompt to manage network printing.

peer-to-peer network: A network in which any computer can be a server if it wants to be. Kind of like the network version of the Great American Dream. You can easily construct peer-to-peer networks by using Windows.

permissions: Rights that have been granted to a particular user or group of users enabling them to access specific files.

PhoneNET: An alternative cabling scheme for Macintosh networks, cheaper than Apple's LocalTalk cables.

physical layer: The lowest layer of the OSI reference model (whatever that is). It refers to the parts of the network you can touch: cables, connectors, and so on.

pocket protector: A status symbol among computer geeks.

port: A connector on the back of your computer that you can use to connect a device such as a printer, modem, mouse, and so on.

PPP: *Point to Point Protocol,* the most common way of connecting to the Internet for World Wide Web access.

presentation layer: The sixth layer of the OSI reference model, which handles data conversions, compression, decompression, and other menial tasks.

print job: A report, letter, memo, or other document that has been sent to a network printer but hasn't printed yet. Print jobs wait patiently in the queue until a printer agrees to print them.

Print Manager: In old-style Windows (Windows 3.1 and Windows for Workgroups), the program that handles print spooling.

print queue: The line that print jobs wait in until a printer becomes available.

print server: A computer that handles network printing or a device such as a JetDirect, which enables the printer to attach directly to the network.

PRN: The DOS code name for the first parallel port. Also known as *LPT1.*

protocol: (1) The droid C-3PO's specialty. (2) The rules of the network game. Protocols define standardized formats for data packets, techniques for detecting and correcting errors, and so on.

punch-down block: A gadget for quickly connecting a bunch of wires, used in telephone and network wiring closets.

QIC: *Quarter-inch cartridge,* the most popular and least expensive form of tape backup. Now known as *Travan drives.* See *DAT* and *Travan*.

queue: A list of items waiting to be processed. The term usually refers to the list of print jobs waiting to be printed, but networks have lots of other types of queues as well.

RAID: *Redundant Array of Inexpensive Disks,* a bunch of disk drives strung together and treated as if they were one drive. The data is spread out over several drives, and one of the drives keeps checking information so that if any one of the drives fails, the data can be reconstructed.

RAM: *Random access memory,* your computer's memory chips.

redirection: One of the basic concepts of networking, in which a device, such as a disk drive or printer, appears to be a local device but actually resides on the network. The networking software on your computer intercepts I/O requests for the device and redirects them to the network.

registry: The file where Windows keeps its configuration information.

repeater: A device that strengthens a signal so that it can travel on. Repeaters are used to lengthen the cable distance between two nodes. A *multiport repeater* is the same as a *hub*.

resource: A disk drive, disk directory, printer, modem, CD-ROM, or other device that can be shared on the network.

ring: A type of network topology in which computers are connected to one another in a way that forms a complete circle. Imagine the Waltons standing around the Thanksgiving table holding hands, and you have the idea of a ring topology.

RJ-45: The kind of plug used by 10baseT and 100baseT networks. It looks kind of like a modular phone plug, but it's bigger.

router: A device that works kind of like a bridge but can handle different protocols. For example, a router can link Ethernet to LocalTalk or a mainframe.

Samba: A program that runs on a Linux server, allowing the Linux computer to work as a file and print server in a Windows network.

ScanDisk: A Windows command that examines your hard disk for physical defects.

scheduling software: Software that schedules meetings of network users. Works only if all network users keep their calendars up-to-date.

SCSI: *Small computer systems interface,* a connection used mostly for disk drives but also suitable for CD-ROM drives, tape drives, and just about anything else. Also winner of the Acronym Computer Geeks Love to Pronounce Most award.

segment: A single-run cable, which may connect more than two computers, with a terminator on each end.

serial port: A port normally used to connect a modem or mouse to a DOS-based computer, sometimes called a communications port. See *parallel port*.

server: A computer that's on the network and shares resources with other network users. The server may be dedicated, which means that its sole purpose in life is to provide service for network users, or it may be used as a client as well. See *client*.

session layer: A layer somewhere near the middle of the beloved OSI reference model that deals with sessions between network nodes.

SFT: *System Fault Tolerance,* a set of networking features designed to protect the network from faults, such as stepping on the line (known as a *foot fault*).

share name: A name that you assign to a network resource when you share it. Other network users use the share name to access the shared resource.

shared folder: A network server disk drive or a folder on a server drive that has been shared so that other computers on the network can access it.

shared resource: A resource, such as a disk or printer, that is made available to other network users.

shielded twisted pair: Twisted-pair cable with shielding, used mostly for Token Ring networks. Also known as *STP*. See *twisted pair*.

smiley: A face made from various keyboard characters; often used in e-mail messages to convey emotion. : -)

SNA: *Systems Network Architecture,* a networking standard developed by IBM that dates from the mid-Mainframerasic Period, approximately 65 million years ago. Used by fine IBM mainframe and AS/400 minicomputers everywhere.

sneakernet: The cheapest form of network, in which users exchange files by copying them to disks and walking them between computers.

SNMP: *Simple Network Management Protocol,* a standard for exchanging network management information between network devices that is anything but simple.

spooling: A printing trick in which data that is intended for a printer is actually written to a temporary disk file and later sent to the printer.

ST-506: An old type of disk drive interface that's obsolete but still found on far too many computers.

star: A type of network topology in which each node is connected to a central wiring hub. This gives the network a star-like appearance.

SUPERVISOR: The top-dog account in NetWare. Log in as SUPERVISOR, and you can do just about anything.

switch: An efficient type of hub that sends packets only to the port that is connected to the packet's recipient rather than sending packets to all of the ports, as a simple hub does.

SYS: The volume name of the system volume on most NetWare servers.

system fault tolerance: See *SFT.*

tape drive: The best way to back up a network server. Tape drives have become so inexpensive that even small networks should have one.

task: For a technically accurate description, enroll in a computer science graduate course. For a layperson's understanding of what a task is, picture the guy who used to spin plates on *The Ed Sullivan Show.* Each plate is a task. The poor guy had to frantically move from plate to plate to keep them all spinning. Computers work the same way. Each program task is like one of those spinning plates; the computer must service each one periodically to keep it going.

TB: *Terrazzo bytes,* imported from Italy. Approximately one trillion bytes (1,024GB to be precise). (Just kidding about *terrazzo bytes.* Actually, TB stands for *terabytes.* It won't be long before you can buy disk drives that can hold a terabyte or more.)

TCP/IP: *Transmission Control Protocol/Internet Protocol,* the protocol used by the Internet.

terminator: The little plug you have to use at each end of a segment of thin coax cable (10baseT).

thinnet: See *10base2.*

three-letter acronym: See *TLA.*

time sharing: A technique used on mainframe computers to enable several users to access the computer at the same time.

time-out: How long the print server waits while receiving print output before deciding that the print job has finished.

TLA: *Three-letter acronym,* such as FAT (File Allocation Table), DUM (Dirty Upper Memory), and HPY (Heuristic Private Yodel).

token: The thing that gets passed around the network in a Token Ring topology. See *Token Ring.*

Token Ring: A network that's cabled in a ring topology in which a special packet called a token is passed from computer to computer. A computer must wait until it receives the token before sending data over the network.

topology: The shape of the network; how its computers and cables are arranged. See *bus, ring,* and *star.*

transceiver: A doohickey that connects a network interface card (NIC) to a network cable. A transceiver is always required to connect a computer to the network, but 10base2 and 10baseT NICs have built-in transceivers. Transceivers were originally used with yellow cable. You can also get transceivers that convert an AUI port to 10baseT.

transport layer: One of those layers somewhere near the middle of the OSI reference model that addresses the way data is escorted around the network.

Travan: A newer technology for inexpensive tape backup that can record up to 800MB on a single tape cartridge. See *QIC* and *DAT.*

trojan horse: A program that looks interesting but turns out to be something nasty, like a hard-disk reformatter.

trustee rights: In NetWare, rights that have been granted to a particular user or group of users enabling them to access specific files.

twisted pair: A type of cable that consists of one or more pairs of wires that are twisted in a certain way to improve the cable's electrical characteristics. See *shielded twisted pair* and *unshielded twisted pair.*

uninterruptible power supply: See *UPS.*

unshielded twisted pair: Twisted-pair cable that doesn't have a heavy metal shield around it. Used for 10baseT networks. Also known as *UTP.* See *twisted pair.*

UPS: *Uninterruptible power supply,* a gizmo that switches to battery power whenever the power cuts out. The *Enterprise* didn't have one of these, which is why the lights always went out until Spock could switch to auxiliary power.

URL: *Uniform Resource Locator,* a fancy term for an Internet address. URLs are those familiar "dot" addresses, such as "www-dot-microsoft-dot-com" or "www-dot-dummies-dot-com."

USB: A high-speed serial interface that is found on most new computers. USB can be used to connect printers, scanners, mice, keyboards, network adapters, and other devices.

user ID: The name by which you're known to the network.

User Manager for Domains: The program you use on Windows NT to manage user accounts.

user profile: The way Windows keeps track of each user's desktop settings, such as window colors, wallpaper, screen savers, Start menu options, favorites, and so on.

user rights: Network actions that a particular network user is allowed to perform after he or she has logged on to the network. See *file rights*.

users' group: A local association of computer users, sometimes with a particular interest, such as networking.

UTP: *Unshielded twisted pair.* See *10baseT*.

VBScript: A scripting language that can be used to add fancy features to Web pages or to create macros for Microsoft Office programs.

VGA: *Video Graphics Array,* the current standard in video monitors. Most VGA adapters these days are actually super VGA adapters, which are compatible with VGA adapters but have extra bells and whistles.

Vines: A network operating system made by Banyan, comparable to NetWare or Windows NT/2000 Server.

virus: An evil computer program that slips into your computer undetected, tries to spread itself to other computers, and may eventually do something bad like trash your hard drive.

volume name: In NetWare, each disk volume has a name. Most NetWare servers have a volume named SYS.

Web browser: A program that enables you to display information retrieved from the Internet's World Wide Web.

Windows: The world's most popular operating system.

Windows 2000: The newest version of Windows NT. Available in four versions: Windows 2000 Professional for desktop users, and Windows 2000 Server, Windows 2000 Advanced Server, and Windows 2000 Datacenter Server for server computers.

Windows 95: A version of Windows that became available in — you guessed it — 1995. Windows 95 was the first version of Windows that did not require DOS.

Windows 98: The successor to Windows 95 introduced in 1998. Windows 98 includes a new user interface that makes the Windows desktop resemble the World Wide Web.

Windows for Workgroups: Microsoft's first network-aware version of Windows, now pretty much defunct.

Windows Millennium Edition: The successor to Windows 98, designed especially for home users and featuring a Home Networking Wizard that simplifies the task of setting up a home network.

Windows NT: The predecessor to Windows 2000. Windows NT is available in two versions: Windows NT Client for desktop computers and Windows NT Server for server computers.

Windows XP: The newest version of Windows, designed for home or professional users.

wiring closet: Large networks need a place where cables can congregate. A closet is ideal.

workstation: See *client*.

World Wide Web: A graphical method of accessing information on the Internet.

WWW: See *World Wide Web*.

yellow cable: See *10base5*.

Index

• J •

FOR DUMMIES®

The easy way to get more done and have more fun

PERSONAL FINANCE & BUSINESS

Investing FOR DUMMIES
0-7645-2431-3

Home Buying FOR DUMMIES
0-7645-5331-3

Grant Writing FOR DUMMIES
0-7645-5307-0

Also available:

Accounting For Dummies
(0-7645-5314-3)

Business Plans Kit For Dummies
(0-7645-5365-8)

Managing For Dummies
(1-5688-4858-7)

Mutual Funds For Dummies
(0-7645-5329-1)

QuickBooks All-in-One Desk Reference For Dummies
(0-7645-1963-8)

Resumes For Dummies
(0-7645-5471-9)

Small Business Kit For Dummies
(0-7645-5093-4)

Starting an eBay Business For Dummies
(0-7645-1547-0)

Taxes For Dummies 2003
(0-7645-5475-1)

HOME, GARDEN, FOOD & WINE

Feng Shui FOR DUMMIES
0-7645-5295-3

Gardening FOR DUMMIES
0-7645-5130-2

Cooking FOR DUMMIES
0-7645-5250-3

Also available:

Bartending For Dummies
(0-7645-5051-9)

Christmas Cooking For Dummies
(0-7645-5407-7)

Cookies For Dummies
(0-7645-5390-9)

Diabetes Cookbook For Dummies
(0-7645-5230-9)

Grilling For Dummies
(0-7645-5076-4)

Home Maintenance For Dummies
(0-7645-5215-5)

Slow Cookers For Dummies
(0-7645-5240-6)

Wine For Dummies
(0-7645-5114-0)

FITNESS, SPORTS, HOBBIES & PETS

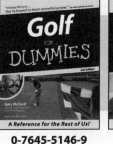

Fitness FOR DUMMIES
0-7645-5167-1

Golf FOR DUMMIES
0-7645-5146-9

Guitar FOR DUMMIES
0-7645-5106-X

Also available:

Cats For Dummies
(0-7645-5275-9)

Chess For Dummies
(0-7645-5003-9)

Dog Training For Dummies
(0-7645-5286-4)

Labrador Retrievers For Dummies
(0-7645-5281-3)

Martial Arts For Dummies
(0-7645-5358-5)

Piano For Dummies
(0-7645-5105-1)

Pilates For Dummies
(0-7645-5397-6)

Power Yoga For Dummies
(0-7645-5342-9)

Puppies For Dummies
(0-7645-5255-4)

Quilting For Dummies
(0-7645-5118-3)

Rock Guitar For Dummies
(0-7645-5356-9)

Weight Training For Dummies
(0-7645-5168-X)

Available wherever books are sold.
Go to www.dummies.com or call 1-877-762-2974 to order direct

 **WILEY**

FOR DUMMIES®

A world of resources to help you grow

TRAVEL

0-7645-5453-0

0-7645-5438-7

0-7645-5444-1

Also available:

America's National Parks For Dummies
(0-7645-6204-5)

Caribbean For Dummies
(0-7645-5445-X)

Cruise Vacations For Dummies 2003
(0-7645-5459-X)

Europe For Dummies
(0-7645-5456-5)

Ireland For Dummies
(0-7645-6199-5)

France For Dummies
(0-7645-6292-4)

Las Vegas For Dummies
(0-7645-5448-4)

London For Dummies
(0-7645-5416-6)

Mexico's Beach Resorts For Dummies
(0-7645-6262-2)

Paris For Dummies
(0-7645-5494-8)

RV Vacations For Dummies
(0-7645-5443-3)

EDUCATION & TEST PREPARATION

0-7645-5194-9

0-7645-5325-9

0-7645-5249-X

Also available:

The ACT For Dummies
(0-7645-5210-4)

Chemistry For Dummies
(0-7645-5430-1)

English Grammar For Dummies
(0-7645-5322-4)

French For Dummies
(0-7645-5193-0)

GMAT For Dummies
(0-7645-5251-1)

Inglés Para Dummies
(0-7645-5427-1)

Italian For Dummies
(0-7645-5196-5)

Research Papers For Dummies
(0-7645-5426-3)

SAT I For Dummies
(0-7645-5472-7)

U.S. History For Dummies
(0-7645-5249-X)

World History For Dummies
(0-7645-5242-2)

HEALTH, SELF-HELP & SPIRITUALITY

0-7645-5154-X

0-7645-5302-X

0-7645-5418-2

Also available:

The Bible For Dummies
(0-7645-5296-1)

Controlling Cholesterol For Dummies
(0-7645-5440-9)

Dating For Dummies
(0-7645-5072-1)

Dieting For Dummies
(0-7645-5126-4)

High Blood Pressure For Dummies
(0-7645-5424-7)

Judaism For Dummies
(0-7645-5299-6)

Menopause For Dummies
(0-7645-5458-1)

Nutrition For Dummies
(0-7645-5180-9)

Potty Training For Dummies
(0-7645-5417-4)

Pregnancy For Dummies
(0-7645-5074-8)

Rekindling Romance For Dummies
(0-7645-5303-8)

Religion For Dummies
(0-7645-5264-3)

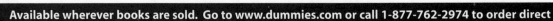

Available wherever books are sold. Go to www.dummies.com or call 1-877-762-2974 to order direct

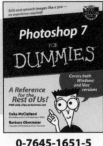